SPITFIRE OFFENSIVE

SPITFIRE OFFENSIVE

A FIGHTER PILOT'S WAR MEMOIR

WING COMMANDER R W F SAMPSON,

OBE, DFC & BAR, TEM, DL, C de G & PALME

with

NORMAN FRANKS

GRUB STREET · LONDON

First published in 1994 in hardback by
Grub Street, The Basement,
10 Chivalry Road, London SW11 1HT

This paperback edition first published 2002
Copyright © 2002 Grub Street, London
Text copyright © R.W.F. Sampson and N. Franks

British Library Cataloguing in Publication Data
Sampson, R.W.F. (Ralph William Frazer)
  Spitfire Offensive
  1. Sampson, R.W.F. (Ralph William Frazer) 2. Great Britain.
  Royal Air Force – History 3. World War, 1939-1945
  4. World War, 1939-1945 – Aerial operations, British
  I. Title II. Franks, Norman L.R. (Norman Leslie Robert)
  940.5′449′092

ISBN 1-902304-84-5

Edited by John Davies

Typeset by Pearl Graphics, Hemel Hempstead

Printed and bound in Great Britain by
Biddles Ltd, Guildford and King's Lynn

CONTENTS

Foreword by

AIR COMMODORE P M BROTHERS CBE DSO DFC & BAR RAF R'td   4

CHAPTER		PAGE
	INTRODUCTION	5
I	FROM KILT TO COCKPIT	8
II	FIGHTER PILOT	17
III	CITY OF GLASGOW SQUADRON	28
IV	ACTION AT LAST	36
V	DIEPPE	45
VI	FLIGHT COMMANDER	57
VII	EXETER WING	68
VIII	SPITFIRE IXs AND TOUR EXPIRED	80
IX	RODEO 194	91
X	SQUADRON COMMANDER, 2nd TAF	102
XI	THE FREE FRENCH IN THE RAF	111
XII	WING LEADER	130
XIII	THE FRENCH FIGHTER WING	143
XIV	VICTORY IN EUROPE	156
XIV	APRES LA GUERRE	170
	POSTSCRIPT	174
APPENDIX A	RAF RECORD OF SERVICE	177
APPENDIX B	COMBATS AND SORTIES	178
	Index	179

ACKNOWLEDGEMENTS

I express my sincere thanks to the following: Air Commodore P M Brothers CBE DSO DFC RAF for his generous foreword; Norman Franks, well known military aviation author for researching the project and putting my notes and recollections into a readable form; Roger Steel ASIA GAVA, Vice President and former Chairman of the Guild of Aviation Artists for permission to use his Spitfire painting, the original of which today hangs in the RAF Club, 128 Piccadilly, London, as dust jacket cover picture; Colin Hodgkinson, now resident in France, for putting me in touch with the following wartime Free French fighter pilots: General J Andrieux, General M Perdrizet, General P Laurent, General V Tanguy, General J Souviat, Colonel L Le Flecher, Colonel F Boyer de Bouillane, Lt Colonel P Lavergne, Commandant M Boisot; Wing Commander R G Kellett DSO DFC and Mr R Parker, son-in-law of M Boisot, for help in translations; my fellow flight commander on 131 Squadron, Tony Pickering; Mrs Jean Holme; Bernard Thompson, County Chairman of the Association of Men of Kent and Kentish Men; and my business colleagues in France and Scotland who from time to time suggested that I had a story to tell.

Finally, I apologise if I have inadvertently overlooked anyone.

DEDICATION

To

Air Commodore P M Brothers CBE DSO DFC & bar

As a squadron commander and wing leader, the most exciting leader on offensive operations I had the privilege to fly with.

FOREWORD

Many are the wartime stories of derring-do which have been written and published extolling the exploits of their authors. Thankfully, these memoirs of Sammy Sampson's experiences do not fall into that oft overweening category. He tells how, as an Army Officer stationed in Scotland in 1940 and imbued with the thought that to fly with the Royal Air Force might offer an earlier and more exciting opportunity to get at the enemy, he obtained a transfer by enthusiastic perseverance and astute wrangling.

By the time he had completed his training and joined a squadron, therefore, he was not among the youngest of fighter pilots, but his comparative maturity was enhanced by his zeal and passion for action. It was these traits which I noticed when I commanded 602 Squadron, in which he was a pilot, and which resulted in my arranging for him to join my Wing at Tangmere in 1942 as a flight commander in 131 Squadron and later in 1944, to fly with me in the Culmhead Wing.

The tale of his wartime career as a fighter pilot contains some errors in detail but these are unimportant, and by not recounting events in dull and factual chronological order he adds interest and spice to the story. My involvement in his life inevitably makes me a biased commentator and his mention of the many friends and acquaintances we shared reminds me of happy days and sterling characters. 'Hoppy' Hodgkinson, the legless pilot who called himself 'the poor man's Douglas Bader', the French 'Jacko' Andrieux and the Norwegian, Martin Gran, both of whom served on my staff at SHAPE, Paris, in the 1960s, to mention but a few.

For my part, Sammy Sampson has related a fascinating story. I leave it to other readers to judge and am confident they will agree.

PETE BROTHERS

INTRODUCTION

In 1989, Wing Commander Paddy Barthropp DFC AFC, a former RAF fighter pilot who had fought during the Battle of Britain, gave me a copy of his updated autobiography—*Paddy*.

Unfortunately, Paddy was shot down by a Me109 in early 1942 to become a prisoner of war, so his war was cut short. However, many of his contemporaries survived the war to become senior RAF commanders and I served alongside most of them. I named some to Paddy with suitable anecdotes and his response was, "You really ought to write a book yourself!" I was reminded that the famous Hollywood actress Mae West gave this advice to a young up-and-coming film actress. "Always keep a diary; one day it may keep you." I didn't keep a diary so have to rely on a combination of memory and notations written in my wartime flying log books.

During the war of 1939-45, I served as a commissioned officer, first in the Army and then on transfer to flying duties with the Royal Air Force. The outstanding difference I found between the two services was that the Royal Air Force, being then only some 22 years old, was to all intents a family business where no jealousy existed between the commands because both officers and other ranks often moved from one to another as they climbed the promotion ladder. The Army, on the other hand, with some of its regiments centuries old, is full of proud traditions, to an extent that there exists a superiority complex. I recollect Brian Johnston, the well known cricket commentator, being asked why he opted for the Grenadier Guards when he was granted a wartime commission. His response was, "Well, it's the best, isn't it?" There is a similarity with Highland Regiments each with its clan background which they guard jealously. My regiment, the Queen's Own Cameron Highlanders, based at Inverness, with the Lovat Fraser and Cameron of Lochiel background, felt it was definitely the best, closely followed by the Black Watch.

When it came to warlike activities, Field Marshal Bernard

Montgomery was well known for relieving Colonels and Generals from their commands because in his opinion they were, as he put it, "..above their ceiling." I never came across a Senior RAF officer who had progressed through squadron, wing or group and above, who was judged above his ceiling. In wartime he simply would not have survived to reach the higher ranks.

I was very fortunate to serve under three brilliant squadron commanders when I was a junior officer fighter pilot. The first was Brendan—Paddy—Finucane DSO DFC & 2 bars, then Pete Brothers DSO DFC & bar and finally James—Orange—O'Meara DSO DFC & bar. If I had to choose one of them as the best, it would have to be Pete Brothers. When it came to leading, first his Squadron and then his Wing, over German dominated skies, it was very often fun! He had what can only be described as instinctive feel for the battle. If our ground controllers were 'on the ball', so to speak, with accurate information regarding enemy reaction to our penetrations into his airspace, Pete invariably led us into an advantageous position before joining combat. His exceptional leadership of No.602 (City of Glasgow) Spitfire Squadron during the Dieppe Operation on 19th August 1942, is described later in this book. In addition to his role as firstly a flight commander, then squadron commander and finally wing leader, he was an outstanding fighter pilot with well over twenty aerial combats in which he was invariably at the right end, with the Hun at the receiving end.

By the 5th of May, 1945 (VE Day in the UK was fixed at 8th May) I was myself a wing leader at Drope, a former German airfield some ten miles east of the Dutch/German border and 15 miles northwest of the town of Osnabruck. This day, which dawned bright and sunny, was to be the day on which Field Marshal Montgomery would officially declare Victory in Europe. At 1800 hours on the previous evening, the Army Intelligence Officer attached to my Wing informed me that 'Monty' had received un-conditional surrender terms from the German Field Commander and that he had ordered the Army to cease fire at 0800 hours the next morning. An hour after hearing this, Flight Lieutenant Crane, the Wing Intelligence Officer, handed me a D-Form (Operations Order) which had been signalled from Head-quarters, Second Tactical Air Force. This instructed me to have all available aircraft carry out offensive operations up to 11 am on the 5th (shades of 11th November, 1918).

My Free French Fighter Wing—No.145—comprised four Spitfire squadrons, as part of No.84 Group, 2nd TAF. We had moved into this recently abandoned airfield on 16th April, flying in close support of British and Canadian troops as they relentlessly advanced east-wards. My immediate reaction upon receiving this order was one of fury and I went straight to the Airfield Commander, who I had known for a long time, Group Captain Loel Guiness (OBE, AE, Legion d'Honneur), who was in his operations caravan. I told him in no uncertain terms that unless he instructed me to the contrary, I had no intention of sending any of my pilots on any dangerous missions, just three hours prior to the victory we had all fought so long to achieve. What a tragedy if, after six years of war, a pilot was to lose his life so short a time before victory and peace. As I expected of Loel Guiness, he totally agreed with me, and with my plan, which at least would satisfy the operational planners at HQ.

At 2000 hours, I instructed all pilots to report for briefing at 0900 the following morning. With Loel Guiness present, I informed them, and especially the 23 young men who would accompany me on this mission, that under no circumstances would they indulge in any war-like activities, unless we were actually attacked. Together with the three squadron commanders, we mapped out areas over which we would fly for just one hour. I would be leading No.340 Squadron which was the first French squadron to be formed, and we would reassemble at 10.45, so that Flight Lieutenant Crane could then report to HQ that we had flown our patrol and that no enemy activity had been encountered.

Thus ended my part in World War Two, and I like to think that after so long flying and fighting a ruthless enemy, we in 145 Wing ended it on a note of humanity. For not only had I not risked any of my pilots at this momentous "11th hour", but equally, we had not risked taking any lives of our erstwhile enemies, so that both could at last begin to enjoy the benefits of a peace bought at the cost of so many lives.

Sammy Sampson
Kent 1994

CHAPTER I

FROM KILT TO COCKPIT

I looked ahead and to the left as I curved round and down towards the grass runway. After four years of flying R J Mitchell's wonderful creation, the Supermarine Spitfire, it came instinctively to me now to approach the landing field in a curve in order to see clearly ahead and around the Spit's long nose. Selecting wheels down and then flaps, I finally straightened up and began to throttle back. The by now familiar sound of my wheels touching the earth, then the bumps and rumbling as my fighter regained the ground, came not so much to my ears as to my senses.

Then the tail wheel touched, just a second later, as I throttled right back and began to lose forward speed. Keeping my goggles on in case dust and dirt were thrown up by the whirling propeller blades, I slid back the cockpit hood and as I pulled off the runway, looked out and behind, seeing the other Spitfires curving round and beginning to land. Like mine, their bomb racks were empty. Another operation had been successfully carried out.

I looked at my watch. We had been airborne just 45 minutes, one of the shortest sorties I'd flown for a very long time, but then the battle front was only a matter of minutes away from our German base at Drope. I had led 345 (Free French) Squadron on a dive-bombing mission on the harbour at Oldersum, just south of Emden. It had been successful despite some quite heavy flak. Results at debriefing were later assessed as excellent, our bombs and strafing runs leaving the place in flames.

I climbed stiffly out of the cockpit, stepped onto the wingroot then jumped down to the ground. My ground crew were around me, with the usual questions. How did it go? Was the aeroplane alright? Had I felt any hits? Meanwhile, the other Spitfires were taxying up to our dispersal area, and with a final burst of engine, each pilot cut his motor and gradually the noise of aero engines died.

Yes, the aeroplane was fine, and no, I don't think the flak touched me. They glanced at the Spitfire anyway, with their loving but very professional eyes. It was not my usual Spitfire, marked "SS" for Sammy Sampson—a wing leader's perogative, having his initials marked on his personal aeroplane. Today, 28th April, 1945, I'd been flying one of 74 Squadron's Spitfire XVIs, coded 4D-A, as I had two days earlier, on mine and the Wing's most successful show. "SS" was being serviced and in retrospect it was a pity that I had not flown it on this day, for as it turned out this was to be my last operational sortie, although I did not know it then.

When I later wrote it up in my log book, I saw that it was my 189th. How long ago sortie number one had been. And in comparison to my last, how peaceful. It had been a convoy patrol to 18 small ships off Beachy Head, and I'd flown as Number Two to Sergeant Bill Loud. At least it had lasted longer than my 189th—a whole hour and 35 minutes! Bill Loud and I had both come a long way since that June day in 1942. He was now a Wing Commander too, until recently commanding No.122 Mustang Wing and had received the DSO DFC & bar.

But now with my French pilots gathered about me, each talking excitedly about the show to Oldersum as we started to walk towards the Flight Hut, 1942 seemed a lifetime ago, as did my time with the Army, way back in 1938.....

When war was declared in September 1939, I had been what was described in those days a weekend soldier in the Territorial Army. As an exile in London, serving a business apprenticeship in an Insurance conglomerate on the sort of salary not acceptable to the youth of today, I had, because of my birthright, joined the London Scottish Regiment of the TA. This was mainly because it was a cheap 'club' (not an inconsequential incentive) offering some gentle soldiering, some shooting at the ranges of Bisley, sports, an annual camp (which might be fun), and an occasional ceremonial march in my native Scotland (including a free journey home), plus a small payment for minimum attendance!

I certainly had no ambition or desire to become either an NCO, nor for that matter an officer, but we had some good times, decked out in our kilts, and sleeping in bell tents at such places as Strathpeffer and Dingwall and marching across the Muir of Ord. There is something warlike about the look of a kilted Scottish Highland Regiment, and when we marched with drums beating, the pipes wailing and kilts swirling, we hoped we looked the part. Whether we would have put the fear of God into a potential enemy, as had our forebares 'going over the top' in 1915, is another matter.

However, we received the military discipline which never really harmed any youth, and I had my brother Victor with me, plus such pals as Sandy Inglis, Jim Campbell, Bob Holman and Halle Muir. Victor, like me, had come to London having obtained a job in the London office of the Peruvian Corpu Railways, sharing the same digs with me.

No doubt things would have continued happily, with me in insurance during the week, while swashbuckling in kilt and sporran at weekends, had not the events of late summer 1939 changed everything. A few days before Prime Minister Neville Chamberlain made his now famous radio broadcast, informing us that we were for the second time this century at war with Germany, the London Scottish Regiment had already been called up and billeted in the Scots Guards Depot, Chelsea Barracks.

'B' Company (my company) was detailed to provide guard duties at the main gate for 24 hours. The Regimental Sergeant Major of the Scots Guards explained all the duties involved and especially when the sentry was on duty. Those of us not detailed for 'Guard' were allowed passes until midnight, and one night six of us decided to go to the Chelsea pubs. Just before midnight we returned, approaching the main gate which was dimly lit by a blue light in deference to the blackout. We heard the well known and familiar west of Scotland accent of Joey Newlands shouting, "Halt—who goes there?" None of us had decided who should answer with the accepted reply "Friend", so Joey again shouted, "I repeat, who goes there?" Jim Campbell, to my surprise, responded, "Och away Joey and fuck yoursel'!", whereupon Joey called, "Pass friends."

Whilst we were at Chelsea Barracks, there was a strong rumour that all packets of tea delivered to the cookhouse were doctored with bromide, the age-old military additive designed to reduce the male sexual urges. George Horsburgh, a large Scottish Rugby International, had received permission plus five days leave, to get married. When he returned there was some good natured bantering, including the 64,000 dollar question, "Did the bromide in the tea make you impotent, George?", to which his reply was, "Not bloody likely—my wife thought I was impudent!"

Within a few weeks, the London Scottish Regiment was designated an Officer Producing Unit, which meant that the majority would be sent off to various Officer Cadet Training Units prior to being

Gazetted as Second Lieutenants. My brother Victor, three years my junior, beat me to it by some six weeks and after OCTU training was, due to our family background, accepted by the Queen's Own Cameron Highlanders, based at Inverness. In due course I was sent to the Royal Military Academy at Sandhurst, which having quickly rushed through the remaining Gentleman Cadets, was now an OCTU but still retaining the Brigade of Guards Instructors.

My instructor was Second Lieutenant, the Hon. Michael Fitzalan-Howard (now Major General Lord Michael, the younger twin brother of Miles, the present Duke of Norfolk). By coincidence, some 30 years later, Michael became chairman of the Council of Territorial, Auxiliary and Volunteer Reserve Associations, when I was a Royal Air Force member of the Council. I reminded him that when I received my commission at Sandhurst in 1940, he would have written my first confidential report and that under the 30 year rule I could, presumably and if I so desired, have sight of that hitherto classified document. With a twinkle in his eye, he strongly advised me not to do so.

When the course was completed, and as I had also opted for the Cameron Highlanders, I was interviewed by Major Grant-Peterkin, which I suppose was a mere formality. Victor by this time, having been married in May 1940, was posted just 14 days after that event to the 2nd Battalion, stationed in Egypt! I was sent to the newly formed 6th Battalion under Colonel Pringle-Paterson MC & bar, who was in his mid-40s, having fought with distinction towards the end of the First War. The Battalion was at Wick, Caithness. 'PP', as he was affectionately known, was a most popular Commanding Officer and if the Huns had invaded, would no doubt have been a first class operational commander.

The thing that really worried me when posted to Caithness, was that we had to guard against a possible invasion from Norway, which had only recently fallen to the Germans. That and the visits of Field Marshal Lord Gort and later General Sir Andrew Thorne. Put in a nutshell, their message to we junior officers was quite simply, 'If the Hun invades now, we shall be defeated.'

I was a platoon commander with a slice of beach to defend, when General Thorne inspected us. After he had departed, a cockney from the East End of London, with their usual sense of humour, said to me, "And what six feet of sand are you reserving for your grave, Sir?" We had certainly not been instilled with any real sense of a future.

*

For the rest of 1940, while the Battle of Britain was being fought by the RAF down in the south, we continued to defend the Caithness coast. Then in February 1941, an Army Council Instruction (ACI) arrived which stated that following the losses during the RAF's Battle, the Royal Air Force was going to expand the flying branches as quickly as possible. It transpired that while they had the capacity to train pilots to an operational standard, they did not have the capacity to teach them to become officers. To an extent this was still peacetime thinking, and in order to overcome the difficulty, pilots and aircrew were being sent to squadrons as NCOs with the eventual possibility of being commissioned in the field. In the meantime, the logic dictated that to fill the immediate void, army officers, physically fit and aged 25 or under, were to be invited to apply and that 2,000 were required. In the event, I gather that some 18,000 applied!

It so happened that I was the Orderly Officer when the ACI arrived. As part of my duties was to open the mail and divide it as necessary, I saw the ACI first thing and immediately filled in an application. Not surprisingly I was quickly sent for by the CO. PP gave me a long spiel about team spirit and building an aggressive fighting battalion, then promptly tore up my application in front of me and tossed it into the waste paper basket.

That, I reluctantly assumed, was the end of any ambitions of mine to become an operational RAF pilot. However, some weeks later the same ACI was repeated, but this time it had a rider. The War Office, having become aware that many COs had, like mine, refused to forward similar applications from their officers, now instructed unit commanders, in no uncertain terms, that applications must not be obstructed.

I immediately put in my application again and this time it was, albeit reluctantly, passed down the line. As I had heard nothing after six weeks or so, and was getting a trifle worried, I took my next week's leave in London. Among many friendly contacts I got in touch with was Joan Brandt, an erstwhile friend of brother Victor. She happened to be the senior female secretary at the Boodles Club. I mentioned to her my worry and she suggested that she could arrange a meeting with Colonel Vaux, whose retirement job from the Regular Army had been secretary of the Club. On the outbreak of war he had been recalled and was a Staff Officer in the War Office.

A meeting was arranged in the Cavendish Hotel in Jermyn Street, off Piccadilly, owned by Rosa Lewis who as a young girl had been in the kitchens at Buckingham Palace, and had been sent to the Cavendish for services rendered. I had been there before, taken by Norman Johnstone, a Grenadier Guards Officer, and his very beautiful girlfriend, Lady Cecilia Wellesly, the Earl and Countess of Cowley's daughter. The only drink served in the hotel was Champagne—by the bottle!

I told the Colonel of my problem and to my surprise he informed me that he was in charge of postings from the Army to the Royal Air Force. I then did two things. Firstly I told Ada, Rosa Lewis' side-kick, to keep the Champagne coming and secondly, I gave Colonel Vaux a written note of my name, regiment, etc. That meeting took place on a Tuesday and when I returned to Wick on the Sunday morning, Ted Dudgeon, our Adjutant, told me that my posting to the RAF had arrived. I was later to learn from Joan that prior to my meeting with the Colonel, my place on the list of hopeful applicants was around the 1800 mark. Who says women don't have any influence?!

My instructions were to report to the RAF Recruiting Centre in Princes Street, Edinburgh, for a medical examination. There I found three doctors, each specialising in different parts of the anatomy. The doctor who was concerned with heart and lungs was young and full of good humour. I recall that at one stage he said, "Now I usually ask the patient to drop his trousers but it your case, please lift the front of your kilt!" During his examination of my nether regions (I was too nervous to remember now if his fingers were cold) he asked me which branch of flying I was opting for and when I said Day Fighters, he remarked, "Fighter pilot in a kilt—wow!!"

Overcoming this hurdle, I was sent to Cambridge to undergo a short initial training course, consisting of navigation, morse code, Air Force law, etc. Thereafter, we—some 30 army officers—having been billeted in Clare College, commenced elementary flying at No. 22 EFTS at Marshall's airfield, near Cambridge, flying DeHavilland Tiger Moths.

It was now August 1941, two months after Hitler had invaded Russia. I clearly recollect the feeling of astonishment when we young officers heard Prime Minister Winston Churchill saying that he had been in touch with Joseph Stalin, promising full co-operation, help and assistance. We were all absolutely horrified as it was Stalin's non-aggression pact with Hitler which had enabled Germany to invade Poland in the first place. I remember clearly that our attitude was, 'It's their war, let them get on with it, whilst we concentrate on ours in the West, in Egypt, Malta and the Atlantic.' I still personally think we would have been better off in the end, by politely ignoring Stalin.

However, I had more basic things to occupy my mind on August 14th, the day I first flew in a Tiger (T7268) for a 30-minute Air

Experience flight, during which I was shown the cockpit layout and the effect on the controls when one moved the 'stick' or kicked the rudder bars. My instructor was Pilot Officer Nigel Bell and I could not have wished for a better one. He was very patient, completely unflappable and never discouraging. His only problem was that he was colour blind! How on earth he got past the medical chaps, I never discovered. Of course, he could not, for obvious reasons, take part in night-flying instruction. He was a VR pilot having joined just before the war. If he had been a regular I imagine the medics would have picked up his colour blindness.

My first ever flight in an aeroplane had been back in 1937, in an Avro Biplane belonging to Alan Cobham's Circus. I had been a guest at some friend's place in Bognor and three of us were taken up for 2/6d (12p) per head, standing in the rear cockpit which had been for an air gunner or observer. There were no luxuries like straps to hold you in, but it proved so exciting (Oh, the innocence of youth!) that we all went back the next day for a repeat performance. So it must have been this experience that had become rooted in my sub-conscious, germinated by that signal that the RAF needed officers to fly.

The Commanding Officer at Marshall's was Wing Commander Peter May AFC, who somehow acquired a Gloster Gladiator fighter which he used to fly during the lunch hour when no pupils were airborne. To see him conduct aerobatics over the airfield was an inspiring experience for us pupils, who wondered if we'd ever be able to do half as well.

I next met Peter May towards the end of my flying course at Kidlington, near Oxford. He was forming a squadron of what can only be described as demoted bomber aeroplanes, such as Stirlings, Manchesters, etc. They were now being used to tow heavy gliders on future invasion penetrations into North Africa, Sicily and so on. He did me the honour of suggesting I might like to join his outfit but as my sights were firmly fixed elsewhere, I politely declined. Sad to relate, he was later shot down and presumed killed as he approached Sicily, towing a glider. I heard it rumoured that he was hit from gunfire from our Navy.[1]

I flew my first solo, which proved quite uneventful, on 29th August. I had already made four brief flights that day, three with Bell and

---

[1] Wing Commander P R May AFC commanded 296 Squadron from October 1942 until July 1943. He was shot down flying an Albemarle, on 12th July whilst engaged on dropping SAS troops into Sicily, during the invasion of that island.

another with Pilot Officer Harrison. After the fourth, which lasted 20 minutes, Bell told me to take off and fly a circuit. Ten minutes later I put N9330 safely back on the landing field. Privately I felt I could have gone off on my own earlier, so I must have felt confident. I had by then made several landings with Nigel Bell and he had not had to interfere or criticise. It was my 26th flight, covering about 11½ hours of dual control.

During September my feet seemed hardly to touch the ground— literally. From the lst till the 20th, I made 69 flights covering the whole range of pilot instruction. Most were solo, but some were with Bell or perhaps another instructor, who would show me how to do something and then send me off to do it. Finally on the 12th came the next hurdle, a 40-minute air test with the Boss, Peter May. With that over I felt even more confident and eager to get on.

Then came night flying. With Bell unable to help me, my first night flight was given to me by an NCO instructor. His name was Sparrow but I secretly wished it had been Owl or Nighthawk! As it happened I had flown with Bell for the last time, and my final flights were with three other instructors, the last being Pilot Officer Pledger on the 20th. During the day I'd flown some aerobatics, steep turns, climbing turns and prophetically, precautionary landings. That evening, Pledger took me up for a 30-minute flight in N6542, then he sent me off alone.

The weather was becoming foggy but I was told it was OK to take off and do a couple of circuits and landings. Mine was the last detail of the evening but I was in no hurry, so took off and climbed to 3,000 feet. When I turned back I noticed the flare path looked decidedly hazy. As I lined up to descend the flare path disappeared, so I climbed again. It reappeared and I quickly realised that while I could see it at 2,000 feet, it disappeared at about 1,000 and below. There was only one thing for it, I had to judge where the flare path would be after sighting it at 2,000 feet, make a blind approach and hope my judgement was correct.

Of course, being inexperienced, I misjudged it and touched down well beyond the end of the path. The Tiger bounced all over the place, entered a ditch and finished up upside down, the poor machine being a write-off. My own damage was a black eye and injured nose. I was not held to blame as it was an admitted briefing error, but it was a sad note on which to leave Marshall's, the course having now been completed.

Our course at 22 EFTS consisted of 65 flying hours spread over some six weeks. About ten days before the course ended we were visited by four WAAF officers who had some rather strange looking instruments, most of which were used in a darkened room. When dimly illuminated they showed, briefly, various objects which we had to describe individually, some orally, some written down. When my session was completed I asked the 'Queen Bee' (Senior WAAF) the object of the exercise, but her only response was, "You have exceptional night vision." I now gather these WAAFs were on the lookout for potential night-fighter pilots.

I might add here that my eyesight did prove quite good, which I put down to being a countryman, used to being out amongst the hills and glens of my native Scotland. When I eventually reached a front-line day-fighter squadron I found I could recognise the 'dots' in the sky a good deal sooner than most of my contemporaries.

My course assessment by Peter May was recorded as 'Good Average' and even my Link Trainer instructor gave me some encouragement. I'd flown about 63 hours plus eight hours on the Link, and from the latter I had "after a mediocre start, improved by leaps and bounds with every session and should continue to do well." With these words of encouragement I proceeded to Peterborough after some leave, to join 17 EFTS where I would spend a week before going on to a Service Training School. I had overcome the initial hurdles of my pilot training; I was on my way.

CHAPTER II

FIGHTER PILOT

When I arrived at Peterborough, one of the instructors there—
Sergeant Trueman—checked my flying log book, then said, "I see
you've recently had a prang and I want to take you up for a test."
Soon after we were airborne he continued, "Climb to 5,000 feet and
give me slow rolls both ways," followed by, "Give me a loop", next,
"Give me a spin and don't pull out till I tell you to!" When we had
landed he said, "Some chaps tend to lose their nerve after a prang,
but I'm pleased to see you haven't lost yours." So was I.

The Officer's Mess at Peterborough was full so a few of us were
billeted out in private houses for bed and breakfast. For this we
needed a daily allowance which in company with pay, was credited
direct to our bank account. After a few days, accommodation became
available in the Mess but in the interim my full allowance had been
paid into my bank account, which in effect overcredited me by £31.
Some two years later, the Accounts Officer at RAF Exeter said I owed
this sum and could the RAF be repaid either in full or by instalments.
I smiled and said I'd look into this but then promptly forgot all about it.

This same question was posed to me on two later occasions at
different stations and I gave the same 'helpful' response. When I was
finally demobed towards the end of 1945, I assumed I had beaten the
system. No such luck! We were all given Post War Credits and these
were eventually paid towards the end of the 1950s. To my utter
amazement not to say disappointment, on the largest credit, some £50
plus, was written, "Less £31 overpaid allowance, RAF Peterborough."

A week after going to Peterborough our postings came through for
SFTS—Service Flying Training School. There were two types of
school, one involving the use of twin-engined Airspeed Oxfords and
the other of single-engine Miles Masters or Harvards. The deduction

was simple. Single-engine for potential fighter boys, twin-engines for bomber or night fighter chaps. My orders were to report to 15 FTS at RAF Kidlington, near Oxford. My heart dropped. I knew they had twins at Kidlington, so deduced that I was being groomed for either bombers or twin-engined night-fighters. I wasn't thrilled at either prospect.

Winter was not far off when I arrived at Kidlington, to join No.31 Course. My instructor was Flight Lieutenant Denis Adams, known, of course, as Fanny. On the outbreak of war he had been an officer pilot in 611 (City of Liverpool) Squadron, Royal Auxiliary Air Force, having fought with a modicum of success during the Battle of Britain. To his personal credit he was philosophical on having been posted from Fighter Command to Training Command. He was a very good instructor, although not quite as patient as Nigel Bell at Cambridge, but he always encouraged and was determined that his pupils would complete the course with better than Average.

Adams never spoke much about his time with 611 and I got the impression he didn't like them too much. Yet he was good and obviously felt, as I did, that I would be better suited in a day-fighter role than the driver of multi-engined machines. I never knew much about his subsequent career but he was a squadron leader by 1944 and survived the war.

Adams took me up in an Oxford for the first time on 20th October, just for 25 minutes of familiarisation. From then on I flew it fairly frequently, going solo on type four days later. At least it was all day flying, and I did not fly at night until Boxing Day when Sergeant Rogers took me up for an hour. War doesn't always take into account Christmas for I flew three times on Christmas Eve, and then made three day and two night flights on the 26th. One of my fellow students on the course was LAC Brignell, and he flew with me on half a dozen occasions. Little did I realise then that Brignell would later become Group Captain J A Brignell OBE DFC MA CEng MRAeS, before retiring in 1968.

The course lasted about four months, delayed no doubt by the winter weather, although it was a rare day that we had no flying at all. I was still flying more by day than night, which encouraged me to think there was a chance of not becoming a fully fledged nocturnal animal, and I survived the Flight Commander's Test in early February 1942. I flew just under 100 hours and when the end of the course was fast approaching I told Fanny Adams that I was not keen to go either onto bomber or night-fighter OTU. To his eternal credit he agreed with my feelings and said he would have a word with the Chief Flying

Instructor, Squadron Leader Jimmy Mackie. In next to no time, Adams took me aside and told me that Mackie would test me himself the next day before committing himself. Fanny's advice to me was to make it all 'split arse' stuff, none of those gentle rate-one turns, "...throw it around as much as possible; in fact, put the shits up him!"

The flight took place on 5th January in Oxford AB698, and we were up for 80 minutes. I can only say that my examination was successful although I still had to wait some weeks to know if I would get single seaters. Mackie had me fly various manoeuvres and although he seemed fairly relaxed about the whole thing, I noticed his hands were never very far away from the control column. When we landed, I followed him into his office as requested and sitting at his desk, he said to me, (more or less). "Sampson, you are not a bad pilot but Christ Almighty, you are not supposed to treat a twin-engined aeroplane like that. It is my opinion that you will be more suited to flying on your own!"

When finally my posting came through, I found to my sheer delight that I was to go to No.53 Operational Training Unit (OTU) at Llandow in South Wales. I could hardly contain myself, for 53 OTU meant Spitfires! I thanked Adams for his help and council and with a course assessment of Good Average by the CO, Group Captain W V Strugnell MC, a first war fighter 'ace', got ready to pack.

What I remember of Victor Strugnell was that he put the 'fear of God' into us pupils and strangely enough he took a very poor view of any fraternising by us with the WAAFs on the Station. Jealousy, we all reckoned! I next heard of him after the war when I commanded the Glasgow and West of Scotland Wing of the Air Training Corps. The Wing Commander of the Devon Wing, Louis Croke (a retired Air Commodore) told me that his Admin Officer was Strugnell. I gather he occasioned many second glances with his flight lieutenant VR(T) rank but with his chest full of medals. Later he rose to Wing Commander VR(T), still one rank below his RAF retired rank.

About three days before leaving Kidlington, we were informed that Winston Churchill would be landing, as he often did on his way to spend a few days with the Duke of Marlborough, his cousin, at Blenheim Palace, Woodstock. On this occasion, however, he wished to inspect all the officers.

Group Captain 'Struggy' Strugnell arranged us in a long line, mixing among us the few WAAF officers we had there. Standing next to me was Flight Officer Bunty Aves, an extremely nice girl if perhaps a trifle on the plump side. The Groupie had taken the precaution of issuing us will small clip-on name tags which were fixed to our lapels, so that the great man could have a name to latch on to. Strugnell, too, could refresh his memory when he had to introduce his people to the PM.

When the PM and the Groupie arrived opposite Bunty, Strugnell said, "This is Flight Officer Aves." Upon hearing this Churchill, with a quizzical smile said in a questioning voice, while gazing at the name tag, "Miss B Aves?" Everyone smiled dutifully as if it was the first time they'd ever heard it.

One other thing happened to me while at Kidlington. At one of the Officer's Mess Dances, I met Doctor Austen's daughter Margaret, who was part of the MI5 set-up, operating within Blenheim Palace. I was completely bowled over by her stunning beauty. We kept in touch, were married in 1946, and she has given me three fine sons, Jamie, Steven and Charles of whom we are immensely proud. We have lived happily ever after.

As soon as the course finished at Kidlington, towards the end of February 1942, we were issued with our RAF Wings and our names appeared in the London Gazette as Pilot Officers RAFVR. I was issued with an all-embracing railway warrant to London and then from Paddington to Cardiff. This allowed me a few days leave before catching the train to South Wales, which would be met by an RAF officer. I duly arrived in Cardiff in mid-March and together with a very mixed bag of officer and NCO pilots, were met as promised by a flight lieutenant. We boarded an old bus that had seen better days and which proceeded to take us on a bone-shattering journey to RAF Llandow.

We were dropped adjacent to our sleeping quarters (wartime huts), told to make our own way to the respective messes for tea at 4 pm, then we were free till 9 am next morning. We should report to the Flight Office on the airfield perimeter, which he pointed out to us from the bus.

Having dumped my gear I headed for the Mess and tea. Entering the anti-room in the Mess, I got the shock of my life for there, sitting on a large oak table swinging his short legs, was the Station Commander, Group Captain J I T Jones, known to everyone as 'Taffy' and to others 'Ira'—but not always to his face, especially we junior sprogs. On his left breast, beneath his RAF Wings, was a formidable row of medal ribbons denoting his not inconsiderable war service, not only during the Great War as even in this war he was known as a fire-eater. Even with my, as yet, limited knowledge of such things, I could make out the DSO, MC, DFC & bar and the MM. I also discovered he had been awarded the Russian Medal of St George. This he had received, together with his Military Medal, when as a ground observer, prior to becoming a pilot, he had rescued two wounded gunners while under fire. In 1918, as a fighting pilot with the famous 74 Squadron, alongside such men as Mannock and Caldwell, he had shot down nearly 40 German aeroplanes. A real-life legend.

Not that I was shocked at seeing the man as war hero and Station Commander, but because I had known him in peacetime, in quite a different context. During the 1930s he had been a rugby reporter for the *Sunday Despatch* newspaper, so I had known him quite well as I had been a player in the London Scottish First Rugby XV. It was well known that Taffy had a pretty severe drink problem and it was also a well known ploy of his to say to a player, "Buy me a Scotch and I'll mention your name in my column." Although I tried to avoid him as I entered the room, his keen eye quickly spotted and recognised me, and he sent an officer over to fetch me to him.

Taffy Jones had a profound stutter and as he looked at me, he said,

"Sammy, I will be a Fa..Fa..Father fi..fi..figure to you while you are here." I said my thanks, hoping it sounded convincing.

Later I was told by one of the staff officers whom I also knew from my rugby playing days, that Taffy was in bad odour at the Air Ministry because he had taken the whole of the previous course of pilots to the mortuary to show them a dead and smashed up body of a pilot who had written himself off whilst doing unauthorised low-flying. The brass at Air House were not amused, but one wonders how many of the pilots got the message, which perhaps saved their lives.

Twice during my time at Llandow, Taffy sent an officer to find me and ask me to join him in the bar, but both times I persuaded the officer to tell Taffy I was off the Station, visiting friends. Sad to relate, Taffy was soon afterwards Court Martialled because a pupil pilot was killed in a flying accident following a drinking session with him. Nevertheless he was a fighter. Once during the Battle of Britain he attacked a Ju88 bomber whilst flying an unarmed Hawker Henley target-towing aircraft, armed only with a Verey pistol, which he fired at the Junkers. He was also known to have flown on a few fighter sweeps over France with his old 74 Squadron when they were at Biggin Hill.

On the first morning following our arrival, we assembled as ordered in the Flight Commander's office. He was Flight Lieutenant A H Corkett and he had with him three other officer instructors and a sergeant pilot instructor. There were 36 pupils on the course and what happened next I shall never forget to my dying day. Allan Corkett was 24 years old and had flown in the Battle of Britain and continued on ops well into 1941. He would later end up as a prisoner of war when commanding a Typhoon squadron in 1943, and become a squadron leader in the post-war RAF.

Corkett looked us over then said that we would be divided into three squads of 12, each under a flight lieutenant senior instructor, he himself being one of the three. First, however, he wished to know on which aeroplane each of us had been trained. Turning to his three instructors, he asked them to take the count of hands, then said to us all, "Hands up all those trained on Masters." Up went 18 hands. "Right, now hands up those trained on Harvards." and up went a further 17 hands. What then made me a trifle nervous and start to sweat was his apparent annoyance with his colleagues.

"Christ, can't you buggers count? Right, start again." The second count was the same, but this time sanity prevailed and Corkett had a bright idea. "Is there someone here who has trained on anything else?" I gingerly raised my hand and his eyes settled on me.

"Airspeed Oxfords, Sir," I volunteered.

"Then what the fucking hell are you doing here?"

"Posted, Sir," I ventured.

"What's your bloody name?" Now as I had always been known in the Cameron Highlanders as Frazer Sampson, and my brother Victor the same, I replied,

"Frazer Sampson, Sir." I thought his reaction rather unkind when he said,

"I suppose one must expect that from a fucking Scot."

Corkett then turned to one of his colleagues, a Flying Officer Walliker, an Australian, instructing him to take me up in the dual control Miles Master before allowing me to fly the single-seater Spitfire Mark II which was the course aeroplane. Out on the airfield, Walliker took me over to a Master (K8636), placed me in the front cockpit and once we were both strapped in, started giving me details of the panel layout over the intercom. He then waved to the ground crew to start up with the battery and to take away the wooden chocks. We started to move forward towards the take-off runway while all the time he kept up a running commentary. Soon we were taking off and he was drawing my attention to the speed at which we came unstuck from the runway, the speed round the circuit, and especially the speeds as we came into land.

When the machine arrived at the original parking spot Walliker said, "As you can see, it's all quite straightforward. Off you go and do a couple of circuits and landings." As he began to depart I asked,

"Don't you think it would be a good idea for you to stay and see me do a couple of take-offs and landings?"

"Not necessary," he casually replied over his shoulder. "If you can fly an Oxford, you can fly any bloody aeroplane!" So much for his regard for Corkett's previous concern.

It was in fact no great problem, and a couple of days later he took me up in a Master III and then I was being briefed as I sat for my first time in a Spitfire II. Unlike the previous three types I had flown, the Spitfire was like a race horse once it was airborne, gathering terrific speed where the others were clambering into the air. As I left the ground, I selected wheels-up and with my eyes glued to the horizon ahead but with an occasional glance at the instruments, gained height. When I reached 1,000 feet I turned my head to look at the aerodrome and it was not in sight. This then was the difference between a fighter aeroplane and the training planes I had flown. Speed and Power.

I flew for just fifteen minutes, thankfully relocated the airfield and landed. It was a tremendous feeling of achievement. I had finally made it.

In addition to our charismatic Station Commander, there was the Wing Commander Flying, Con Donovan and the Chief Flying Instructor, Squadron Leader Alec Edge, for some unaccountable reason known as Paul. Both men from time to time flew in formation with a pupil, but usually with pupils who for some reason or other were having difficulty in making the grade and were becoming possible candidates for transfer to Transport Command.

Squadron Leader Edge spent the majority of his time leading formations on low-flying exercises but this would be when pupils had some 50 flying hours. Likewise, Edge was keen on very close formation flying exercises because, as he rightly said, there would be a lot of clambering through cloud as squadrons on offensive operations require heights above cloud. He later received the AFC for his work. He was, as well as being brilliant at handling a Spitfire, very approachable, very patient and generally admired by his pupils.

The senior instructor of my Flight was Flight Lieutenant Geoffrey Baynham, a Welshman like Taffy. I formed a high opinion of him, and he stuck his neck out a bit, when he confided to me that I would do well. It was an encouraging remark for one such as me just starting along the road to becoming a fighter pilot. What made it more convincing was that he had been in the Battle of Britain and on offensive ops over France in 1941. On one occasion in July 1941, he claimed three Me109s in one sortie. I later heard he'd been posted to North Africa, took part in the Tunisian campaign, then the invasion of Sicily, winning the DFC. He married Claude-Bertrand de Colasse, but the marriage later broke down and Claudie went on to marry Peregrine Worsthorne after the war. She died in 1990.

There was no doubt that the 'Powers' at the Air Ministry were determined that fighter pilots should have at least 60 flying hours on Spitfires, and had flown the complete range of exercises similar to what might be expected on warlike operations. The Commander-in-Chief of Fighter Command at that time, was Air Chief Marshal Sir William Sholto Douglas KCB MC DFC, later to become Marshal of the RAF, Lord Douglas of Kirtleside. Fighter Command was now at the stage of conducting round the clock offensive fighter sweeps over German-dominated France, Belgium and Holland, and we were told that we were expected to be able to cope with being, proverbially speaking, 'thrown in at the deep end'.

The mention of Sholto Douglas reminds me that when he was appointed C-in-C, he had made the extraordinary statement that in his opinion a fighter pilot over the age of 25 was senile. That, of course, was rather a stupid statement, which I am sure he must have regretted making, especially when one remembers that Harry Broadhurst, (later ACM Sir Harry) Victor Beamish, Sailor Malan, Ronald Kellett, Douglas Bader, and so on, were all over 30 years old. Johnnie Johnson, who was to become the RAF's top scoring fighter pilot in Europe, was himself 26 in 1941! Of these men, only Beamish was to lose his life in action, having survived a tremendous amount of operational flying between 1940 and 1942.

Whilst at Llandow I had a slight accident which put me in hospital for a few days. We had to take our parachutes with us when we were to fly or after we'd finished. This meant we invariably had it strapped on when getting in and out of the Spit. I had the misfortune to jump off the wing into a pothole and strained my ankle to such an extent that I was whisked off to the RAF Hospital at St Athan. Because I couldn't walk they decided to keep me in for the night and to be examined by the midicos the next day.

The Sister in charge was the comparatively young, certainly under 30, and very good looking Averil Godsell who had been in St Thomas Hospital when war broke out and had volunteered for the RAF Nursing Service. The next morning at about 6 am a sergeant orderly entered the four-bedroom ward and looking at his paper work said, "Pilot Officer Sampson, you are for the Ops Theatre at 0800, so pyjama jacket off and put it on back to front, and pyjama trousers discarded." I said this was OK except for the trousers but that as it was only my ankle discarding the trousers was not necessary. At this the sergeant got very up-tight and said,

"It is a Hospital rule regardless of the injury or complaint." To which I still replied in the negative and told him to "Buzz off!"

He went but soon reappeared with Sister Godsell who asked what the problem was. The sergeant confirmed,

"This officer refuses to remove his trousers." To this she said,

"Don't worry sergeant, once he's under the anaesthetic I'll whip them off!" My three ward companions naturally got a lot of mileage out of this and quizzed Sister Godsell for full details.

In the event they put my ankle in plaster and I was told, "Limited flying only and report back to the Hospital in three weeks." Paul Edge told me to proceed as normal, as I only used my foot on the rudder bar for taxying.

Sister Godsell, I remember, was very broad minded. In my tiny ward, with its four occupants, I had next to me an RAF doctor with some minor ailment. Now the Sister had some sort of problem with one of her legs—just a niggling pain. She asked this doctor chap if he'd mind looking at it for her. He agreed but asked why hadn't she seen one of the hospital medics; the place was stiff with doctors. She explained she didn't want to be involved with any of them.

So he said he'd take a look and asked the three of us to be gentlemen and avert our eyes, while she stood by his bed with her skirt raised well above thigh level. I recall that rather than averting our gaze we were all practically breaking our necks and almost falling out of bed to help with the diagnosis!

Soon I had reached a stage where a posting to an operational front-line squadron was not far off. I reflected on the outlook of the Royal Air Force. Unlike the pessimistic views we heard from Lord Gort and Sir Andrew Thorne, we pupils on the various courses were given pep-talks by carefully selected officers with strong operational backgrounds. They always gave the same message—we were going to defeat Germany because we are relentlessly winning the war in the air. I particularly remember Group Captain Basil Embry (later ACM Sir Basil GCB KBE DSO & three bars DFC AFC), telling us that the RAF's standard of technical excellence was way ahead of the Germans. Our organisation was based on sound principles with no interference from either the Army or Navy—thanks to Lord Trenchard. Embry stressed the point that we pilots were better trained and superior to our German counterparts. To emphasise this he reminded us that the opening rounds of the war had been won against great odds. This I assumed meant the Battle of Britain and not the Battle of France.

All that now remained for me was the final exercise with Geoffrey Baynham, covering air fighting. Aerial combat, known as "Dog-

Fighting" would be the final test, for the next time it would be for real. Pupils who had preceded me all had the same dismal experience to recount. Each confirmed that no sooner had the dog-fight commenced, then Geoff and his Spitfire were on their tail, and each knew that if this had indeed been the real thing they would have been promptly shot down. A sobering thought for us embrionic air fighters, keen to get to our squadrons and at the Germans!

When my name was posted on the notice board, indicating examination by Flight Lieutenant G T Baynham at 14.30 hours, I had some 2½ hours in which to think about it. I consulted Flight Sergeant Payne, another of the instructors, to see if he had any advice to give me. In the event he gave me some very bad advice because it involved a manoeuvre which, to date, I had not attempted. His advice was, and I quote: "The moment he gets on your tail, roll the Spitfire onto its back, open the throttle wide, pull the stick hard back into your stomach and just before the vertical, slam the stick hard to one side. The aeroplane will then go into a series of barrel rolls, gathering speed all the time, especially if you hold it just before the vertical. This manoeuvre makes it impossible for another pilot to follow, let alone get in any telling shot."

Armed with this 'gem', at 1430 I found myself in front of Geoffrey Baynham who briefed me as follows. "We will take off in formation and I shall be on your starboard side. Once we are airborne, move in as close as possible with your wing tip no more than two feet from my port wing tip and a few inches behind. We will climb to 32,000 feet and when you see my left hand raised, drift to about 500 yards to the left and as soon as your are ready, try to get on my tail." I responded that I understood, then we made our way to our respective Spitfire, climbed in and taxied to the runway. It was 29th April and I was in a Spitfire I. The previous day I had had my port tyre burst in another machine when landing with a 40 mph cross wind, and had damaged that Spit's prop. It was now my second flight on the 29th, having already flown Number Three in a three-man formation flight, led by Flying Officer Denville.

As the two of us climbed southwards over the Bristol Channel, I tucked my Spitfire as close as possible and he gave me the 'thumbs up' sign to indicate his satisfaction. Soon after passing 32,000 feet, we levelled off and Geoff raised his hand. As agreed, I swung my Spitfire off to the left until I was about 500 yards out. I was now ready, so I closed the throttle a bit in order to fall some 50 yards behind him, and then slamming the thottle right forward, I quickly climbed to turn towards his tail. Equally as quickly he dived towards me and passed under me, turning hard to the left. The situation had developed so quickly that he was now turning very steeply to his left and although I turned hard to my left I could see that he was gradually tightening the circle which would take him just moments, to position himself below and behind my tail!

Now was my moment to apply the 'gospel according to Flight Sergeant Payne'. I did exactly as he had advised and in no time, although tightly strapped in, I was being unceremoniously tossed from side to side in a most uncomfortable manner. After a few seconds I glanced at the sensitive altimeter. To my astonishment, what had started at 32,000 was now 15,000 feet, with the hands rapidly unwinding like those of a clock. I quickly decided to cancel the manoeuvre and see where Geoffrey was. To my horror I found I could not move the stick to the central position—it was stuck solidly to one side. In my gathering panic I forgot to close the throttle and I did what I suppose every pilot does when he wants to arrest the downwards dive. I got both hands on the stick and with all my strength, started to pull it back into the pit of my stomach.

To date, I had no real experience of the force of gravity and as I presumably succeeded in getting the stick back, all the blood went to the extremities, that is, my legs and feet. With that, I completely blacked out, in fact, passed out.

Some moments later I gradually regained consciousness to find the Spitfire flying straight and level some 150 feet above the sea! I was shivering and my teeth were chattering. I could hear Geoffrey calling me on the intercom radio but it took me some moments to be able to respond to the effect that I seemed to have lost him. He now instructed me to return to base and land. As I approached the circuit I could see that he had already landed and was taxying to the dispersal point.

When I entered his office some minutes later, I apologised for losing him. "That's alright," he said, "That was a good escape route, but if you want to avoid the dreaded Reaper, make sure you have got plenty of height or you will surely hit the deck." Later on I saw Flight Sergeant Payne who told me that I had done well, being the only pupil not to be 'shot down'. I thanked him but quietly hoped I would never find myself in a position where I should have to use it again.

CHAPTER III

CITY OF GLASGOW SQUADRON

In mid-May the OTU moved from Llandow to Roose, but my training days were now numbered. I had progressed onto the Spitfire II, flown several more dog-fighting sorties, formation flying and low-flying details. Then, towards the end of May my posting came through. I was to go to No. 602 (City of Glasgow) Squadron, a Royal Auxiliary Air Force unit, based at Redhill as part of the Kenley Wing, in 11 Group.

Geoff Baynham told me that 602 was commanded by Paddy Finucane, one of our top scoring fighter 'aces' of the time. He wished me luck, adding, "Keep your finger out and you should do well."

I had in fact met Finucane when I was on a few days leave from Kidlington. An Australian pupil pilot had taken me to 'Codgers', a pub behind Fleet Street in London, which was a meeting and watering place for Australians. Paddy was there with a red-headed Aussie named Keith 'Bluey' Truscott, as both were flight commanders with 452 Australian Spitfire Squadron.

I spent the first week of June 1942 flying dog-fight and aerobatic sorties, and then, with an Above Average assessment written in my log book and signed by Paul Edge, headed for Surrey. I had 'amassed' what I thought was an impressive 236 flying hours, and the 'deep end' was fast looming up!

By prior arrangement I was to go direct to Kenley, being met at Whyteleafe Railway Station. Kenley was on the top of a hill, the train station at the bottom, so I was pleased to be met at 3.30 pm and driven up the hill to the airfield. I was dumped at the dispersal area to meet both the Squadron Adjutant and Intelligence Officer. I was told that the CO was flying but was due to land at any moment. I wondered if he would remember me and sure enough, when he did land, he greeted me warmly with, "I hope you brought your kilt!"

He led me into an office where the paper work from my OTU was already on the desk. "I see you've done well," he commented, "there aren't many 'Above Averages' dished out by OTUs, and I'm glad to see that your Dog Fight assessment is even better than above average." "Can I see that, Sir?" I asked. He handed me Geoff Baynham's report. The piece dealing with aerial combat read—"An exceptionally good performance; the pilot is not afraid to throw his aircraft around the sky." I did not, of course, appraise Paddy of the truth but thought to myself, "How wrong you were, Geoff!"

I soon received the heartening news that the Squadron was short of pilots, having suffered severe losses over recent weeks, and that in consequence I might have to become 'operational' within a few days. It was, therefore, with a mixture of excitement and apprehension that I was introduced to the two Flight Commanders, John Niven DFC, from Edinburgh, whose Flight I was to join, and Eric Bocock DFC. Both had seen action, Johnny having joined the Squadron as a Sergeant Pilot, while Eric had flown previously with 72 Squadron prior to his promotion.

My impression then and one I had no reason to alter, was that both men were battle-hardened, experienced, fighter pilots. Bocock was the senior in that if for any reason the CO were not flying, then he took over.

I also met John Dennehey and a French chap, Roland de la Poype, nick-named 'Popeye', with whom I was to share a large bedroom. We all then went off to the Officer's Mess at Redhill for tea. The Mess was a large, magnificent red brick house belonging to Mr Benson, the watch maker. 'Barnbridge' was the name of the house and it had been requisitioned for the duration of the war. It was famous for the excellent food provided by a Czech cook by the name of Decmar. How he managed it on the rations available was one of the war's unsolved mysteries. His 'piece de resistance' were his marvellous cakes, usually produced when word reached him that the Squadron had shot down one or more Huns by lunch time.

After tea, John Dennehey took me off to another magnificent requisitioned house which was the sleeping quarters. There were five beds in our room and Johnny said, "Apart from Popeye's and mine, help yourself to any of the other three." I noticed one bed with the name tab—F/O C K Tait. "What happened to him?" I asked. "All three were shot down a few days ago," was his somewhat casual reply.

The Commanding Officer of the Sector and based at Kenley, was one half of the RAF's irrepressible Atcherley twins. This was Richard

'Batchy' Atcherley OBE AFC, who had been one of the famous Schneider Trophy Team in the early 1930s. (His twin brother was David.) Batchy was very keen on dining-in nights and the less formal 'drinks' evenings. He was famous and well known for his particular version of the hunting song "Do you ken John Peel". Now he had one arm in a sling because he had been shot down by a Focke Wulf 190 and had to take to his dinghy in the Dover Straits.

The Wing Commander Flying was a New Zealander, Edward Wells DSO DFC and bar, and due to his amazing eyesight and shooting ability was known to everyone as 'Hawkeye'. His Wing consisted of two Squadrons at Kenley, 611 (City of Liverpool)- another Auxiliary outfit, led by Douglas Watkins DFC—and the 485 (New Zealand) boys commanded by Squadron Leader Reg Grant DFC DFM. Grant was, I remember, under a bit of a cloud for he had been flying as wingman to Victor Beamish when the latter was shot down over the Channel on 27th March. He was later to die himself in a flying accident while his younger brother failed to return from a show over France, Reg actually shooting down the Hun who got him.

The other two Squadrons in the Wing were both at Redhill. 602 of course, and 402 Canadian Squadron commanded by R E 'Bob' Morrow DFC. All in all, it seemed, I was amongst some highly experienced fighter pilots and air leaders.

Paddy had told me that that evening we would all be going to the White Hart in Reigate (not to be confused with the Biggin Hill's local, the White Hart at Brasted) where we would be joined by our Sergeant Pilots. Amongst those were two outstanding fighter pilots, Bill Loud and Arthur Strudwick. I've already mentioned that Bill Loud was later to become a Wing Leader, and Strudwick too later won the DFC, and eventually retired as an Air Commodore, CB. Perhaps I should mention here that our Frenchman, de la Poype, later went to Russia to fly with the French volunteers in the 'Normandie Groupe', with whom he shot down some 16 German aircraft. After the war he was to settle down in Paris, married to the daughter of the wealthy English Paget family.

That evening Johnny Niven filled me in on what was happening. Paddy had put me in his Flight, he had said, because being a Scot, I, along with all other 'foreigners' went to A Flight, while Eric Bocock had all the English types. John also filled me in on some of the gossip which included the fact that 602 Squadron's claims in air combat, and those of Paddy Finucane himself, had been under official scrutiny. This episode has been well covered by author Doug Stokes in his biography of Paddy (*Paddy Finucane—Fighter Ace*, published by Wm Kimber Ltd, 1983).

The previous Wing Leader, Wing Commander R Finley Boyd DSO DFC, one of the original AAF members of 602, had instigated the investigation and in the event, to quote a legal term, the case was "not proven". It is also interesting to relate that apart from 602's claims being investigated, other squadrons, notably Sailor Malan's old 74 and the first Polish Squadron—303—commanded at one time by Ronald Kellett, had also been 'looked at'.

The result of the 602 investigation made Paddy rather bitter and so upset him that from then on he refused to involve himself in a half share if another member had also fired at the same Hun. He also refused to put in a claim for damage to an enemy aircraft. I recollect one incident when the Squadron bounced four FW190s. Paddy got many hits on one of them and then told Sergeant Francis, his No.2, to finish it off. When the boys returned to base, Francis was told to put in a claim for the destruction but Paddy himself made no claim at all.

At the fairly frequent Mess parties held at Kenley, Batchy Atcherley used to invite officer friends from other Stations and I soon met Adolf 'Sailor' Malan DSO & bar DFC & bar, and Jamie Rankin DSO DFC & bar, the Biggin Hill Station Commander and Wing Leader respectively. Jamie, another Scot, had a repertoire of bawdy Scottish ditties. I was able to help him out on one occasion when he got stuck for a verse of 'The Ball at Kirriemuir'!

Very soon after arriving at Redhill there was an Officer's Mess Party. Free drink, a spectacular Buffet and dancing to the Station Band. I decided to play it all 'low key' being the new boy so I spent some time chatting to Flight Officer Broadhurst, Harry Broadhurst's wife (they divorced later). She was in her thirty's and considered by us a very nice and charming 'mother' figure.

Eric Bocock eventually came up saying, "Sammy, your glass is empty; come and have a refill." I suspect he thought I needed to be rescued.

Some few minutes later we were standing in a corner chatting, when a beautiful young girl, not unlike the future Marilyn Munroe, came up to us. Looking at me she said, "I haven't seen you before, who are you?" Eric then interrupted, saying, "This is Sammy and without doubt the most famous chap in the room. He played Rugger for Scotland." I detected a slight clouding over of her face, confirmed when she looked at me and said, "You Rugger Buggers aren't worth a fuck!" and promptly walked away. At the time I was more shaken by her language than by the brush-off.

A topic sometimes discussed by Atcherley, with Watkins, Malan and others, was just referred to the 'Unholy Alliance'. Later on when I got to know Douglas Watkins well, I quizzed him on it and he told me it referred to Air Marshal Trafford Leigh-Mallory and Air Marshal Sholto Douglas, who had got together and bull-dozed the rather weak Air Minister, Sir Archibald Sinclair, into forcing the retirement of Air Chief Marshal Sir Hugh Dowding from his post of C-in-C Fighter Command. The result was that Sholto Douglas got Fighter Command, while Leigh Mallory got 11 Group. The erstwhile boss of the premier 11 Group, Sir Keith Park, was posted away.

It has often been thought that Churchill must have agreed with these sorry changes, Dowding and Park being cruelly treated after winning the Battle of Britain. However, Churchill's biographer, Martin Gilbert, in a letter to *The Times* in 1986, made it clear that Sinclair was suggesting Dowding go as early as July 1940—ie, before the Battle began. Churchill managed to resist that, in fact had his full confidence. Undoubtedly, Churchill was remembering the recent gallant stand which Dowding made when Churchill was wanting to pour more fighters into the Battle of France, at the possible expense of the defence of Britain. Dowding had stood up to Churchill and it seems the great man respected him for it.

Finally in late 1940, Sinclair and the Air Staff unanimously urged that Dowding be removed as C-in-C, and with such weight behind them, Churchill had to agree and accept their advice. Churchill still stressed his admiration for the man and even suggested Dowding later be given an operational command but Sinclair and the Air Staff refused.

It seems to me that the Unholy Alliance was indeed very powerful and by virtue of having both the Air Minister and the Chief of the Air Staff under control, so to speak, they were able to deny Churchill's wishes that Dowding should still be retained in another senior post.

However, all this occurred before my time in Fighter Command, but the scandal of it still rankles in the minds of many of Dowding's fighter boys from the Battle of Britain era.

My first job was to settle into the operational routine of both 602 Squadron and of the Kenley Wing. I had my first flight in one of the Squadron's Spitfire Vbs on June 10th, flying for 85 minutes on what every pilot knows as a Sector Recce; ie, flying around for air experience and to become familiar with the surroundings to the airfields, in my case both Kenley and Redhill. For the next few days

I flew a variety of practise sorties, and by the 18th I had added a further 13 or 14 hours to my meagre flying hours total.

Having spent these first few days getting used to the feel of the Vb and testing the armament, which consisted of two 20 mm cannons and four .303 machine guns, I took my turn at Readiness—waiting close to the aircraft to Scramble in case enemy aircraft were reported. I was with John Dennehey at 10 am but just 15 minutes later we got the Scramble. As soon as we were airborne the Controller came over the radio telephone (R/T), telling us to climb to 30,000 feet in a north-easterly direction as an unidentified aircraft was coming into Essex from Holland.

Soon after take-off we entered cloud at 4,000 feet above the ground and knew from information supplied by the weather people that this would be solid up to 20,000 feet. As we climbed I had tucked my Spitfire right in close to John's—I suppose some two feet away from his wing tip, in order not to lose contact with him. The turbulence got worse as we headed up and suddenly Johnny made a violent lurch dangerously towards me. As I took avoiding action I lost him and then I was spinning down. I closed the throttle and looked at the altimeter which showed 12,000 feet. I remembered that at 4,000 I should come out of the cloud and when I saw daylight I quickly adjusted the controls to come out of the spin, then looked around to see if I could recognise the land below.

Suddenly, when I had sorted things out and I was at 2,000 feet, I noticed with horror that balloons were slightly above me. I was in fact on the eastern end of the London Balloon Barrage! I could see the River Thames so dived down to it as there were no cable anchors in the river. I then flew down the Thames until I was out of the barrage, then set course for Redhill. (I was to have a similar experience in 1945 over Antwerp.) In the meantime, I had heard the Controller saying, "Return to base—it's a friendly." There were no repercussions when I landed as Johnny had also been buffetted to such an extent that he almost lost total control.

Then came my first real operational sortie. Nothing very glorious or glamorous, merely a routine convoy patrol to 18 ships in the Channel just off Beachy Head. I flew as No.2 to Bill Loud for 1½ hours, our role being to intercept any would-be attempt at a hit-and-run raid on our charges. The next day I flew wingman to Arthur Strudwick on a similar sortie but again nothing interfered with our peaceful pursuit.

Then came my first real taste of war flying. On June 20th, Fighter Command and 2 Group of Bomber Command mounted Circus

No.193. A dozen Douglas Boston light bombers (actually only 11 turned up) of 88 Squadron were to attack the power station at Le Havre, and the Kenley Wing were to provide Target Support. This meant that we would fly direct to the target area to intercept any enemy fighters which decided to interfere with the Bostons, while other Wings provided both Close Escort and High Cover.

As the Bostons came to the target area, we were flying Top Cover for the Wing and over the radio we could hear that enemy fighters had indeed been spotted but the brief battle went on 5,000 feet below us and of course, we could not go down and leave the other units unprotected from above. Wing Commander Wells was leading 611 Squadron below and the intention was that if fighters attacked, some of us would hopefully be able to surprise them from behind. It didn't work out like that because the Huns were in two separate formations.

One attacked the bombers and the other came after 602. Paddy warned the Wing Leader who with another 611 pilot, each shot down a Focke Wulf, then our only hope was to scream for home. I had great difficulty in keeping my eyes on my own friends *and* the FW190s which were gradually overhauling us. Eventually when I saw one of them firing his guns, I reacted so viciously that I got into a spin and when I had sorted that out at about 1,000 feet above the water, I was on my own, so headed for home. Paddy wasn't too pleased at me losing the formation but I was not alone as two other pilots were also guilty.

The next thing I knew was that Paddy Finucane was leaving us. He was promoted to Wing Commander, and given the Hornchurch Wing. We said our farewells and good lucks, and awaited our new Boss. In the interim we had a number of farewell drinks parties and the morning after one of these, I was down for a Convoy Patrol and seeing Johnny Niven told him I was not looking forward to it with my thick head. His advice was to go to my Spitfire, switch on the oxygen before take-off and it would clear my hangover. This I did and it certainly worked.

The normal procedure for using oxygen was that for Convoy Patrols or Scrambled for tip-and-run raiders, the oxygen was not switched on before take-off. For Sweeps etc, and certainly when knowing we'd be flying above 8,000 feet, oxygen was switched on before take-off. After the advice from Johnny I invariably switched on the oxygen regardless. It did cause comment from the Stores Officer who remarked on my consumption but I took no notice!

Our new CO turned out to be Squadron Leader P M Brothers DFC, another Battle of Britain veteran. I had been very proud to be in the Squadron commanded by Paddy. Unfortunately when the only warlike activities were being conducted by the RAF, the press latched onto Paddy and he was subjected to some extravagant journalese, to such an extent that there was quite a lot of jealousy from pilots in other squadrons, not to mention other commanding officers.

However, Pete Brothers was a very different type of pilot and leader to Paddy, and one whom I was to admire greatly. We would see much of each other over the next two years of war. He was, of course, a good deal more experienced operationally than Paddy. When the Battle of Britain commenced in the early summer of 1940, he was already a flight commander in 32 Squadron and his personal score of enemy aircraft destroyed during the Battle was well into double figures. He was then promoted to Squadron Leader and put in command of a newly formed Australian squadron. When Pete arrived to take over 602, he made no bones of the fact that there had been a clash of personalities between him and the Australian Parlimentary Minister who was in the UK looking after the interests of the Australian Military.

The Minister had been Dr H V Evatt, who had come to arrange for 457 and 452 Australian Squadrons to return home to help defend northern Australia against the Japanese. Pete had no wish to go with them and complained to Air Vice-Marshal Hugh 'Dingbat' Saunders, the SASO of 11 Group, only to be told that Winston Churchill had said how splendid it was that a Battle of Britain veteran should lead the squadrons in the coming Battle of Australia! As Pete knew he would never get to see Churchill, he was as rude as possible to Evatt but to no effect, leaving Pete no choice but to pack and be ready to depart. Two days before sailing, Evatt returned home, which was what Fighter Command had been waiting for, and Pete was promptly taken off the boat.

Pete then came to us, where he arrived with a score to date of 10 enemy aircraft destroyed. Personally I felt that the Australians' loss was certainly our gain.

Now we could hopefully look forward to some more action, or in my own case, 'some' action!

CHAPTER IV

ACTION AT LAST

Two days after my inglorious exit from France, we were off again, escorting 12 Bostons who were going after a 4,000-ton ship in Dunkirk harbour. 602 Squadron led the Wing at 18,000 feet, but we saw nothing except some flak off to our starboard side over Gravelines. Then on the 26th we swept the French coast from Cap Gris Nez to Dieppe in support of a Roadstead, but again nothing was about for us.

In between these major ops we, along with most other fighter squadrons, were tasked with routine convoy patrols and anti-rhubarb patrols, in order to combat the ever-present danger of bomb-carrying Me109s to FW190s, in hit and run raids on coastal towns and targets. These latter sorties were usually flown by a section of two Spitfires, a few thousand feet above the sea. High enough for us to spot and have a chance of diving on any would-be raiders, and I suppose, high enough for enemy radar to pick us up and know we were there waiting for their fighters to try something. By the same token, I guess, they could try and pick us off, but I don't think they ever tried that trick too often—thankfully.

I flew one each of these patrols on the 26th and 27th. On the latter date Bill Loud and I were on an anti-rhubarb patrol and after becoming airborne we were told that a plot showed two bogeys approaching Beachy Head at low level. We headed towards them, out to sea, and were later told they were two Me109s, but we failed to find them. These sort of shows had all the makings of a dangerous situation, for often more than one section were either Scrambled, or were on standing patrols, and at low level and high speed, with everyone looking for that fleeting sight of a couple of single-engined fighters, mistakes in identification could easily occur.

It was only a couple of days later that just such a situation developed, which cost the life of the Biggin Hill Station Commander,

Group Captain P R Barwell DFC. We had all been active with these hit and run raiders and Bobby Oxspring, the CO of 91 Squadron, whose unit was often concerned with these Germans, went to 'Dickie' Barwell to try and sort out a plan to curb their activities. On 1st July, Barwell, a very press-on type despite his rank and position, and who had often flown with Sailor Malan and the Wing on shows over France during the summer of 1941, Scrambled as Number Two to Bobby, to go after a couple of Hun fighters. However, the Controllers also sent out a section from Tangmere, who, unfortunately, were not experienced. The upshot was that the two sections met in poor visibility. The Tangmere boys came out of the glare of a setting sun, fully expecting to find 109s, and seeing fighters ahead of them, convinced themselves in those fleeting moments that they had indeed found the enemy. Barwell's Spitfire was shot down and he was killed.

There was a massive inquest of course, and anyone flying that evening was subjected to intense examination by Group Captain Atcherley. I remember him saying over a drink in the Mess, "There is an official questionnaire procedure for these occasions and if there had been a dog in the cockpit with a pilot, it would also have to answer some questions!"

It was back to first league stuff on the 20th—Circus 193. The target for Bostons from 88 Squadron was the power station at Le Havre and the Kenley Wing was again assigned as Target Support Wing.

Soon after the Bostons had dropped their bombs we were below two separate formations each of about ten FW190s. They were definitely stalking us but we were in no position to take them on. Eric Bocock was leading the Squadron this day and he called the Wing Leader that he was going to dive away at right angles to the bombers, towards the coast, with the idea of drawing off the two gaggles of 190s. I was flying Yellow 4 at the back of the Squadron, the position known as 'Arse-end Charlie'. I must say I was very frightened, for the moment we dived I could see about 20 black and white crosses, not to mention those evil looking swastikas, all diving towards us. As we had the initiative in the dive we momentarily left them behind but soon they started to overhaul us.

Eric shouted to me to tighten my turn and get ready to break as there was a Focke Wulf starting to menace me. That was really more than I could bear and taking my eyes off the Spitfire in front of me, I turned my head to look back and to my horror there were in fact two 190s on either beam. Whichever way I turned I would give one of them a straight shot at me.

Part of the 190's armament is the equivalent of two 20 millimetre cannon (MG/FFs), one in each wing, in addition to two MG17 machine guns, plus two MG17s firing from the upper part of the engine cowling. The cannon shells were set to explode at 450 yards or upon impact. Suddenly I saw shells exploding, puffs about the size of a large orange, some ten feet to the right of my wing—so I knew at once they had the range. As I pulled hard to the left I felt a most earth-shattering explosion just behind my cockpit and the whole of my perspex canopy disappeared. Without further ado I was tossed willy-nilly into a spin.

I reckoned I'd been shot down because with no hood to deaden the sound and with the atmospheric elements pouring in, I feared the worst. As I was spinning down I weighed up the two alternatives facing me. I could bale out at 1,500 feet and float about in the dinghy attached to my parachute pack, or I could endeavour to regain enough control to make a belly landing on the water—ditching as it is called. At about 1,500 feet on the altimeter I took the necessary action to get the Spitfire out of the spin and to my utter surprise it reacted perfectly, so perfectly that I decided to try for England.

Dropping down to zero feet I set course for the south coast, making landfall near RAF Tangmere where I landed. An examination of the Spit showed that I had in fact only received one bullet which had hit the external release pin of the canopy—hence its sudden disappearance into space. I later rang Eric who told me to get a new canopy fixed at Tangmere. He also said that he had managed to get some shots at the two FW190s menacing me which, I reflected, had stopped them finishing me off.

The Engineering Officer at Tangmere suggested I should go to the Mess and have a drink—it was 2 o'clock. When I entered the bar I saw Jamie Rankin talking to Sailor Malan. Jamie remembered me from the Mess party at Kenley and invited me to join them for a pint of beer. Over this I described my somewhat dismal experiences to date, as it seemed to me I was continually on the wrong end of the 190s. When I finished, Sailor turned to me and in his slow South African accent, said, "Think nothing of it, Laddie. You're obviously not destined for the chop!"

I got to know Jamie Rankin very well in the early 1960s when, having retired from the RAF, he was appointed Commandant of the Air Training Corps in Scotland. He had ended the war as an Air Commodore, with the DSO & bar, DFC & bar, Belgian Croix de Guerre, and 21 Germans shot down. Sadly he did not last long. He was a latent victim of the war years during which time he proved to be one of the outstanding Wing Leaders in a period when our Spitfire Vb was a little behind in performance to the FW190. Some of his close friends say that he did not really treat alcohol with the respect it deserves.

I had survived these first actions more by luck than judgement and soon came to realise what men like Johnny Niven and Eric Bocock had been telling all us junior pilots. Both men possessed an air of confidence and both drummed home the fact that as the Spitfire Vb could always out-turn the Me109F and FW190, there was no reason to be defeated in aerial combat. The Huns usually relied on the Jump or Bounce and if they saw the Spitfire break at 500-600 yards, they immediately half rolled and quickly disappeared. The odd Hun pilot who did have a go was usually somewhat inexperienced and more often than not paid the penalty. As a completely inexperienced pilot officer, I found both Johnny and Eric helpful and encouraging.

Under Pete Brothers, the Squadron continued operations in July. I flew as No.2 to Flight Lieutenant J S Fifield on the 2nd, Scrambled to chase a couple of 109s over the Channel, but the plot faded and we saw nothing. We also flew a couple of Roadstead shows, Hurribombers of 402 RCAF Squadron looking for enemy shipping off the French coast, but I was not unhappy when we found an empty sea, for German flak ships were notoriously accurate with their defensive fire. However, on the second show we were fired at by the flak gunners in Boulogne harbour.

Our last show was a Diversionary Sweep to Circus 199. Bostons from 107 Squadron were attacking the Boulogne marshalling yards, so we headed for nearby Abbeville in the hope of catching German fighters coming up from the airfield there. We collected some flak from the Somme area and then four FW190s passed over us at about 2,000 feet higher, and they chased us back, giving our Number 4's the usual testing few moments. Then about 20 more 190s were spotted sitting above and behind us, just waiting to pounce if we began to turn, but we didn't. Upon landing, however, Flying Officer Innes-Jones was missing, nobody seeing him go.

Then on the 15th came the disastrous news that our recent CO, Paddy Finucane, was missing believed killed. He had led the Hornchurch Wing on an attack on a German encampment just inland from the French coast, and coming out at low level, his Spitfire had been hit in the radiator. He attempted to ditch but his Spit dug its nose in and went straight down. Paddy probably hit his head on the gunsight and was knocked out, so went to the bottom of the sea with his fighter, some eight miles off Le Touquet.

I was particularly sad, for he had been my first CO, and although

I had known him for only a short time, admired him greatly.
I remember one Op we flew when he led the Squadron off the French
coast and we were fired at by shore guns. With shells hitting the water
all around us, Paddy's somewhat risky comment was, "Bloody awful
shooting!"

I reflected on Johnny Niven's earlier prophetic remark that
"No Hun fighter will ever get him." On subsequent reflection, as I
progressed, gaining experience, my one and only criticism of Paddy
Finucane was that he still stuck to the line astern formation for the
squadron. This meant that the squadron commander leading from
the centre had three Spitfires in line astern and likewise the flight
commanders, one to his left and one to the right. All this added up
to the fact that if the Huns got the Bounce (you see the enemy and
are ready for their attack)—or worse still, the Jump (the enemy is not
seen and the first you know is one or more of the Number 4s is shot
down). The wretched three Number 4s were always the first potential
victims.

Flying 'Arse-end Charlie'—Number 4 in a section—was always
a dangerous position, especially in the line astern formation.
I remember there was a RAF Doctor, Group Captain H W Corner
AFC, who amongst other things, specialised in pilot stress etc.
He used to fly as a guest occasionally to get some first-hand experience
of what fighter pilots endured. When I joined 602 Squadron, I was
told that he had recently been on a Sweep with 602, flying as Number
4 and had been shot down and lost. Paddy and the Squadron were in
poor odour on that score.[1]

Referring back to the many controversial opinions as to Paddy's
ability and his score of 32 enemy aircraft destroyed in aerial combat,
those who flew with him on many occasions, such as Bluey Truscott,
Bocock and Johnny Niven, were quite adamant that he did in fact
destroy that number and probably more. Bocock and Niven had been
furious when there was a claims query. They knew what outsiders
didn't, that Finucane always got in very close to his victims before he
opened fire, very often as close as 100 to 150 yards. In the whole of
my subsequent experience I enjoyed two separate occasions when I
got as close as 150 yards to a FW190 or Me109, and there is no doubt
whatsoever, that although we were taught that our guns were
harmonised to converge the bullets and shells at 250 yards, I found

---

[1] Group Captain Hugh Corner AFC, killed in action on Circus 137, 25th April 1942.
Shot down by a FW190 over the Channel, he baled out but was too late for his
parachute to open before he hit the sea. He was due to be promoted to Air
Commodore.

150 yards eliminated all doubt as to whether you damaged or destroyed the opposition.

It would be invidious to compare Paddy with Pete Brothers; they were both quite different in their brilliant ways. Pete was more mature, of course, having been commissioned into the RAF at the beginning of 1936. He was also more reserved. Paddy, being Irish, was inclined to blow his top if an operation had not gone according to plan, whereas Pete never did and was always calm and self-controlled. I flew under the command of five squadron commanders and six wing leaders and I have no doubt in my mind that the best all-round leader was Pete Brothers.

The very next day we were ordered to move to Peterhead, Aberdeenshire—out of the Front Line—for a rest! The evening before we left Kenley, we attended a Mess Dinner at which Batchy Atcherley bade us farewell and also welcomed a new Wing Leader. This was Brian Kingcome DFC & bar, who had arrived to take over from Hawk Wells.

I felt I hardly needed a rest, having been with the Squadron for such a short time but to the north I went, grateful perhaps, in the knowledge that I might live a bit longer, and that I was going back to my native Scotland. However, the first day at Peterhead, Flying Officer Rippon and I were Scrambled after two bandits were plotted way out in the North Sea, and although we chased ahead for 15 minutes, they stayed about 60 miles out and then they faded from the radar screens.

Peterhead is about 25 miles north of the City of Aberdeen, and although officially on rest, our job would be to defend that eastern stretch of the Scottish coast, especially from German long-range recce aircraft that would be watching for convoys or major Naval ships in and around Scapa Flow Naval base.

The one thing, however, that most of us with a Scottish background knew was that Peterhead, being mostly bog, had been chosen as an escape-proof prison for dangerous criminals. Needless to say, the airfield had been constructed on the bog! We spent our time practice flying and doing convoy patrols, plus, of course, maintaining a Readiness State in case the Huns decided to raid Aberdeen where, incidentally, B Flight, under Eric Bocock, was based at the RAF Station at Dyce, just to the north west of the City.

One amusing and interesting officer was Flight Lieutenant Duncan Brown, the Station Intelligence Officer. Before volunteering he was the Headmaster of a junior secondary school at Lockerbie, Dumfrieshire. He was a raconteur, a piano player, a performer off the

cuff at parties and a very good Bridge player. A piece of poetry by
Duncan is worth recording:

Wanderings of a Wingless Wonder

At Inverness where I have been
The mighty on their thrones I've seen,
Wing Commanders by the score
Squadron Leaders too galore,
An odd Flight-Loot, an odd F-O,
The 'Bog Rats' in that dazzling show.
Amidst that glittering troop,
That galaxy of Fourteen Group,
I there appeared, believe or no,
A humble, lowly, young P-O.
I viewed the world with niery a care,
I admired the Highland scenery there,
Enjoyed the wine, the WAAF, the song,
Did all things right and nothing wrong.
Said "Yes Sir", "No Sir", morn and noon,
Then packed my bags for Castleto'on,
Where Pentland's Firth roars cold and grey
And Orkney lowers across the way,
Midst storms and tempests, wind and foam,
Stands Castletown's muddy aerodrome,
'Twas there that I came face to face
With Britain's foremost fighter ace.
In treeless Caithness wide domain,
One felt the hand of death had lain,
The countryside I well recall,
Just miles and miles of bugger-all,
A weary lonesomeness was found,
And every mother's son was browned.
And so to pass the time of day,
A game of Bridge we used to play.
Ye Gods, the pangs of deep depression,
They led to many a drunken session.
And lads in normal times demure,
Would sing the 'Ball of Kirriemuir',
At midnight hour the rafters rang,
As bawdy songs we oftimes sang,
Then barely conscious, nearly dead,
We'd slowly stagger off to bed,

They didn't have to ask me twice,
To pack my bags and make for Dyce.
Six miles from Aberdeen,
As fair a town as e'er I've seen,
For wine, women, love and laughter,
Forget old boy, the morning after.
'Twas a veritable paradise,
The coastal aerodrome of Dyce.
The boys in 'A' Flight, Six-Oh-Two,
You'll never meet a finer crew,
Sad day for me, and others,
The parting from Peter Brothers.
It fairly made my heart to bleed,
The thought of going to Peterhe'ed,
For Peterhead it beats them all,
There's nothing there to see at all.

Per Ardua Ad Nauseam....

The weather in that part of the world was variable and usually blowing a gale. Looking at my flying log book I see that between the 29th of July and the 15th of August I was airborne on only twelve occasions for a total of just seven hours flying. Despite the enforced inactivity, there were moments when we were reminded of our task, such as the evening of August 7th, when we were Scrambled. It was just on dusk when two Ju88s decided to bomb Aberdeen harbour. Visibility was poor and although the Controller told us we were very near the Hun bombers we could just not obtain any visual sign of them, although we quickly became aware of the Aberdeen 'ack-ack' fire! We landed after nearly an hour of chasing about, the last 20 minutes being logged as night flying.

There was greater excitement when on 15th August, we received instructions to move down to Biggin Hill the following day and that the reason was Top Secret. I had personally been flown up to Peterhead in a Harrow transport 'plane, but now I flew back down in my Spitfire, marked LO-K, which was the machine I invariably flew. I was no longer the squadron 'Bog Rat', so was deemed sensible enough to have my own aeroplane. We refuelled at Kirton-in-Lindsay and the next day we found ourselves being briefed by the Biggin Wing Leader, Wing Commander E H 'Tommy' Thomas DFC, for a Sweep over the Dunkirk area. Thomas would be leading the Wing, which comprised 602 and 222 Squadrons, with 165 Squadron making rendezvous over Canterbury.

However, something went wrong because 165 failed to rendezvous and 222 were late taking off. There was a lot of belly-aching from Thomas as we headed for Le Touquet and meantime, the Group Controller was reporting strong Hun reaction behind Dunkirk, so Thomas called the show off when we were about 15 miles out and we returned to base; not a very impressive effort.

Next day Pete asked permission to repeat the show, but as a two squadron Wing, and the necessary permission for 222 Squadron to join us was granted. We had an early lunch and then Pete briefed us. We were to take off and fly at zero feet until we were half way across the Channel, where we would then climb rapidly to 20,000 feet to reach the French coast at that height. We would then turn and fly down the coast and when near Calais, turn inland towards St Omer, the strongest German fighter base, with the object, as Pete put it, "To stir them up!"

As was to be expected, there was in fact a quick reaction from St Omer and the Controller kept giving us the position and height of some of two separate formations of Huns, one of 6+ and the other of 10+. Thanks to Pete's leadership, it seemed apparent that if contact was made we at least had the height advantage by some 1,500 feet. Suddenly Johnny Niven on the right of the Squadron reported six FW190s coming towards us from below our starboard quarter and ordered his Yellow Section of four to break. Sergeant Gledhill, flying No.4, was a bit slow and was shot down, finishing up as a prisoner of war.

Both Johnny and I got bursts at the turning 190s but neither of us made any claim. I shoot pheasants from time to time so I knew I was behind. The other gaggle was apparently concentrating on 222 Squadron to our left and as they came between our two squadrons both a pilot in 222 and Pete Brothers got killing bursts so two 190s finished up in the sea. Pilot Officer Peter Davey, a New Zealander in our Squadron, was hit but managed to struggle back and force land at Hawkinge.

We were not sure about the CO's kill and it was not until our missing pilot turned up that he asked who had got the 190 that went into the sea. Apparently after being hit he had spun down and as he recovered, saw a Focke Wulf splash down. Pete asked if anyone else was claiming; certainly Johnny and I weren't, so Pete was rightly credited.

Whilst at tea, still chatting excitedly over the afternoon scrap, we were told that there was a briefing in the Intelligence Office at 1800 hours. At first we thought there was going to be a late show put on but then the base was sealed off, so we quickly realised that something big was on. We must, of course, been brought down from Peterhead for something specific, so this seemed to be it. We marched off to the the briefing with a mixture of excitement and apprehension.

CHAPTER V

DIEPPE

We assembled noisily in the Intelligence Office until silenced by the arrival of the Station Commander, Group Captain J R Hallings-Pott DFC AFC, Tommy Thomas and the Station 'Spy'—Squadron Leader B E de le Torre. Spy de le Torre stunned us into silence as he outlined the plan for dawn the next day, the plan of 'Operation Jubilee'—a commando-style raid on a grand scale upon the French port at Dieppe.

It was a Combined Operation, involving Army, Navy and Air Force. British commandos, including the Lovat Scouts under Lord Lovat himself, would storm ashore just on dawn at either side of the port, while the main assault would be in the hands of Canadian troops whose job it was to take and secure the harbour, hold it for most of the day while its installations, and a nearby airfield were blown up, then retire by mid-afternoon. It all sounded pretty risky to me, but I supposed that the planners had done their homework.

The Navy would take the men in, and a huge air armada would provide smoke, bomb and cannon attacks as well as a mighty air umbrella throughout the period of the raid. One thing was certain— the German Luftwaffe would react in force. With our offensive Sweeps, Circuses, Rodeos, Ramrods, Roadsteads, etc, reaction from the Luftwaffe was never certain, but they wouldn't sit it out on the ground on the morrow. We were in for a fight.

De le Torre warned us that each squadron would probably fly as many as four sorties and that he would later inform each squadron commander the take-off times and the areas we were to patrol, and patrol for one hour, 45 minutes. If for any reason (and the possibilities seemed endless) we ran short of fuel, arrangements had been made for pilots to land at Friston, by Beachy Head, to refuel before returning to Biggin. A more sobering arrangement was that if for any reason (and the chances seemed even more endless) a pilot had to bale out or force land over Dieppe itself, there was a small landing ground just inland from the port where we would find a jeep ready to drive us into the harbour—four miles away—and put us on a ship which would bring us back to England. With all this ringing in our ears, we adjourned to the Mess for a drink, having been told the base was now secure and that we could not leave nor make any telephone calls.

Later Pete told us of our patrol timings. Our first take off was scheduled for 5.30 am, our second at 9, the third at 11.30, and fourth at 2 pm. Breakfast would be available at 4.30, thereafter hot snacks would be served at our Dispersal points in case any of the timings had to be altered through circumstances. Johnny Niven remarked to me, "I hope the shithouse is in good order at Dispersal!" I asked why. "Because," he said, "every time I am scheduled for an offensive Op I get the equivalent of a dose of salts and it's no different if it's a lavatory or a cemetery, when you've got to go, your've sure got to go!"

Pete told us that he'd brief us before each show to decide our height and positions over the ships. He also made certain we were aware that the Navy had orders to fire at anything flying below 8,000 feet, so told us to be careful when over the convoy. We all went to bed early and were awakened at 3.30. It was still dark but the Batman told us that the skies were clear and cloudless. We were up and ready very quickly, 222 Squadron actually being at Readiness by 3.15! Already the armada of small ships taking in the commandos and the Canadians to a day they would never forget, were within a few miles of a very hostile coast.

We of course knew that all our front-line airfields were 'chock-a-block' with aircraft and squadrons in order to provide a continuous air umbrella over the Operation. As we assembled at our Dispersal area, Pete told us that we would be on the north side of the ships and the harbour, and that once we reached the area we would separate into our fours and keep a wide circle on the look-out for any enemy activity which he reckoned would probably come from a northerly direction.

Whenever now I think of the Dieppe Operation I have, believe it or not, 'nightmares' because during three of our four sorties, I was presented with four 'sitting ducks' in the form of two FW190s and two Dornier 217 twin-engined bombers. And on three of the four occasions, I fell into the trap of the most inexperienced fighter pilot, namely the desire to fire one's guns immediately and unnecessarily at too great a range.

We were airborne at 5.50am, 402 and 611 Squadrons also at Biggin, having left half an hour earlier. As we headed out over Beachy Head the sun was just appearing over France although it was still quite dark. We could see ships below us on the dark sea, and ahead of us flashes of gunfire on the enemy coast. It had started.

When we arrived at the north end of Dieppe and to the north of the main convoy of ships, we began, as previously arranged, to patrol from south to north while always keeping the ships in view and being ready to expect reaction from the north. Our section led by Johnny was to patrol at 8,000 feet, the other two at 9,000 and 10,000. Half way through our patrol which was to last one hour, dawn finally disappeared and the sun began to show itself.

I was looking down and behind at the ships when I suddenly saw two FW190s climbing away in a northerly direction from them. I reported them to Johnny saying that they would, if they didn't see us, appear to our front. Well, they didn't see us and nicely presented themselves about 500 yards ahead. It was obvious that Johnny would take the one on the left and I would take the one to the right. As soon as the 190 was the same height as myself, I opened fire with a quick burst which certainly woke them up and they quickly dived towards the land. I saw one strike on my 190 before it dived, pouring white smoke, indicative of damage to its petrol tank as the high octane fuel vapourised in the cool morning air. Johnny saw it go down, confirming it for me.

When we landed back at Biggin Hill, I claimed a damaged but as the Intelligence Officer was writing it down, he said, "We'll have a look at the camera gun film." In the event the damaged was upgraded to 'probably destroyed'. I was told to fill out my first combat report, which read:

> 19 August 1942.   Time: 0635 hrs.   8,000 ft. Dieppe.
>
> "I was flying Yellow 2 in 602 Squadron when Yellow 1 reported two FW190s flying north east. I followed Yellow 1, turning with EA starboard. I saw Yellow 1 pick out the port aircraft so I took the starboard aircraft and delivered a short burst of one second each of cannon and machine gun. The EA went into a spiral to starboard, diving down towards Dieppe emitting very thick white smoke. Yellow 1 ordered me not to follow down and I broke away at about 4,000 ft."

Pete had, I discovered, also had a go at another 190 and also claimed a damaged. 611 Squadron had been bounced and had lost one of its Free French pilots, but Douglas Watkins had shot down a 190 which was seen to crash land west of Dieppe. Some of the boys were also reporting seeing a ship blow up.

We had little time to reflect on all this, for we were told that we would soon be off again, and already our ground crews were busily engaged in rearming and refuelling our Spitfires. Pete briefed us once more, telling us that we would be flying south of the ships and at heights of 4-5,000 feet as it was expected that Hun bombers would soon be operating. Our second take-off was timed for 8.30, but in fact we did not take off until after 10. We were on patrol with 133 Eagle Squadron and about half way across to our patrol area we spotted a He111 flying in the same direction as ourselves about 1,000 feet above us. The Germans saw us too and quickly disappeared into some cloud which was adjacent to it.

Pete took us to about midway of the convoy which stretched about five to six miles from the harbour and we started our patrol, flying in a square, always keeping the ships in sight. Over the R/T came sounds of combat, so we knew things were warming up. Then, as we completed our second square and were flying towards Dieppe, I saw three Dorniers which I rapidly reported to Johnny, as they headed towards the harbour.

This was reaction indeed, for it was rare for anyone to see German bombers in daylight at this stage of the war in the West. They were usually confined to night bombing or perhaps the odd attack on shipping but here were twin-engined bombers out in force. As we now know they were from KG2—Kampfgeschwader No.2.

The Dornier which was furthest away from us was attacked by Eric Bocock and we saw it jettison its bombs and go down sideways on fire. Johnny said he was going to attack the one nearest to us and instructed me to take the one further ahead. As I started to overhaul it I was completely put off by the rear gunner opening up on me and what looked like red tomatoes passed by me on either side. The result of this was that I opened up far too early and too far away again. However, I saw hits on the port wing and petrol started to pour out of the port wing tank. Then Johnny warned me of two 190s above and behind so I quickly broke off and rejoined him.

A few minutes later we came across another Dornier and Johnny went in first, but he was put off by the defensive fire. I then went in and again, before I was in killing range, I ran out of 20 mm shells and was just left with .303 cartridges. I saw several hits on the bomber's fuselage and port wing but .303 bullets were not powerful enough to penetrate armour and destroy. Another 'damaged' was the best I could claim for this and the first Dornier, and my cine gun camera film confirmed the damage and the probability that both would get back to their base. The patrol had lasted more than two hours, so we were glad to land back at Friston to refuel.

I made a note that I had just four gallons of petrol left!

We hadn't done too badly. Three Dorniers were claimed as destroyed, Bocock and Sergeant P L Hauser each got one, and Bill Loud and Sergeant W E Caldecott the third. Caldecott also claimed a probable. A further six Dorniers, a Ju88 and two 190s had been damaged. However, we were one short on landing, Pilot Officer Mike Goodchap being reported missing, whom we later heard was a prisoner. He had been flying No.2 to Pete and went down during an attack on the bombers when jumped by two FW190s.

Once again I found myself writing out a combat report for the Intelligence Officer:

19 August 1942.   Time: 1100-1115 hrs.   10,000 ft. Dieppe.

"I was Yellow 2 in 602 Squadron. Yellow 1 reported two Do217s flying in a SW direction about 2,000 feet above. The Section climbed to attack as they turned to port and I picked out the rear EA, giving him two long bursts of cannon and machine gun. I observed strikes on the port wing near the port engine and saw petrol flowing out. As FW190s were in the vicinity, I broke away to starboard.

"A little later I reported another Do217 to Yellow 1, flying about 10,000 feet in a SW direction over the convoy. Yellow 1 made an attack from starboard, breaking to port and I went in after him, firing a three second burst at 300 yards and then a further four second burst of cannon and machine-gun from 150 yards, closing to 50 yards. I observed both cannon and machine-gun strikes on the main fuselage and port wing root. I overshot this aircraft and climbed away to starboard."

Our third Dieppe sortie came in the early afternoon, by which time the main battle on the ground had not only ended, but had been lost. The gallant Canadians, pinned down by murderous gunfire, had been unable to establish any kind of beach-head and had been cut to ribbons. We in the air had no knowledge of their sufferings, although it seemed that there was still much fighting and gunfire too near the water's edge to think that, as planned, the raiding force had moved right into the town itself.

Most of the morning, light bombers and Hurricane fighter-bombers had been flying low level attacks on the guns on the nearby headlands, while we Spitfires had been engaged in several prolonged air battles high above.

We now reached Dieppe as the withdrawal began. The heavy

bombers had retreated, hurt badly by our fighters, but now the Jabo units of the Luftwaffe, the bomb-carrying staffels of FW190s and Me109s, were making their presence felt and going for the ships. We were still to patrol to the south of the ships but nearer to Dieppe itself. Pete added at the briefing: "Don't forget to keep clear of the ships because they have been attacked by single seaters and are now firing at any aircraft regardless of height, if they are over them."

With this warning, we found ourselves over the convoy to encounter a tremendous amount of anti-aircraft fire taking place from the ships, so one presumed that they were again being attacked by bomb-carrying FW190s. Our section was again led by Johnny Niven and had completed one square search and we were on our way towards the ships at about 4,000 or 5,000 feet when two FW190s appeared no more than 100 yards in front of us, climbing away from the ships and crossing us, going away to our left. I was to Johnny's left and, as I reported them, said I was taking the one on the left.

I don't think the Hun pilot saw me for very conveniently, he turned to starboard which enabled me to give him a three second burst from 150 yards and he went down on fire to the sea, very close to the ships. I quickly turned to see where Johnny was and I got a nasty shock. First I saw the FW190 in front of him on fire and then saw his Spitfire pouring white smoke, which indicated that he had been hit in the glycol coolant tank. Bocock reported that more FW190s were behind us so I lost sight of Johnny as I turned to look. It so happened that his engine seized up as he turned away from the ships and he baled out. In the sea he was able to climb aboard his dinghy where he was spotted by Pete Brothers, who stayed in the vicinity until he saw Johnny picked up by the Navy.

I was convinced he had been shot down by the fire from the ships, indeed, I myself flew through a barrage of Naval flak as I turned away. When Johnny later returned to our unit at Peterhead, after having been in hospital for a few days—he had lost one finger on his left hand—he quizzed me as to how he had got clobbered, because when he attacked the 190s, there were no others behind us. I think I was non-commital but long afterwards an airforce pal of mine with connections at Air Ministry, said that it was understood that quite a number of RAF aircraft had been lost that day due to Naval gunfire.

Despite the number of fighters about, and 602 engaging several of them, mine was the only combat success of this our third trip to Dieppe; but the day was not over yet. Our fourth sortie began shortly after 5 pm. Most of the ships were well on their way back by this time bringing home the survivors, many of them wounded. As far as we were concerned there was no enemy air activity in our area and we landed back at Biggin after one hour, 15 minutes, to be told we were released until 9 am the next morning. That good news was given to us by Squadron Leader Bill Igoe, Biggin's Senior Fighter Controller. We quickly laid on transport to the West End, which was easy for us to do, but totally impossible for the poor Canadians who had (those who survived) endured an horrendous day. Many more lay cold and still on the beach or at the water's edge at Dieppe while more still were having their first night in captivity.

Incredibly I found myself writing out my third combat report of this equally incredible day. It read:

19 August 1942.   Time: 1350 hrs.   10,000 ft. 5 miles from Dieppe.

"I was flying Yellow 2 in 602 Squadron at about 6,000 feet. I saw two FW190s above at 12 o'clock, travelling in a northerly direction over the ships, doing an orbit to port. I reported these aircraft and Yellow 1, who closed to attack with the Section. I was on the left of Yellow 1 and observed strikes on one FW190 from, I imagine, Yellow 1. I opened up at the other aircraft with a three second burst of cannon and machine gun, and closed to about 150 yards and fired from about 30 degrees for two seconds with cannon and machine-gun. I observed cannon strikes on the engine and cockpit and the machine went into the sea near the ships, shedding pieces as it went down and apparently on fire."

In the debriefing excitement of having shot down my first FW190, I forgot to put in a claim for Johnny Niven. I last saw the Focke Wulf he attacked flying away from land smoking heavily and not very fast. When Johnny returned some days later and discussed the affair with me and Eric Bocock, he declined to make an official claim of any sort as he said it was too late. He was far more concerned as to how he had been shot down when I had not!

It has been recorded that after three or four sorties on this very busy day, some pilots were feeling very tired. On a personal note I think it depended on how and where the sorties had taken place and the reaction of the Luftwaffe. We in 602 Squadron had, thanks to the meticulous briefings plus the brilliant leadership of Pete Brothers, been involved in aerial combats with the Luftwaffe on our first three sorties. We were raring to go on our fourth sortie and it was very disappointing for all of us when we were allocated an area near the front of the returning convoy and consequently saw no further action. As we were able to whoop it up in the West End of London till after midnight, I think it suggests that we at any rate were not the least bit tired.

Whilst I was getting rid of my flying clobber, Wing Commander Thomas passed by with Group Captain Harry Broadhurst, who was the SASO at 11 Group HQ, but who had himself been flying in a Spitfire IX over Dieppe. In fact he had flown five times during the day, in order to witness for himself how the air and land battle had been going. Indeed, he had personally destroyed one FW190 and damaged three more. Thomas asked me if I'd had any luck, to which I replied, "Yes, Sir, I clobbered an FW190 which most of the Squadron noticed as it finished up about 10 yards from the ships of the Navy." "Well done," he said, "that will be a drink later on."

I suppose the change from our Battle Dress into our Number One uniform took about ten minutes and in no time at all we were in Chez Nina, a club in Denman Street, near the Regent Palace Hotel, Piccadilly Circus. There were six of us and when we arrived we had the club to ourselves. We were looked after by Nina and her three very attractive hostesses who drank with us. One of the girls, whose name I can't remember, which is probably just as well, drank a lot of brandy and was thin enough to be able to stand on the mantle piece above the fireplace, which had been boarded up I remember.

Then some late editions of the evening papers started to arrive and naturally all the headlines were dominated by the news of the Dieppe Raid and the part Fighter Command had played during the day's activities. "More than 600 sorties flown," ran one headline, "Tremendous Air Battle—Many German Aircraft Destroyed", ran another. Due to the secrecy of the Show we had not mentioned one word about it, so it was rather hurtful when the girls suddenly froze and one of them said, "You lousy bastards, whooping it up in the West End whilst your pals have been in the largest battle since 1940!" Nothing we could say or do would let them believe us when we said we had been there.

Later that evening, Johnny Checketts, a New Zealander, and other 485 Squadron pilots arrived and immediately started saying things like, "Did you see the Ju88s? Well we clobbered them," to which we replied, "No, we were involved with the Dorniers, and clobbered those!" etc, etc. After a bit of that type of 'line-shooting', Nina and the girls forgave us and to show there was no ill-feelings, we all got large ones on the house.

It had been arranged that a full de-briefing would be made the next day at 9 o'clock by the Station Intelligence Officer, de le Torre. All he could tell us was the Canadians had taken an awful beating and had suffered many casualties. From Fighter Command's point of view it was thought to have been a total success. A large number of enemy aircraft had been claimed as destroyed, but the Command had also suffered severe losses. There was only one report of a pilot making a forced landing on the airfield near Dieppe, but he found no transport so made it back to the harbour on foot.

The 602 Squadron score for the whole period of our detachment to Biggin, was the 190 Pete shot down on the 18th, while over Dieppe itself on the 19th, we had destroyed four, probably another and damaged ten. We had lost three Spitfires with two pilots taken prisoner (one on the 18th, one on the 19th) and had had Johnny Niven wounded.

As I became a member of 131 Squadron later in the war, I was interested in their showing at Dieppe. They had, like us in 602, flown on four sorties during the day, plus two defensive patrols and an air sea rescue mission. They had shot down four enemy aircraft with two more damaged for no loss, which was pretty good arithmetic for this day.

The day after the Dieppe Raid, Pete got permission to do one more Fighter Sweep before returning north. We flew out on our own to Le Touquet then headed in behind Dieppe but we had no reaction from the Luftwaffe. As we now know, they had operated their maximum strength the previous day and were in no state to fly operationally. Indeed, most of its cannon ammunition had been exhausted and extra supplies had urgently to be flown in from Germany. I see I wrote in my log book—"In at Le Touquet and out by Dieppe area. One or two [EA] plotted but not near us. Smoke and shit in Dieppe hanging about."

The next day we flew back to Peterhead via Kirton, where it was back to the old routine until 10th September, when we were transferred to the Orkney Islands, to the RAF base at Skeabrae, swopping with 164 Squadron. I was involved in just two operational sorties, one on the 30th, when Scrambled to intercept a bogey which turned out to be a Coastal Command Wellington, and another on the day before our move to the Orkneys. Bill Loud and I attempted to intercept a German weather 'plane which we called 'Weather Willie'. We flew 120 miles out over the North Sea and actually got to within one mile of it. We were told he was at 15,000 feet, but we could see nothing. It was always difficult to get the height right on radar at these distances and I suspect he was either much higher, or lower, possibly in some cloud at 6,000 feet. These chases invariably ended in bitter disappointment and frustration.

At the end of September, Pete Brothers was promoted to Wing Commander and became Wing Commander Flying at Tangmere. 602 was taken over by Squadron Leader Michael Beytagh, who had been in the Battle of Britain, and at the defence of Tobruk in North Africa, and had just finished a rest tour at the Spitfire OTU at Annan in Dumfrieshire. Some years after the war I was asked to help author Gil Thomas on his biography of Mike, which was published in 1959 under the title *Shoulder the Sky*. Mike was always reticent about his background and when I read the book I realised why. With a sister and brother, he had been abandoned in the Far East when his mother and father separated. He soon fitted in with the Squadron, and although quite different from Pete Brothers, was a pretty good commander. I recall he was very keen on a variety of training exercises, so the Squadron, apart from the Readiness Section or the Section flying convoy patrol, would always be training.

Very little of note took place while we were at Skeabrae although we did have the opportunity of flying a Spitfire Mark VI, used for high level work—interception of high level German recce aircraft, because it had a pressurised cockpit. However, we could only get to 40,000 feet in them and the photographic German aircraft were usually at 43,000, but at least we frightened them off, or so we hoped. Later, after I left the Squadron, they were equipped with Spitfire VIIs which could reach 45,000 feet and one of the Hun photo boys was shot down.

Meantime, on October 7th, we were told over breakfast that Flight Lieutenant Carlson, who was in charge of the De Havilland Dominie—a twin-engined biplane of mid-30s vintage—allocated to Major General Kemp, the officer in charge of the Orkneys, Shetlands and Faroe Islands—had been taken to hospital suffering from appendicitis. Our adjutant was in a terrific flap for apparently the General was due to arrive at Castletown airfield on the Caithness mainland where he expected to be picked up and taken to Sumburgh in the Shetlands.

The Station Commander wished to know if any pilot had experience of flying twin-engined aeroplanes, but there were no rush of volunteers. However, the adjutant later re-appeared having checked our records to discover that I had flown Oxfords in training, so I was detailed for the job, which pleased me no end!

I finished my breakfast and made my way round to dispersal. The fitter and rigger corporals were both standing by the Dominie (W6455), which they said was in order. I asked them to come into the cockpit with me and explain the various knobs and tits, as I had never flown the type before. I don't recall if they looked apprehensive at me taking 'their' aeroplane up, but I said I'd fly a circuit and a landing and take off, for experience. As a friendly gesture I asked them if they'd like to accompany me, as most ground crew like the chance of a ride. I don't think I have ever seen two people get out of an aeroplane so fast in my life!

Anyway, I took off and flew across the Pentland Firth to Castletown, where I landed and taxied to the Airfield Control Tower. As I did so I could see about six army people waiting with the Station Commander, Wing Commander Saunders. He was pretty short to start with. "Why are you late? These brown jobs have been waiting for more than half an hour!" When I filled him in with all the facts, of which he was not aware, he said, "Good God, don't repeat that! You'd better say you had a spot of engine trouble but it's OK now." Off he went to the clutch of army bods, consisting of the Major General, one Colonel, two Majors, a Captain and a corporal.

No sooner had Saunders spoken to them, than one of the Majors came over and asked if the engine trouble I'd had was OK now? I confirmed that to my knowledge both engines were running satisfactorily, but then the Colonel came over and asked the same thing. He got the same answer and then, just as they were about to get on board, the General posed the same question! Anyway, all went well and I landed them safely at Sumburgh where they were to stay for a few days, and I flew back to Skeabrae. Fortunately a replacement pilot arrived the very next day so I did not have to fly the General back again. However, having been once volunteered, I had occasion to fly the old machine from time to time to various parts, including Inverness, Wick, Tain. I even had to fly the General again towards the end of the month—twice!

A story worth telling here began after I dropped the General and his Staff at Sumburgh. I noticed six Spitfires on the edge of the runway, which turned out to be from another Spitfire squadron based at Grimsetter (east of Kirkwall). Two pilots were at Readiness in the Watch Tower, and over a cup of tea I quizzed them about the social life—if any. They said it was great because as most of the local men had been called-up and sent away there was a surplus of girls about.

Apparently, if you dated one you were invited to meet the parents and as there was only one room with a fire, the pair were accommodated in one of the bedrooms (no fire) and were supplied each with a large woollen sock-like garment which when worn correctly, covered the whole body, right up to the shoulders! A candle was then lit and placed on the window sill so that neighbours would know that

'Bundleing' was taking place, which was the island name for official courting.

The two reasons for the sock was warmth and to hinder any personal contact below the face. To my $64,000 question, the response was that 'shot-gun' weddings were fairly frequent!! For some strange reason not all pilots were invited to partake of Bundleing.

There was another amusing episode while at Skeabrae which involved a 'brown job'. There was a Colonel, who'd been recalled from retirement, who had been put in charge of Airfield Defence. He was very over-powering and more or less ran the Mess, especially any parties. One day an invitation to Buffet, drinks and dance came from the Naval Air Station some five miles north of us, for two RAF officers and one army officer. Two of us, Johnny Niven and I were detailed and the Colonel detailed himself.

We were told that the female WRENS were few and far between so to lay off. Johnny and I therefore decided to spend the time in competition, seeing which of us could down the most pints of beer. This we proceeded to do, interspersed with sandwiches, etc. He finally beat me by downing 22 pints to my 21.

Meanwhile, the Colonel had taken over and was organising every-one and telling the band what to play. This was more than the Navy lieutenants and sub-lieutenants could take, so they invited him to go outside to look at the static water tank, which they said had a problem. Whilst he was on the top step looking down at the open top, the tank being full, they tipped him in.

It was quite a sight to see the dripping Colonel at the anti-room door, saying, "I will never enter this Mess again!"—loud applause! He stomped off and later put in a formal complaint to the C-in-C and all lieutenants and sub-lieutenants had to appear in front of him. The spokesman informed the C-in-C that the Colonel must have slipped and fallen in. As none of them would alter the story, the Admiral said (we were told), "I don't bloody well believe you but as there are so many of you and all telling the same lie, you are dismissed."

On 15th December, Mike Beytagh sent for me and told me that Pete Brothers had requested my posting on promotion to Flight Lieutenant, to take over a Flight Command vacancy in No.131 (County of Kent) Squadron, commanded by Squadron Leader J S Fifield, whom I knew because when I first joined 602 at Redhill, he was a Supernumary Flight Lieutenant awaiting a Flight Commander vacancy. 131 was based at the Tangmere satellite airfield at Westhamptnett, not far from Tangmere itself, near Chichester, Sussex. So for me at least, it was back to the South, back to 11 Group and back to the war.

CHAPTER VI

FLIGHT COMMANDER

Arriving at RAF Westhampnett, I discovered I was to command 'A' Flight of 131 Squadron, while my brother flight commander was Flight Lieutenant Chris Doll. He was one of the most amusing characters I have ever met, with an exceptional sense of humour. I learned that he had been with 258 and 610 Squadrons, and with the latter had fought over Dieppe.

We had a very mixed bunch on 131, and among my flight members was a Czech, Otto Smik, A W 'Bill' Bower from South Africa and Henri de Bordas, a Free French pilot. The other Squadron in the Wing was 165, commanded by Squadron Leader H J L 'Darkie' Hallowes DFC DFM and bar, one of Fighter Command's high scorers with over 20 victories.

The Squadron had been formed in 1941, consisting initially of a high proportion of Belgian pilots, who then went off to form 350 Belgian Squadron. 131 began operations in 1942 and was involved in the Dieppe Show. It was equipped with Spitfire Vb fighters, still Fighter Command's standard war-horse. Our CO, J S 'Fifi' Fifield had also seen action over Dieppe, while with 616 Squadron. He was shot down by a FW190 and had a nasty experience when he baled out, as his neck became entangled in his parachute lines. He was rescued from the sea by a minelayer with, fortunately, nothing more serious than a stiff neck.

John Fifield was a brilliant aviator, really finding his metier when he commenced a second tour flying Intruder Mosquitos. He was later a test pilot of note, flying with the Martin Baker Company on their ejection seat program. When I joined 131, it had been in the Wing for a long period and was soon to be rested. The offensive operations were fairly few and far between as the weather was pretty foul most of the time. I had taken the place of Ray Harries who was promoted to Squadron Leader. He too was destined for a high placing in the top scorers, ending the war with 20 victories.

The Squadron had a bit of history. Following the Battle of Britain, the Lord Lieutenant of Kent, Lord Cornwallis, decided that Kent County, over which most of the fighting had taken place, must show its appreciation to Fighter Command by providing a new Spitfire Squadron. The cost of a Spitfire in 1940/41 was approximately £5,500. He appealed to the various towns and in next to no time enough money was raised to provide 21 Spitfires. The aircraft, which I usually flew as A Flight Commander, was coded NX-B, and named 'Bromley'.

Today, there is a painting of NX-B hanging in the downstairs corridor of the Royal Air Force Club in Piccadilly. Roger Steel, the artist, was commissioned by the British Aircraft Corporation, when Jeffrey Quill was the Managing Director, to paint a Spitfire for the 50th anniversary of the RAF and he found a Spitfire marked NX-B at the entrance to RAF Manston, which he used as his 'model'. The original painting, which he entitled *Evening Sortie* was in fact stolen from the Club, but he had kept his original sketches, etc, and was able to paint it again in 1967. I have a copy, one third the size, which Roger did for me. It is a reproduction of this smaller version which appears on the cover of this book.

The origins of the Kent County Squadron idea began back in August 1940, when no less a person that Bob Stanford Tuck brought down his shot-up Spitfire to a forced landing near Lord Cornwallis's home, at Plovers, Horsmonden. Tuck was taken to Plovers where he was given a bed for the night. Next morning, Cornwallis said to Tuck that he had just received a cheque for £5,000 from a Mr Stanley Johnson of Bearstead, which he was going to earmark towards a new Spitfire.

There followed an appeal to everyone in Kent, through local newspapers, by Lord Cornwallis, for money to form an Invicta Flight of Spitfires. Within a short space of time, no less an amount than £29,370 had been sent in for the County of Kent Fund. The first three Spitfires purchased with this money were named 'Man of Kent', 'Kentish Man' and 'Fair Maid of Kent'. The Fund was taken up by the various towns in Kent each of whom raised their own separate Spitfire Fund. By March 1941 the amount raised reached £67,677 and by November it topped the £100,000 mark.

During December 1942 and January 1943, with the weather so bad, we only managed to fly nine offensive Sweeps as Wing formations and three as a Squadron. We also flew weather recce sorties up the Channel as well as Scrambles, for German hit and run raiders were still being a nuisance. Just before Christmas I was Scrambled to help a section of Typhoons of 486 Squadron go after a couple of Me109s, but they put both into the sea 20 miles out from Selsey Bill and didn't need our help.

Just a few days before Christmas, as a portent of things to come, we escorted American B17s to Le Havre at 22,000 feet—officially Circus 244. In fact we flew twice on this day, the 20th, as a Wing, seeing nothing on the first show. Flying as Rear Support on the second Op, a few FW190s put in an appearance, two passing beneath us and they seemed to be in a good position for a perfect bounce by 165, but the 190s dived away before they could be engaged.

Our next Circus—249—didn't take place until 13th January. The Tangmere Wing was "bouncing Wing" crossing in at the Somme, penetrating as far as Amiens. One FW190 dived on 485 Squadron who were at 21,000 feet but they broke successfully. Two more were spotted right under us but they saw us and went away, going like hell. I led the Squadron twice during the month, which was quite a thrill.

Chris Doll left us at the end of December, his place taken by a Czech pilot, Flight Lieutenant T Kruml, in from 66 Squadron. I remembered him as one of our instructors at Llandow and Rhoose, so it was interesting to be his operational senior. I missed Chris. One example of his sense of humour, and one which I swear is totally true, concerned our CO.

It so happened that the CO had a very young WAAF batwoman and to say she was innocent and no doubt first time away from a closeted home would be a true statement. Fifi told us that the Squadron was to be released from duty the next day and so he was going to have a lie in. As he was rather dissatisfied with our formation flying he instructed Chris and myself to spend all the morning practising. When we arrived at dispersal it was pouring with rain, with bags of low cloud, so flying was out. At 11 o'clock, the dispersal 'phone rang and the orderly corporal, answering, told Chris that the CO's lady batman wished to speak to him. The young WAAF said that as the CO had not heard any aeroplanes flying, he wanted to know the reason why. Chris replied, "Give the CO my compliments and tell him that the weather is bad and that is it raining."

Some minutes later the 'phone rang again and this time the WAAF said the CO wanted to know just how bad the rain was. Chris said, "Give the CO my compliments and tell him that it is raining like fuck!" We saw Fifi at lunch time and with a broad grin said to Chris, "I fully understood your message!"

On another occasion the Squadron was scheduled for dusk

Readiness. As was normal, a WAAF Officer from the Operations Room 'phoned to ask the state of Readiness. Chris Doll replied, "Please tell the Controller that there is a problem. The lift at the end of the runway which gets us airborne has broken down!" Two minutes later, she came on again, saying that the Controller fully understood, but apart from that, presumably all was well. "Unfortunately, No," replied Chris, "Please tell the Controller that the night-flying petrol hasn't arrived yet!" The Controller then came on the telephone himself and said, "OK, Chris, you have had your childish fun, I presume that we can now get on with the war?"

I was sorry to see him go. He was a very sound pilot and flight commander; completely unflappable. During January, Fifi told us that we were getting Colin Hodgkinson, a legless pilot similar to Douglas Bader. He had lost both legs in a flying collision when he was training with the Fleet Air Arm. The fault was entirely due to his instructor as Colin was under the blind-flying hood when the two aircraft hit. I told Fifi I knew Colin, having met him when he was still in Naval uniform at 'Victor's' Night Club, in Carnaby Street, London, so Colin was assigned to my Flight.

'Hoppy', as the other pilots immediately nick-named him, was in his early twenties. He had thick, very fair, wavy hair and bright blue, crystal clear eyes. He wasn't very tall, but no doubt this was due to his artificial limbs being made deliberately shorter than his original legs would have been. Probably as a result of being unable now to take violent exercise he was very thick-set with unusually powerful hands and wrists. He had, I recall, an amazing capacity for beer drinking, and it was said that he filled his hollow legs with the liquid!

He absolutely refused to be treated any differently from anyone else and anyone mistakenly endeavouring to make friendly allowances for his apparent disability invoked the full brunt of some very forthright invectives.

For the occasions he was on Scramble-Readiness, he had evolved a technique with his ground crew for getting him into his Spitfire smartly. As soon as the bell or siren sounded, they would immediately start the engine for him. His parachute and helmet were already laid carefully out in the seat and on the gun-sight respectively, with the various safety straps and harness arrayed in readiness. All his crew, therefore, had to do once he'd stomped to the machine was to help shovel him into the cockpit and do up the straps. He was never behind on a Scramble, in fact, invariably ahead of the majority.

The only story I can remember of Colin was that I had made the list for the next day's early morning Readiness and it was Colin's turn

Top left: Under canvas with the Territorials in 1938; Halle Muir is behind me.

Top right: Brother Victor (second from the left) with Bob Holman and Jim Campbell, Dingwall 1938.

Bottom: At No.53 OTU 1942. Front left to right: Me, unknown, WC Donovan, GC Taffy Jones DSO MC DFC MM, SL A R Edge AFC.

Top left: Bright-eyed and bushy-tailed: ready for the fray.

Top right: 602's two flight commanders, Johnny Niven DFC (left) and Eric Bocock DFC, A & B Flight respectively. I was in A Flight.

Middle left: Squadron Leader Pete Brothers DFC was my CO after Finucane. He was later my Wing Leader too, and the best fighter pilot I flew with.

Bottom: Flight Lieutenant Chris Doll was B Flight commander of 131 Squadron when I arrived to take over A Flight.

Top: With 131 Squadron as flight commander. Front left to right: Cy Smith, Sampson, SL J J O'Meara, Tony Pickering, Bill Bower; Rear: Doc Rycroft, -?-, -?-, Earl Smith, Dunsford, Ede and Jongblood.

Middle left: 'Orange' O'Meara DFC in Spitfire F. VII, 'Spirit of Kent'.

Middle right: We had a mix of nationalities on 131. This is FO Rene Mainguard, a pilot with the Free French in NX-Z.

Bottom: Spitfire NX-K, 131 (Country of Kent) Squadron, 1943.

Top: 131 Squadron A Flight pilots: Front row left to right: A V N Ede, myself, O'Meara, Cy Smith, Jongblood; Rear: -?-, -?-, Turnbull, Ken Parry and Foskett.

Middle left: Flying Officer Bill Bower, 131 Squadron.

Middle right: Clipped-wing Spitfire V. 610 Squadron in the distance.

Bottom: I look a bit leg-less drooped by the cockpit door, but the chaps with Mae Wests are on stand-by.

Top left: I've looked happier; obviously I needed a cigarette!

Top right: I was happier when I met Margaret, who later became my wife.

Bottom: My NX-B at Castletown, 1943. Note parachute on wing-tip ready for a quick Scramble.

Top: Seated in my Spitfire, 131 Squadron.

Middle: Two Squadrons of the Wing returning to Culmhead as the sun goes down.

Bottom: One for the Press. Culmhead Wing 1943, left to right: F/Sgt Morris, Tony Pickering, myself, WC Cam Malfroy (Wing Leader), Sgt Williams, F/Sgt Clatworthy, FO G Smith, Sgt Turnbull, Sgt Hirst and F/Sgt Parry.

Top left: Joe Holmes DFC AFC, whose job as Sector Gunnery Officer at Exeter I took over in 1944. He is supposed to have wounded Rommel during a strafing attack in July of that year.

Top right: Rolf Berg, our Norwegian Wing Leader. Killed in action 3 February 1945.

Bottom: Commanding 127 Squadron late 1944, France. Note camouflage netting over the Spitfire brick-built dispersal.

Top: Pilots of 341 FF Squadron at Antwerp just prior to me taking over the French Wing. SL Jacques Andrieux stands centre rear, with Pierre Laurent 4th from right. Roger Borne stands second from left.

Middle: Jacques Andrieux DFC, CO 341 Squadron. Note he has named his Spitfire 'Commandant Mouchotte' in memory of Rene Mouchotte who was killed in action in 1943.

Bottom: 341 and its leaders. Front row, left to right: Roger Borne, GC Loel Guiness, Jacques Andrieux, self, Dorrance, Victor Tanguy.

to be one of the two pilots on duty. During the evening he told me that he was going to some Navy party at Portsmouth and although he didn't spell it out, the hint was there that perhaps he could do a swop. For umpteen reasons it wasn't possible and all I said was "Enjoy yourself but be sober when you take up your duty at 0700 hours."

At about 0730, I thought perhaps I had better check and when I arrived at dispersal I could only see one pilot. I asked where Colin was, and was told he was in the Engineering Shop in the hangar some few yards from the dispersal hut. When I arrived there I found the legless Colin sitting on the ground with two engineers hammering away at his metal legs which were somewhat bent. In as calm a voice as possible I asked what he thought might happen if we had an immediate Scramble? "Not to worry," he said, "These boys will whip these on in no time and I will be in the Spit pronto. The legs are 90% OK and its the final 10% they're working on." I stuck around until he was properly dressed and then left him fit to get airborne if necessary.

"What happened at your party?" I later asked him. "Oh, we were playing one of those silly games and I forgot about my tin legs and spun in from a great height. But I have been on to the leg people at Roehampton and a replacement pair is on the way."

There was another Czech pilot I remember meeting at Exeter, by the name of Kimlichka, who visited us as he had a WAAF officer friend on the Station. He showed us a trick which involved taking a small mouthful of cigarette lighter fuel and after rolling it around his mouth, mixing it with some saliva, asked someone to stand approximately three feet away and flick on a cigarette lighter. He then blew out the contents of his mouth and produced a long sheet of flame. The secret was to blow hard enough and long enough to keep the flame away from the mouth!

Although I suppose I should have known better, I decided to try it but unfortunately ran out of breath and got my lips burned after which there were no more takers!

Quite unusually too, we had two brothers on the Squadron. Cy and Earl Smith were Australians and arrived in mid-December.

On 19 January 1943, we received the unwelcome news that 131 Squadron was to move to Castletown (not far from John o'Groats) to swop with 610 Squadron commanded by Johnnie Johnson, the eventual top scoring fighter ace of Fighter Command. Colin Hodgkinson asked me if he could stay at Tangmere to join 610 and this was arranged for him. So for the rest of January and February, it was back to the old routine of long periods of training, as new pilots from OTUs arrived.

Flight Lieutenant Kruml also left us in February, going to 122 Squadron, his place taken by Flight Lieutenant T G Pickering. Tony Pickering had seen action in the Battle of Britain, and later became a test pilot at an MU at Hawarden, and was destined to stay with 131 for almost a year. Tony recalls:

> "I remember when the Squadron was at Castletown, the airman's mess hall was the nave of the local church. I was the leader of a flight of pilots trained to land and take-off from aircraft carriers. This was to be a cover for the Anzio landings but thankfully we were not required, as the Fleet Air Arm losses were very low."

I had another Czech pilot in my Flight, by the name of Hlado. He had been a test pilot in his native country and had amassed some 1,800 flying hours. I vividly remember standing at Dispersal with Fifi one day, who was singing Hlado's praises, as the man came into land. In the event the Czech bounced three or four times before the Spitfire settled. Fifi then instructed me to tick him off, which I did, and which he took very well.

It was about this time that Fifi Fifield made the bad mistake of trying to take the Station Commander's, (still Wing Commander Saunders) personal Spitfire, which was part of the Squadron's strength, from a parking spot near Saunders's office, so from that moment there was a clash of personalities. I was due for a week's leave and when I boarded the train at Wick I found that the Wingco and his wife were also travelling south. They very kindly invited me into their sleeping compartment to have a drink. The Wingco quizzed me on Fifi's background and I could detect there was no love lost.

Early in March, Fifi had an engine failure while flying over the Pentland Firth. He was much too low to glide to land, so had to ditch in the sea. Unfortunately his dinghy failed to inflate so that he had to tread water for almost half an hour before he was rescued by a small fishing boat. The temperature of the water, as can be imagined, was pretty low, so that both his lungs were in a collapsed state when they got to him. It says a good deal about his overall fitness and the efficiency of the hospital, that in a few days he was rapidly on the way to recovery. I suppose plenty went on in the background because within a fortnight we heard that Fifi was being posted and the new Boss was to be Squadron Leader J J O'Meara DFC & bar. I was very sorry to see Fifi leave. He was a decent squadron commander and an immaculate aviator.

Jimmy O'Meara was Irish and a devout Roman Catholic, so his RAF collegues nick-named him 'Orange'. He was very much more demanding than Fifi had been and flew the Squadron from dawn to dusk. He too had fought in the Battle of Britain, and in fact shot down his first German over the Dunkirk evacuation. A very experienced fighter pilot, he had definite ideas on formations to be used in Sweeps and when flying close escort to bombers.

The Station Intelligence Officer was Flight Lieutenant Duncan Brown who, it will be remembered, was our poet at Peterhead when I was with 602. Wingco Saunders was keen on Mess parties and often members of the local gentry were included. We used to see a lot of Katherine, the charming and good looking daughter of Sir Archibald Sinclair, the Air Minister, whose family seat was at nearby Thurso Castle. Not surprisingly she attracted a number of admirers, and it was said amongst us cruel sceptics that if you wanted to get posted away, then let it be known you were dating her!

Sinclair himself frequently flew up to Castletown for a few days break and often took the time to inspect some area of the Station and occasionally the officers. I personally found him rather unimpressive and felt sure he was only in the job because of the Coalition Government. He was a senior liberal who had been included in the wartime Cabinet.

One story I recollect from our time at Castletown went the rounds. Our local pub was in the hamlet of Dunnet and one of the regulars was Willie Mackenzie from Rona, in the Hebrides. He was acting foreman on a large farm whilst the other locals (all Territorial soldiers) had been called-up. Willie was quizzed about a story that a German U-boat had been seen off the island.

> "Aye, it's true—a German intelligence officer with fluent English was landed by dinghy in one of the bays at dusk with orders to wait till dawn and then climb to the top of the bay and to go to the white house. Once there, Mackenzie would take him in and keep him until dusk when he would return to the water's edge, plus a package, and be uplifted by the dinghy.
>
> "At first light, the German made his way up to the top, but no house, let alone a white one. He started to walk inland and came across a herdsman leading a cow by a rope. He stopped the man and asked 'I am looking for Mr Mackenzie,' to which the herdsman replied 'But we are all Mackenzie's here.' 'Oh,' said the German, 'he lives in a white house at the top of the bay.' 'Och weel, that will be Mackenzie the Spy.'"

I remember another quite amusing incident while we were at Castletown. I was acting CO, as O'Meara was away on leave. We had to provide fairly frequently, one section of two Spitfires to be at Readiness, in case of hostile aircraft coming into our area. Sunday, quite naturally, was the most unpopular day to be assigned this task, because for one thing nothing ever happened, and secondly the Mess cook usually excelled himself with a spectacular curry on Sundays, which went down well after a lengthy session in the bar.

On this Sunday one of our pilots was due to take over Readiness at 2.30 and he was having quite a 'few' with Duncan Brown. I stopped this and sent him to lunch, then suggested he have a snooze at Dispersal. However, when he arrived at Dispersal, like a bloody fool, he decided to do an air test! Coming in to land he undershot and managed to whip off both legs of his undercarriage on a concrete fence, and ended up putting the Spitfire down onto its belly. I had to telephone the Station Commander at his house and he quickly arrived. He interviewed our pilot and could see that he had been drinking, so sent for the Bar Book. From the entries he could see that Duncan had also sunk a few, so he took me to one side and said, "I think at all costs we must avoid a court martial. It's a long and tedious operation so I'll put in a report, explaining the turbulent conditions which resulted in an error of judgement."

He then sent for Duncan Brown and banned him and the pilot from the bar for one month. A few days later, Wing Commander R P R Powell DFC & bar, a Staff Officer at 14 Group HQ, arrived for a few days visit which coincided with the Officer's Mess being challenged to a cricket match by the NCOs and Other Ranks. We all knew that Wing Commander Desmond Sheen DFC, the Officer Commanding, Skeabrae was a cricketer, so he was invited to take part. When the selected team was placed on the notice board, the Games Officer (quite a wag) penned it like this:

> Wg Cdr D F B Sheen DFC & bar
> Wg Cdr R P R Powell DFC & bar
> Fl Lt D Brown (No Bar)
> etc, etc,

I first met Peter Powell in early June 1942 when he visited Kenley to brief the Wing on practice attacks on targets at RAF Ford and Tangmere. On the fringe of the conversation which he had with Batchy Atcherley, I gathered that on the outbreak of war he had been a flight commander in 111 Squadron, commanded by Harry Broadhurst. He later commanded the Hornchurch Wing, probably because Broady had been an earlier wing leader there, and then Station commander.

When 131 was at Castletown, we saw Peter fairly often. He told a story against himself as follows. He was walking around the perimeter at Hornchurch whilst a Spitfire was coming in to land. The pilot was too low and hit a gun emplacement, knocking off his undercart and then slithered along on its belly. At the subsequent Court Martial, Peter was called as the main witness and was asked if he had seen the accident, to which he replied, yes. The defending officer, Mike Peacock, said, "You have said you were walking round the perimeter and you heard the impact. Did you actually see the impact?" Peter said, "No". "Then," said Peacock, "you are not correct when you say you saw the accident, you only saw the result of the accident!" Peter concurred, so Peacock turned to the Chairman and claimed, "The evidence of this officer in unreliable and should be stricken from the record." The Chairman agreed. Later, Mike Peacock said, "Sorry Peter, but I am a lawyer and that's the way it goes!"

Peter Powell had quite a serious wound which definitely affected him and gave him a great deal of pain in the back and neck and probably contributed to his early death. He once let me look at his log book and the most interesting thing to me was that in all the courses he had attended, such as Central Gunnery School and so on, he invariably received 'Above Average' passes. He was a most charming and likeable person, good looking, tremendous sense of humour and very popular with the opposite sex.

After the war I got to know him much better and in fact I was Best Man at his wedding to Joan Sanders, which took place at Marylebone Registry Office, followed by a Champagne lunch at the Savoy, including my wife, who had been Lady in Waiting. The four of us often played Bridge together. Joan's brother James Sanders had also been in 111 Squadron before the war, and had a fine fighting record in France and the Battle of Britain with 615 Squadron. Peter retired from the RAF in 1963 as a Group Captain and died in 1970, at the age of 53.

Our rather dull routine continued at Castletown until 20th June 1943 when we heard that we were to become part of a new wing formed at RAF Exeter under the leadership of Wing Commander C E Malfroy. We had spent the first half of 1943 maintaining constant and unrewarding Readiness states, patrolling over Royal Navy ships and practice flying.

On one occasion we had escorted HMS *Scylla* from Scapa Flow to Thursoe, its main VIP passenger being King George VI, and in April some of us had been the guests of the Royal Navy, when invited for lunch on HMS *Anson* in Scapa itself, then had tea on the carrier HMS

Furious as well as having a look over HMS *Duke of York*. I guess all this was as a thank you for our ever ready, if rarely needed, protection.

The Naval C-in-C was, if I remember correctly, Admiral Sir Bruce Fraser. He had, we were told, advised the sailors against bathing in Scapa Flow owing to the temperature. He was to join us for lunch one day but he apparently missed his step when boarding his Admiral's Barge and fell into the 'drink'. A signal was received by the Captain saying he would have to miss lunch but would come to tea. The Captain immediately responded—"To C-in-C in Sea. Bathing is not recommended in the Flow."

Soon after this I was at Readiness and was Scrambled to try and intercept an in-coming photo-recce He111. It was all 10/10ths cloud and unfortunately the course took my No.2 and I over the anchorage. We received a barrage of Navy gunfire at all heights. When we landed unscathed I complained to the Controller in Ops, who put me on to the Naval Commander Ops Officer. His reply to my belly-aching was, "Oh, really! What was it like for accuracy?" I replied, "Bloody awful, thank God—they need a lot of practice!"

The only bit of real excitement was in April when the Luftwaffe bombed Aberdeen. Four of us took off into the dark night sky but the show was over by the time we got there. All we saw were three large fires burning in the city.

In early June Gerry Jongblood, a Dutchman on the Squadron, had to use my personal Spitfire for some reason or other and preparing to land he found that the undercarriage, when he selected 'down' would not lock, which meant it would probably collapse on landing. The Control Tower alerted me and I instructed them to keep him airborne whilst I took off in another Spit and give him various instructions in the air. This situation infrequently arose and the locking could be achieved by various ham-handed manoeuvres, such as selecting wheels down and then putting the Spit into vicious barrel rolls or flying inverted whilst selecting the lever, or spinning, or pulling up into a blood-draining loop.

Anyway, whilst flying within a short distance of Gerry, I put him through all these manoeuvres but with no success. One thing I did discover was that his aerobatics left much to be desired and his spins were far too gentle. I later spent a lot of time making all the pilots spin, etc. Eventually, however, I had to admit to failure and it was with heavy heart that I ordered Gerry to put my NX-B down on its belly. I wrote in my log book: "A frantic endeavour to assist by advice, F/O Jongblood how to get the mighty 'B's undercart, which had stuck, down. All in vain—he pranged her wheels up. MY HEART BLEEDS."

Our last 'action' in Scotland occured on June 24th. We frequently tested our guns by firing them into the sea. The local fishermen asked us to fire at some basking sharks because they were interfering with their nets and curtailing their catches. We did this using mostly high velocity incendiary armour-piercing 20 mm cannon shells. We found the sharks in Dunnet Bay and I claimed one destroyed and one probable, with three more likely to beach themselves in due course.

However, we later paid for this bit of 'sport' because a number of the sharks, and they were about 20 feet long, did in fact finish up on the beach, not far from the Officer's Mess, and the stink of rotting fish was appalling and lasted for a long time!

Two days later we headed south for Exeter. The boys flew down in their Spitfires while I drew the short straw and had to accompany the men and equipment in a 'Sparrow'—a converted Handley Page Harrow transport. But at least we were down where the action was, and under Orange O'Meara, raring to go.

CHAPTER VII

EXETER WING

Exeter was in 10 Group and situated in a nice part of the world. The officer commanding the Exeter Sector was Group Captain A B Woodall, the former famous Fighter Controller in 12 Group, and later 11 Group and on Malta. However, not long after we arrived, he took up another appointment and Group Captain Loel Guiness took over. He was married to the beautiful Lady Isabel Manners, the Duke of Rutland's daughter. Loel Guiness had been a pre-war member of the Auxiliary Air Force, serving with the famous 601 (County of London) Squadron, which he later commanded at the beginning of the war.

The Wing Leader, Camille Enright Malfroy, 'Cam' for short, was a New Zealander, a well known tennis player before the war and former Davis Cup player. In the 1930s he had been a member of the Cambridge University Air Squadron, and then joined the RAF when war came. He had flown in France, then after a period on instructing, had commanded 417 Squadron RCAF, then 66 Squadron before becoming CFI at No.61 OTU.

He was a staff officer at 10 Group when he heard of the formation of a new wing and immediately asked Air Commodore Basil Embry for the command of it. Basil Embry, being a sucker for anyone wishing to be operational, agreed, so despite the fact that Cam was in his 34th year, he got the job. The extraordinary thing we soon discovered about Cam, was that while he could volley a tennis ball in the centre of his tennis racket, regardless how high or fast it had been struck, he had great difficulty in seeing enemy fighters which were any distance away!

There was a famous occasion when the Wing had to rendezvous inland from Cherbourg to escort flying Fortresses coming back from a raid south of Paris. As we crossed into France, I spotted and reported 12 Focke Wulf 190s to our right and approaching towards our rear. His response was, "Can't see them, keep your eyes on them." Seconds later he called me, asking, "Where are they now?" Before I could answer, the slow, bored voice from an obvious Australian pilot, was heard to say, "You'll fucking soon find out, chum!"

A story which Cam used to tell against himself was the time he was flying a Hurricane to Boscombe Down in 1942. As he came into land he was distracted by an aircraft taking off from the runway. As it was almost airborne he reckoned that by landing right at the start of the runway there would be no danger. Unfortunately he undershot and in doing so, his undercarriage ripped the top off a Blenheim housed in a bomb-proof pen. The damage to the Hurricane was confined to the undercart but was severe to the Blenheim.

He was told to go to lunch in the Mess and then to report to the adjutant at 1400 hours. He was standing at the bar having a pre-lunch beer and noticed a number of men in civvies all clustered around each other and obviously very upset. Cam spoke to another officer who had just approached the bar, enquiring who the civvy types were. It turned out they were radar Boffins, engaged in testing Airborne Radar for nightfighters. Unfortunately some clot had just written off the equipment housed in a Blenheim, putting progress back months!

Our main job at Exeter was to escort day medium bombers to targets in Brittany and Normandy, mostly airfields, marshalling yards and ports. Altogether, apart from defensive Scrambled and convoy patrols, I completed 71 offensive sorties over France between 10th July 1943 and 1st February 1944, when I was rested. Added to my previous sorties with 602 at Redhill and 131 Squadron at Tangmere, my total offensive operations over enemy held territory amounted to 135. Our sister Squadron in the Wing was again 165, but now commanded by Squadron Leader H A S Johnston DFC, recently back from Malta. Tony Pickering again reminds me:

"In mid-1943 we moved down to Exeter where our Spitfire Vs were no match for the Me109s or FW190s. However, we soon moved to Culmhead where we were re-equipped with Spitfire IXs, and were then able to cope with the Messerschmitts and Focke Wulfs.

"I recall too, when later at Redhill, that Lord Cornwallis and reps of 'Men of Kent' and 'Kentish Men' visited us. Flags were

handed to Sammy and myself and we all appreciated that the
Spitfires were donated by the people of Kent.

"Ten tons of apples arrived within a few days and many of us
suffered the usual ailment after eating too many of them."

I must say we didn't get off to a very auspicious start, for our first two
shows were cancelled and when about to start out for a third, my
engine went u/s. I was now flying NX-K, 'K' being the letter of my
usual Spitfire with 602 Squadron.

On one of our early Wing shows, led by Malfroy, we had been
detailed to meet returning Fortresses between Rennes and Laval.
We failed to make rendezvous because the Forts were earlier than
expected and the Controller informed Cam who immediately turned
for home. We were at about 8,000 feet when Sergeant N A A
Turnbull, an Australian, reported some parked aircraft on what
turned out to be a satellite landing ground. Cam took us down on
a strafing run.

It was a grass field but heavily defended so we only made one pass.
However, we damaged about four Me109s and I came down on another
which was being taxied prior to take-off. My cannon fire set the fighter
ablaze whereupon it blew up, engulfing the unfortunate pilot.

On July 10th, we actually got as far as Le Havre before the weather
over the target was reported bad and we and 72 American B17s had
to return. We finally completed a mission on the 13th, an escort to
two boxes of 12 Mitchell bombers attacking the airfield at Brest
Guipavas. We didn't see any enemy fighters but the flak which came
up from Brest was pretty spectacular.

The next day it was an escort to some 200 Fortresses which bombed
the airfields at Le Bourget and Villacoublay. It was an early show and
we met them on the way back. Some fighters had tried to interfere
with the Forts but they had broken off by the time we picked them up.

I recall that same day we attempted to fly an Air Sea Rescue search,
but had to return because of bad weather. We later heard that the
search was in case Wing Commander John Nettleton VC had come
down in the sea on his way back from Turin. He had won his VC
for a daring daylight raid on a diesel engine factory at Augsburg, in
April 1942.

On occasions the Wing would fly into other Sectors to fly an Op or
several Ops. One such was a Circus we flew towards the end of July
from Coltishall, Norfolk, escorting 12 Bostons bombing the Focke
Wulf works in Amsterdam—bags of flak on that one. Then on the last
day of July we took part in an 11 Group Ramrod from Manston,

escorting 21 Marauders attacking the German airfield at Merville. Again we met plenty of flak the whole way across France. Sometimes enemy fighters reacted, sometimes not. On this day they did.

We were, of course, as Tony has mentioned, still flying Spitfire Vbs which meant that we had to do all the close escort stuff while the squadrons equipped with the newer and better Mark IXs were used as High Cover or Target Support, so they usually got all the fun when the Luftwaffe did react to our incursions. However, some Huns inevitably got through and our job was to engage them but under no circumstances to follow them and leave our charges unprotected.

This day turned out to be my lucky day, for I would have been shot down if the marksmanship of two FW190 pilots had been up to scratch. Orange O'Meara was on a day's leave so Cam Malfroy decided to lead 131 Squadron. He said he would be slightly above and more or less in front of the bombers with five other Spitfires, and I should be at the back with the others, and slightly below.

It was a cloudless day with unlimited visibility except for some ground haze. Our six were flying line abreast and soon after the bombing we were north of St Omer and homeward bound, when I saw about ten FW190s coming in fast from behind with black smoke pouring out of their exhausts. I reported these to the Wing Leader and warned my lot that we were about to be attacked and to be ready for the 'break' before they got into range.

I was a little worried because I had two not so experienced pilots in my formation and rather stupidly I lagged a bit behind the line. Also I misjudged the speed of the attacking 190s because suddenly I saw the explosive cannon shells showing just to my right, which indicated that they were now just 450 yards behind me—in range—and closing fast.

I immediately took the riskiest option, but sometimes the best, and firmly closed my throttle so the two 190s attacking me overshot and were then about 100 yards in front of me and trying hard to turn. One presented a straight shot and my three second burst of cannon and machine gun fire severed his tail unit completely. I then lined up on the other but had meantime forgotten in all the excitement, that I had throttled back, so my Spitfire, helped also by the recoil from my guns, now stalled and I went into a sharp spin, which was just as well for there was someone else shooting at me. Sorting that out I found myself way below the formation. So I went on down to zero feet and headed back to Manston on the deck.

After everyone had landed, Flying Officer Cyril Smith, who had witnessed my combat, thought I had got both Focke Wulfs because he said he'd seen the second one go spinning down. However, I had to disappoint him by confirming that I had had no chance of firing at the second 190.

Flight Sergeant N A A Turnbull returned with some holes in his Spitfire while Pilot Officer L Luckhoff, a South African we had on the Squadron, flying as Red 3, claimed two 190s damaged.

A few days later, after examining film and so on, Fighter Command stepped up my damaged claim to one of Destroyed.

Our Intelligence Officer on 131 was Flying Officer C S Flick. He usually took down our reports after an action, then wrote up a combat report, which was then counter-signed by Duncan Brown, now the Redhill Intelligence Officer. Mine, for 31st July, read:

31 July 1943.   Ramrod 179.   Time: 1140 am.   Place: St Omer

"Flight Lieutenant Sampson flying Yellow 1 in the eight aircraft by Wing Commander Malfroy behind and above the bombers. Then turned left after bombing for the return journey via Gravelines. When about a third of the way from the target to the French coast, Flight Lieutenant Sampson noticed about 10 aircraft a long way behind at the same height (14,000 ft). They gained on the Spitfires and he identified them as FW190s. He reported them to the Wing Commander and warned Yellow Section that they were about to be attacked from dead astern. This attack came when just north of St Omer.

"Flight Lieutenant Sampson found two FW190s firing at him out of range from both quarters. He broke port into the nearer one and as it was gaining rapidly without deflection he closed his throttle and it overshot. The Hun also throttled back and started turning to starboard very slowly. Flight Lieutenant Sampson gave a one second burst of both cannon and machine-gun fire, 1½ ring deflection from 250 yards without any observed result. The FW190 now appeared to be hanging on its prop. and the Spitfire was practically on the stall. Flight Lieutenant Sampson gave a second burst of one second at the EA's nose and observed a few strikes on its tail unit. The EA is claimed as damaged. Flying Officer C Smith (Yellow 3) observed the combat and confirms the damage.

"At that moment Flight Lieutenant Sampson noticed explosive shells bursting past his port wing so he pulled the stick back and spun down, returning via Gravelines at 8,000 feet and then at 100 feet to Deal, landing at Manston at 1155 hours.

"The camouflage of the FW was bottle green with black spinner. The black and white cross on the fuselage was scarcely distinguishable. Rounds fired: 62 x 20 mm; 80 x .303."

It was back to a 10 Group Circus (No.49) on 3rd August, the Wing escorting eight Whirlwind fighter-bombers to Brest Guipavas aerodrome. Bags of flak again and about 20 FW190s engaged us. 131 got fairly mixed up but claimed a probable and five damaged. I had a quick squirt at one 190 but it was ineffective I'm sure. When we got back we found that we had lost Earl Smith. Brother Cyril was naturally pretty upset, but the good news later was that Earl, shot down by one of the 190s, had got away with it and was a prisoner.

The Whirlibombers went back to Brest a few days later and again the 190s had a go at us—they obviously didn't take kindly to us hitting their air base at Guipavas. A 190 made an attack on our Blue Section—unsuccessfully and my Section was menaced. We chased them and they chased us, but in the end neither of us did much harm to each other. However, the others in the Wing claimed one destroyed, two probables and a damaged, so we got something out of it.

The main problem for us with these operations from Exeter, was the amount of water we had to cross to reach the enemy coastline. Back in 11 Group it might be anything from between 20 and 60 miles, but down in the southwest, Cherbourg and Brest were a couple of hundred miles or more. For instance when we escorted 40 Bostons to the marshalling yards at Rennes, we covered 450 miles over the sea. Apart from all the other dangers, the slightest hiccup, or odd note from our engines helped to concentrate the mind amazingly. It says much for our hard-working and conscientious ground crews that we rarely, if ever, lost a man through engine failure during the summer of 1943.

Our main types of sorties were Ramrods, Circuses and fighter Sweeps. A Ramrod was a bomber operation with a principal objective, whereas a Circus, while similar, was designed primarily to entice the Luftwaffe fighters up so that a large Spitfire escort could shoot as many down as was possible. A pure fighter Sweep was flown in the hope of mixing it with enemy fighters but quite obviously, the Luftwaffe saw us as no danger by ourselves and generally left us alone.

Guipavas was back on the menu for 15th August, Whirlwinds again, but 10/10th cloud over the target saved the airfield. Part of the raiding force comprised the Typhoons of 266 Squadron, who got some attention from the 190s, and had their CO, Squadron Leader A S MacIntyre, and two other pilots, shot down and killed.

We were not sorry, therefore, during the middle of the month that we moved to Redhill in my old Kenley Sector, now commanded by Peter Wykham-Barnes (later Air Marshal Sir Peter Wykeham KCB

DSO & bar, OBE, DFC & bar AFC), a young Group Captain who
had a brilliant operational record in the Middle East and in Greece.
We were to spend a month there, our main tasks being as escorts
to frequent bombing raids on airfields, railway junctions and other
strongpoints, obviously as a build-up to possible invasion, and a
Dieppe-type operation in early September, of which we knew nothing
at this stage. Later we were to become involved in the early attacks
on the strange construction sites in and around the Pas de Calais,
which turned out to be the launching pads for V1 rocket bombs, but
that was still some months away.

We arrived at Redhill on 16th August and the very next day we were
flying Ramrod 207, close escort to 36 B26 Marauders attacking Poix
airfield, but once again the weather beat us. The next day we went
for Woensdrecht in Holland, another airfield. Some FW190s menaced
us and made some passes but were ineffectual. However, we lost Cyril
Smith who developed engine trouble over the target area. He too
ended up in the bag like his brother, but at least they both survived.

The Germans almost got me again on the 19th—exactly one year
after the Dieppe Operation it will be noted! Ramrod 209 saw us flying
escort cover to 36 Marauders bombing Amiens/Glisy airfield. Orange
was leading the Squadron and Cam Malfroy decided to lead my Flight
so I said I would be his wingman. His briefing included the usual, "....
our job is to stick to the bombers at all costs and not to leave
them for anything." But HE did and as his Number Two, I had to go
with him.

We were on our way back just to the north of Dieppe (yes Dieppe!)
when we could hear over the R/T that the top cover wing of Spitfire
IXs was obviously in contact with many FW190s and Me109Fs. Then
some of these started to appear below and behind us and apparently
taking no part in the main action. Guessing Malfroy would not see
them, I reported one FW190 to him which I had spotted below and
ahead of him, some 250 yards, and with his, "I see him!", he promptly
winged over and went after it.

I began to wonder if he was so surprised at seeing something that
he lost all thought of his briefing orders, for to my surprise he kept
going down with me in tow trying desperately to see if we were being
sucked into a trap. We started down at 14,000 feet and it didn't take
us long to lose all the precious height and be down almost on the deck.
What was also alarming was that I could now see two 190s, not one,
so the first had been joined by a wingman, or perhaps we had been
chasing the wingman who had caught up with his leader. I reckoned
the only hope for us was to despatch both of them quickly, so we could

break off and get out without them turning after us, but these turned out to be very good Hun pilots who skidded and yawed as we went in.

Malfroy was blazing away but whether he was hitting anything I couldn't tell. My fire seemed to be doing some damage, and the wheels dropped on one of them and then a single undercarriage leg flopped down on the other, but they just wouldn't crash. I soon ran out of cannon ammunition and then my .303 magazines were empty. At least the 190 pilots were in no shape to chase us as we broke off and rapidly headed for the coast. When we arrived back, Orange asked me where the hell I'd got to. When I told him he made a very rude expression concerning our Wing Leader.

Once again my words were taken down and written up on a formal Combat Report:

19 August 1943. Ramrod 209. Time 1100 hrs. Place: Amiens.

"The Squadron (with 504) was escort cover to 36 Marauders bombing Amiens/Glisy aerodrome (11 Group Ramrod No.209). They were up at 1035, made rendezvous over Rye and proceeded uneventfully to the target which was accurately bombed. A few minutes after leaving the target, the formation was attacked by about six FW190s and at least one Me109F which came up behind from the south east. The only interesting details concerning the remainder of the operation were provided by Wing Commander Malfroy and his No.2, Flight Lieutenant Sampson of 131 Squadron, whose personal combat report follows here:

"Flight Lieutenant Sampson flying at 14,000 feet a few minutes after leaving the target, saw several FW190s and one Me109F with Italian wing markings, below and behind him. A few moments later he saw and reported another 190 with its port wheel down below and slightly ahead. Wing Commander Malfroy went down after this EA, Flight Lieutenant Sampson following 500 feet above. At about 10,000 feet they found themselves behind two more FW190s one of which also had its port wheel down. Flight Lieutenant Sampson fired several bursts; he saw strikes on fuselage and port wing and claims this EA damaged.

"The 190s were skilfully piloted. Despite the fact that one had a wheel down, they stuck closely together although making violent evasive manoeuvres at 'O' feet. Their speed is estimated at 300 mph in the dive and 240 mph on the deck.

"The return journey was uneventful except for slight light flak north of Dieppe and a column of black smoke, suggestive of a crashed aircraft 2/3rds of the way from target to coast."

No sooner had we debriefed than we were told we were to fly a second Ramrod (210), this time escorting Marauders to St Pol. The 190s were up again and on the way back my Yellow Section were bounced by six of them near Boulogne. My Flight was at the back and flying in line abreast. We had been warned by the Controller that 'Bandits' were in the vicinity, but the weather had turned hazy and visibility was down to 200 yards or so. Unfortunately the whole formation went over the middle of Boulogne and we received a lot of attention from the flak gunners, both at 8,000 feet, slightly below us, and some heavier stuff above. This diverted our attention somewhat and we were weaving like mad to avoid the explosions.

Although we had started in line abreast, Flight Sergeant Ken Parry, a Welshman and a very good, experienced and fearless pilot, lagged behind. We were then jumped by these 190s, the leader picking off Parry who because he was weaving, received the shells underneath his engine, which immediately burst into flames. I shouted, "Break"— which was too late for Parry, and the 190s then half-rolled and went into their usual disappearing routine. I then saw Parry's Spitfire going rapidly down on fire towards the sea.

In the event he was lucky and managed to glide towards an Air Sea Rescue boat (these boats were usually around when a show was on waiting for customers) where he baled out and was quickly pulled on board. He was greeted by the Captain with, "Thank God for you; you're our 100th pick up!" Parry, to my surprise, telephoned me from Dover and I arranged for him to be collected, quite unharmed, but merely furious with himself for having been jumped.

We were certainly having a busy time. During the last week of August, we flew no fewer than nine more shows, eight Ramrods and one Circus. Seven of the operations involved American Marauders, one with Mitchells and the last with B17s. We encountered flak on every mission, fighters on four of them, and we lost two pilots.

Our two losses occurred on one sortie, to Rouen on the 27th. About 20 enemy fighters engaged the formation and we lost Pilot Officer Bateman and Flight Sergeant Andrew. They were flying in Cam's Section as Yellow 3 and 4 when they were attacked by eight FW190s. In another fight, Ken Parry, still fresh from his dip in the Channel, knocked some pieces off a Me109G, but it was little recompense for our loss or his recent hurt pride. The bombers of course, had, in the main, to take the flak, and we saw some shot down and others damaged. One B26 we saw heading across the Channel trailing smoke but they made it to Shoreham where they crash landed. On the escort to the Forts we were shot at by the Yank gunners, which didn't please us, but then of course they were usually guided by the thought that, to be on the safe side, anything without four engines—"..ought to get it!"

September began where August left off for in the first 16 days we flew 15 Ramrod missions with Marauders, Mitchells and Venturas. Flak was a constant companion, fighters made sporadic attacks, some Huns making head-on attacks at the bombers, and some of the top cover boys shot a few 190s down.

In the midst of this came Operation "Starkey". Unknown to us, our recent intensive bombing of enemy airfields was part of this operation. The plan was to make the Germans believe that another full scale Combined Operation, just like Dieppe the previous year, was about to be mounted upon the French coast. They even had large troop concentrations assembled, including assault craft, in the south of England. The object really was to bring the Luftwaffe to a full scale battle in the air and inflict maximum damage upon it.

It finally took place on September 9th. Quite unexpectedly on the afternoon of the 8th we were told that everyone was confined to the airfield, no leave passes were permitted and nobody was allowed out that evening. An amusing story came out of this. I happened to be in the small dispersal office allocated to the Flight Commanders, after hearing this news, and Sergeant Desmond Leslie came in and told me that he had a very important dinner date which he couldn't cancel! It seemed so stupid that instead of immediately booting him out, I remarked, "Oh yes, and with whom?" To this he replied, "With the Prime Minister, Winston Churchill! You see, my father, Sir Shane Leslie, is a first cousin."

To say I was surprised is a bit of an understatement but I kept my reason, and apart from telling him to say nothing about anything he'd heard or seen this afternoon, said, "Say no more, off you go." The next morning I asked him how he had got on and he replied, "When I was shown in, Winston came along and said, 'Ah, Desmond, so glad you could make it because I've got another airman coming to dinner.' Oh, I said, who is that?, to which Winston replied, 'The Chief of the Air Staff, Air Chief Marshal Sir Charles Portal.'" I would have loved to have seen Portal's face, when Churchill introduced him to a mere Sergeant Pilot who would be joining them for dinner.

Meantime, we were briefed and told that on the morning of the 9th, a fairly large convoy of ships was to sail towards Boulogne but would not attempt to make landfall. Hopefully it would cause a reaction similar to Dieppe, from both German bombers and fighters and with our superior escorting numbers, we would exact a large toll on their aircraft resorces. We were never told what went wrong but there was simply no reaction by the enemy.

We were airborne early as cover above the ships but when nothing happened we were then switched to escort bombers to airfield targets inland from Boulogne, St Pol being one I remember. It was disappointing and I still wonder if German intelligence was smarter than we thought.

I remember at Exeter we had some RAF chap down to talk to us about Escape and Evasion should anyone be unlucky enough to be shot down, which was all pretty interesting. What intrigued us more, however, was the man's own evasion story. He'd been shot down and had been picked up by the French underground movement who eventually arranged for him to be sent along an escape line.

At one stage he was to catch a train which was due to leave just after midnight but as the local curfew began at midnight, he and his guide, a young woman, had to judge it just right in order to be at the station just before curfew began.

They were making their way along the darkened streets but as they neared the station, a detachment of German soldiers came into sight at the end of their street. They couldn't chance being stopped so near to midnight, so the RAF chap, being quite smart, quickly pulled the girl in through the door of a small hotel. Once inside they knew they would now miss the train, so not wanting to chance the curfew, he decided to stay where he was. He suggested to the girl, who was also now in danger from the curfew, that she stay too. She agreed and he booked a room. The punchline to the story was that he caught the midnight train—but five nights later! We liked that story.

One of our pilots, Flight Sergeant Morris, was later shot down in the same area as our story-teller, was also picked up by the underground and got back down the line, but he didn't have such an 'interesting' tale to tell when he got back.

Following Ramrod 223 on the 16th, another close escort job to Marauders hitting Beaumont Le Roger airfield—the High Cover Wing got six fighters but lost two—we were told we were returning to 10 Group. It had been an exciting month, which I suppose was all for the abortive Starkey 'Do'. In the event, the build up had scored infinitely more successes in our normal offensive operational role, than had the 'great day' itself, which I seem to remember hearing netted just two Hun fighters, despite over 1,200 RAF and American sorties.

While we were at Redhill, our AOC in 10 Group, Air Vice-Marshal Charles Steele, visited us and we also arranged for the Lord Lieutenant of Kent, Lord Cornwallis to pay a call (as Tony reminded me earlier), as it was through his efforts that 131 Squadron had been raised. I am sure he appreciated it.

Also, during a visit to Manston, Cam Malfroy met Pam Barton, the famous pre-war lady golfer who was a WAAF officer, very charming and good looking. He introduced her to the officers in the Mess much to our joy. Sadly she was later killed in a flying accident.

CHAPTER VIII

SPITFIRE IXs AND TOUR EXPIRED

We returned to Exeter on 17th September 1943, whereupon three things happened. First Cam Malfroy was taken off operations, second he was replaced by Wing Commander Denis Smallwood DFC (known to everyone as 'Splinters'), then third, we transferred to a new airfield which was known alternatively as Church Stanton or Culmhead.

Culmhead was situated on the Blackdown hills some few miles to the east of Taunton. It had originally been intended as an emergency airfield by Trilkey Warren Farm. In its early days it had been the home of some Polish squadrons for the defence of Exeter and Bristol. It was still known as Church Stanton when we were there but became better known as Culmhead towards the end of 1943 to avoid confusion with a number of RAF airfields throughout the country which have 'Church' in their name.

The most important thing, however, was the news that we were about to hand in our Spit Vs and re-equip with the Mark IXA. After two final flights in my old 'K', I took over a new Spit IX coded 'K', flying it for the first time on the 21st. It had a Merlin 63 engine and it felt a lot racier than the old Mark V.

Mind you, the Mark V was a beautiful aeroplane to fly but by the summer of 1943 when I flew it most it did not match up to the Me109F or FW190. There was nothing much different in speed, but the Spitfire was inferior in both dive and climb. It was, however, superior in the all important turning circle.

The IXA and then the IXB was designed to operate in excess of 30,000 feet where it had the edge on both the 109 and 190. Unfortunately when the IXs came into more general use in 1943, operational heights seldom reached beyond 25,000. The Spit IXB which came along later was in full use by 1944, had all the answers and was superior in all conditions to the Messerschmitt and Focke Wulf fighters.

For the rest of the month we flew our new aircraft, broke them in and generally got used to them. We flew our first Sweep on 3rd October but nothing interrupted our quiet sojourn above the French countryside. We were soon back in the old routine of bomber escorts to targets in Brittany and the very occasional Fighter Sweep which raised no reaction. The Germans were no fools and knew that fighters on their own posed no danger, and only when we escorted bombers would they deem to react, and even then not always. Even when they did engage in combat the best we could hope for was to inflict some damage as they made their sweeping passes, for we could not follow them down or give chase, as this would leave the bombers unprotected and vulnerable to other enemy fighters just waiting for just such a chance. This was a pity because both Smallwood and Orange O'Meara were both aggressive leaders and only on very rare occasions were they able to show their qualities as top rate fighter pilots.

I must say I held both men in high regard. Smallwood was a very competent leader and his briefings were always meticulous and what is more, he stuck to them. He later became Air Chief Marshal Sir Denis, GBE KCB DSO DFC. Orange I rated very highly too. He was brave, a very good marksman and like most Irishmen, had a very quick temper which would disappear just as fast. I got on very well with him and was very sorry when I had to leave the Squadron on rest.

The Ramrods continued into October—I recall the flak when taking Bostons to the Lanveoc Poulmic airfield and seaplane base on the 8th. We were at 24,000 feet, totally alone—except for the flak. Christ!

A Rodeo on the 15th—a straight Fighter Sweep in company with the Typhoons of 257 Squadron, took us to the Brest Peninsular. Some Huns were reported way below us at 2,000 feet off Guernsey but the Typhoons, being much lower than us, got to them first and put one into the sea. All we saw was the splash.

We also flew the odd weather recce up the Channel, and the occasional 'Jim Crow' mission, low level, looking for any signs of enemy shipping. Towards the end of October I led a four-man section to the Sillon de Talbert point, and then headed in up the river as far as Peimpol trying to locate any ships but it was empty. There were no fighters or flak—almost like peacetime.

November was a most disappointing month, for the weather had begun to curtail our operations and those we did fly did not budge enemy fighters. It was not until the 26th and Ramrod 107 that we received some attention at last. I led the Squadron as Top Cover to three lots of bombers attacking the Martinvast Works south of Cherbourg. Suddenly the Wing was attacked by about 15 FW190s and a fight developed.

It was one of those rare occasions when we received absolutely no warning that enemy fighters were even near us. The first we knew was a shout from Smallwood that we were under attack from head-on and that he had received a hit in the wing—fortunately not serious. These 190s were without doubt an experienced bunch and came in at three different levels. I saw four of them about 1,000 feet below me apparently just asking for it but I knew enough about the game by now to smell a rat. Checking about me, I soon picked out four more sitting 1,000 feet above ready to pounce if we went down.

The very experienced Ronnie West, flying as my No.3, who had collected a DFC & bar over Malta, plus several kills, both German and Italian, came to the same conclusion as me. He called and suggested that he and his wingman should climb up towards those guys to which I agreed. As the two Spitfires headed up, the 190s above immediately half-rolled and came down in front of us, levelling off as they did so. I pulled round and made a head-on attack on one 190 from 500 yards just as the pilot saw the danger and began to half-roll. I managed three good bursts on it, totalling five seconds of fire which was witnessed by Ronnie, who later suggested that in his opinion he didn't think that 190 would be operating for some time, if at all. My wingman, Flight Sergeant Wood, who stayed with me, also reported seeing strikes on the fighter's starboard mainplane and fuselage. However, all I could claim was a damaged as the camera film did not show any bits flying off or other signs of lethal damage, so that was that.

If the Controller had given us some warning and had we not been taken by surprise, I think that by the way we were so well spread and with the enemy in rather closed formation, although at different levels, we might have taken a bigger toll. In the event the Wing was able to claim two destroyed, three probables and six damaged, including mine, so Splinters was well satisfied, considering the surprise we endured. If luck had been against us it could have easily been a reverse score!

It was always the same game. If the Germans came up at all, they usually just sniffed around and unless they felt they could take us by surprise, they more often than not just left us alone. I imagine I was showing my frustration on December 1st, after an 11 Group Ramrod—No.343, which we flew from Ford on the south coast. Again we flew as Top Cover to Marauders, myself leading 131, going to the airfield at Cambrai. Thirty plus enemy fighters were soon reported near us, and we anxiously started to search the heavens, but nothing happened. Upon landing, I wrote in my log book that they had

"...pissed off when near enough to see us first!"

But occasionally we got in and did some damage. On the last day of 1943, we and 165 flew to support American Forts and Liberators coming back from a raid on Bordeaux and Chateaubernard. I was leading 131, crossing the coast at Morlaix. The Wing saw and jumped four German fighters carrying rockets, and the boys of 165 shot them all down.

Nevertheless, we all felt we were doing a worthwhile job. After all we were hurting the enemy with our bombing and knew that protecting the medium and heavy bombers from attack was of paramount importance. It was not always exciting, unless as some-times happened the bomber leader opened the throttles for home making the formation straggle, which made life more difficult for us and a lot easier for the Huns, who were past masters at picking off stragglers.

I suppose from the German pilot's point of view, certainly in the West, their tactics were sound. After all they were fighting a defensive kind of war, with limited numbers of fighters. The main fighting was in the East or over the German homeland. Our bombing might disrupt captured French industry, but if civilians did get hurt they were French and not German. If they could pick off a bomber or two or even a Spitfire or Typhoon, without putting themselves in too much danger, then they probably saw it as good arithmetic.

It was now that we began to have a new sort of target although at first we were not told too much about them. Rumours were rife, however. We now know they were the V1 rocket launching sites that seemed to be springing up like mushrooms in Northern France. They consisted of just a bit of cleared ground, a launching ramp, each facing England, and nearby a concrete hut used by the launching crew. They were small targets, too small in the main for large-scale bombing unless we found a clutch of them, so more often than not it was the Hurricane or Typhoon fighter-bombers that had to attack them. As they and ourselves found out very quickly, they could be highly dangerous as the Germans protected them with any amount of 88 mm guns and light machine-gun emplacements.

I was leading the Squadron quite a bit at this time and our first recorded operation against these new targets—we called them 'No Balls'—was flown on 4th January 1944. Typhoons were doing the dive bombing and we merely provided a diversionary sweep nearby in case enemy fighters came up. In 11 Group these targets began to take up a good deal of operational time, whilst we kept busy with those appearing in the Cherbourg area. All during January we flew escort to bomb-carrying Typhoons or Mitchells and Bostons going for these No-Balls, so HQ must have thought them important, which of course they were. Bearing in mind the first V1s were not fired until June, it took six months of effort to try and keep them down. Like painting the Forth Bridge, it seemed a never ending job. No sooner had you destroyed one than another appeared, and then the first was repaired or rebuilt.

In between, we flew along into 11 Group and took part in one of their operations, flying from Manston, Ford or Tangmere. Then suddenly my tour was up. I had flown over 135 sorties, covering something like 275 operational flying hours and was told it was time for a rest. I was a bit sad at leaving, but if I am honest, I was beginning to feel tired. It had been a busy summer and long winter. I flew my last Op with 131 on February 4th, a two-hour fighter Sweep in support of Forts and Libs into the Ghent area, Ramrod 504, and that was that. According to my log book I now had a total of 773 flying hours, which was a lot more than I had when I joined 602 back in May 1942.

I now received a signal to proceed to HQ Fighter Command at Bentley Priory near Stanmore where I was interviewed by a Squadron Leader in the Postings Department. He suggested that I would be a useful instructor at an OTU and there was a possibility of promotion to squadron leader. I told him that the idea didn't really appeal to me, to which he added, "You've really got no choice."

When I got back to Exeter my luck was in. Group Captain Tom Dalton-Morgan DSO DFC & bar, a high scoring fighter pilot in the early war years (17 victories) and now the Senior Plans Officer with 10 Group, happened to be visiting the Station. I told him about my interview and he promised to have a word with the AOC, Air Vice-Marshal Charles Steele, a former fighter pilot in the Great War. Tom thought there was a chance that I could take over from Squadron Leader Joe Holmes DFC AFC, the Sector Gunnery Officer at Exeter. Tom asked if I knew the AOC. "No," I replied, "but I see from the Preparatory School Magazine that he was at the same Prep School as me, but, of course, quite a few years earlier." "That should do no harm," smiled Tom. In the event I got the job—and promotion to squadron leader.

The job involved being in charge of two Drogue Towing Martinet aeroplanes and a dual-control Miles Master. The idea was to give both Spitfire and Mosquito pilots practice at firing at a towed drogue and some instruction on the Master. Before settling in I was sent on a month's course at the gunnery school at Sutton Bridge which then moved to Catfoss, near Hull. It was commanded by another former fighter pilot, Wing Commander Archie Winskill DFC & bar, later Air Commodore Sir Archie Winskill, Captain of the Queen's Flight, who had just taken over from New Zealander Al Deere DSO DFC & bar.

We flew Spitfire IIs at Catfoss which was quite a change from the Mark IXs I'd been flying recently. There were quite a number of prominent fighter pilots continually going through the School, and I recall meeting, and indeed flying with such men as Johnny Checketts DSO DFC, another New Zealander, who had gained some fame by being shot down over France commanding 485 Squadron. He managed to evade capture and was back in England five days later. Another was Squadron Leader John Beard DFM, who had fought in the Battle of Britain, and Martin Gran DFC, a Norwegian pilot who like me was between tours. Also like me he was later to get back onto operations, commanding a squadron. He ended the war with three DFCs.

When I was later with the Norwegian Wing, whom incidentally I consider to be the bravest of the brave, Martin was one of the squadron commanders (331 Squadron). He was leading his squadron on 29th December 1944 on an armed reconnaissance at 4,000 feet, adjacent to the clutch of German occupied airfields of Hengelo, Almelo and Enschede, when some eight Me109s and FW190s took off in a hurry, but still as a unit. They must have been aware of the Norge Squadron and were turning very hard to port, so much so that it was, as Martin said, impossible to get the dot and the cross together on his gunsight. He then told me that he had to apply the lesson taught at the CGS, and that was to pull through the target and start short bursts when the target was out of sight. He managed this on three of the fighters, which left two 109s and one 190 burning on the ground. He got a bar to his DFC for this effort.

The course was designed to suit a dual purpose. The first, to teach pupils how to become instructors on the various aspects of Fighter tactics, and the second, to teach pupils how to lecture, using blackboard diagrams and thus either at OTUs or squadrons put over the lessons to operational pilots, especially those still inexperienced.

Obviously the set-up had to be well staffed and indeed it was. One of the three flying instructors involved in demonstrating the various methods of attacking enemy aircraft in addition to Johnny Checketts and Martin Gran, was Flight Lieutenant Scott, a former 603 Auxiliary Squadron pilot and a brilliant aviator. Apart from a lot of flying, including Drogue shooting, we had to prepare and lecture each other on given subjects. We were then criticised, first by fellow pupils and then by the instructor in charge. I thought it was an excellent course, and very well conducted.

There were some twelve of us and all with one tour of Ops behind us so we were treated as equals and perhaps one or two new points might emerge for us. The whole atmosphere was one of relaxed friendliness and co-operation. As I was distined for Exeter I was told that I would have to be very persuasive with the various COs to obtain their co-operation to get some extra tuition for pilots as second pilot to me, flying the Master with one machine gun firing at the Drogue towed by a Martinet.

The Flight consisted of myself as Squadron Leader/CO, two pilots, two Martinets and one Master for instruction purposes. The two Martinets also carried an NCO in the rear seat, controlling the Drogue, ie: letting it out when airborne and drawing it in before landing.

Loel Guiness, who had been Station Commander at Exeter, handed over to another former 601 Squadron pilot from the earlier days, Group Captain Sir Archibald Hope Bt DFC. Under my command I found I also had three Air Sea Rescue boats at Exmouth, Torquay and Dartmouth, so part of my duties was to go out with them whilst they practised with their fixed Bren gun on the towed Drogue.

I started my job at Exeter towards the end of April 1944, and apart from overseeing the various training aspects, spent some time flying about the countryside in a Master, visiting such places as Culmhead, Bolt Head, Fairwood Common, sometimes taking Orange O'Meara with me, etc. I must say I found the standard of gunnery of some of the junior pilots left a lot to be desired and on at least two occasions the Martinets received a bullet in the tail unit. Understandably, I received some forthright complaints from the airmen i/c Drogues.

Another of my responsibilities was the appointment as Officer's Mess PMC (President of the Mess Committee) which involved looking after the Mess bar and the 1/6d per day, per officer, for the odd extra, by way of food. I had to check bar stocks, bar takings and ensure that 10% over cost was showing and then transferred to the Dining Room Fund. The only three people entitled to sign for free drinks were the CO, the Senior Admin Officer and the PMC, and then only for drinks ordered for visiting senior guests.

The Profit and Loss Account I found was in fact showing minimal profit so I spent hours going over the 'chits' with the two barmen, a corporal and an LAC. Finally, in desperation, I asked, "Is there anyone who gets anything from the bar without a 'chit'?" "Oh yes," was the reply. "The officer's mess cook gets a bottle of whisky, a bottle of gin, a bottle of port and a bottle of sherry once a week for cooking purposes." I quickly put a stop to that, ordering the cook in future, to see me with the recipes which required so much alcohol. I never heard a word. Obviously, without a single drop of alchohol I had well and truly 'cooked his goose'.

The airfield was also used by an American outfit flying Dakotas and gliders. They had their own Messes but, of course, there was friendly liaison between us all. Colonel Krebbs, their CO, asked if an ENSA party could be organised. They would fly the party from RAF Northolt and back the next day and transport could also be arranged from a point in the West End of London to Northolt. Group Captain Archie Hope got clearance from the PR people at 10 Group and I was asked to make arrangements with the famous Jack Hylton.

I flew up to Northolt and then by transport to the Cafe Royal where we finalised a date and numbers. Jack said it would be most of the Crazy Gang, plus Tommy Trinder and a bevy of beauties. We were to arrange accommodation in the Royal Clarence in Exeter and have an Officer's Mess Party in our Mess. The AOC, AVM Charles Steele, plus family, were also invited to attend.

All went very well although Tommy Trinder was a bit near the bone with his jokes. He told the Americans that he was the English Bob Hope and sang all the riskiest songs, including 'Yank my Doodle its a Dandy'. Afterwards the AOC congratulated me for the arrangements and with a twinkle in his eye said, "You should have vetted Mister Trinder's script!"

I remember too that for the party we needed some extra eggs and I was told that a small holding, literally on the side of the airfield, had some hens. I went over to it and upon my arrival I spotted two men digging and asked, "Which of you is the husband of Mrs.......?" They replied, "We both are." When I mentioned this to an officer who had been at Exeter for some years he confirmed, "Oh yes, one of them was her first husband and never came back from Europe in 1918 and was presumed dead. In due course she married again but eventually her first husband returned. He was taken in and all seems to be OK."

All in all, I must say I enjoyed the short time I was OC the Sector Gunnery School before going to 10 Group Plans. I'd certainly seen a bit of life.

Whilst I was at Exeter, Tony Pickering, now the senior flight commander on 131 Squadron, gave me the sad news that Flight Lieutenant Ronnie West DFC & bar, who had risen to command my Flight, had been killed when making a wheels-up landing at the satellite airfield at Bolt Head. It appeared that his undercarriage failed to come down and he forgot to release the 45-gallon slipper petrol tank held underneath the Spitfire's belly. Therefore, as he bellied in, he landed on the tank which exploded, engulfing the Spitfire in an appalling fireball.

As mentioned earlier, Ronnie had been on Malta where he had proved to be a first class fighter pilot and a very good marksman. There is no doubt in my mind that he should not have been posted back onto operations so soon, as he was battle weary.

Ronnie had told us of one or two experiences which are worth recording. He had arrived on Malta after flying off with the first batch of Spitfires, from the carrier HMS *Eagle*, joining 249 Squadron. He told us that as the Spitfires only had flaps which were either fully up or fully down—no half or partial flaps as with bombers—they had to overcome the problem of really needing partial flap when taking off from the carrier. They achieved this by selecting flaps 'down' prior to take-off, then inserting bits of wood which were held in position whilst the flaps were selected 'up'. Thus partial flap was achieved. Once height was made, flaps were selected down, which released the bits of wood, then 'up' again before flying on to Malta.

They arrived on the island by early evening but by the morning there were only six of the new Spitfires serviceable and ready for the first German raid from nearby Sicily, which he said, normally took place around 11 o'clock.

When the sirens sounded, the six Spitfires took off, led by Ronnie. The Controller reported fifty bombers escorted by an estimated 100+ fighters. As the six Spifires approached the German formation, they suddenly all turned round and went back. As the policy was to conserve the defensive resources of the island, an attack or pursuit was not pressed home so the Spitfires broke off and headed for base. Upon landing, Ronnie was informed that the island's listening service had overheard on the German radio frequency, the voice of the German fighter leader, which, roughly translated, said—"Christ, Spitfires! Why haven't we been told that Spitfires are on Malta? Back we go." When I heard that story I said aloud, "We can't possibly lose the war now."

Two things happened at this time: firstly came the pleasing news that I had been awarded the DFC, and early the following month—6th June—the tremendous Invasion of Normandy began. I was at the Central Gunnery School, doing a course at Southend, in fact on D-Day itself I had to content myself with flying two air-to-air firing practices as my sole 'contribution' to the greatest invasion of all time. At least I can say I was flying a Spitfire on D-Day, so long as nobody asks me where and why.

My job at Exeter, while enjoyable, had its frustrations. I see for instance that on the 15th, I took four flight sergeants up for individual dual instruction on air-to-air firing in a Master. My log book comments read: "I am supposed to teach these boys how to fire their guns. Some of them could do with a little more flying tuition and NOT by me!"

I remained at Exeter until the middle of July when Splinters Smallwood arrived one day for lunch. He had become tour expired some weeks after me and been posted to Group as Senior Day Ops Officer. (There were Ops Day and Ops Night staff.) He told me that the Ops Section at 10 Group Headquarters was to be increased by an additional squadron leader and that both he and Orange O'Meara were in the team and would like me to join them. I didn't have to be asked twice, so off I went to Rudloe Manor, Box, near Bath, where the Headquarters was situated. I did, however, remind Splinters that Tom Dalton-Morgan had promised me that I could return to Ops after my rest period was up, and Splinters said he would not stand in my way when the time came.

The Group had a fairly large establishment of WAAF cypher girls and operations room plotters. The Group was well known for its very good looking WAAF Officers and if I only mention Helen Wooler and Pauline MacGuire, it is because they were stunningly beautiful and full of charm.

Our job in the Ops Section was to liaise with Fighter Command HQ and 11 Group, to see if either of our two Spitfire Wings, the Culmhead Wing, commanded by Pete Brothers, or the Harrowbeer Wing at Perranporth, commanded by Wing Commander H A C 'Birdy' Bird-Wilson DFC & bar, were to operate. As Pete Brothers later explained it to me:

"On posting in April 1944, my Wing consisted of 610 Squadron (Spitfire XIV), Squadron Leader R A Newbury DFC; 616 Squadron (Spitfire VII), Squadron Leader L W Watts DFC; 131 Squadron (Spitfire VII), Squadron Leader J J O'Meara all three based at Culmhead. At Bolt Head I had 41 Squadron (Spitfire XII), Squadron Leader R H Chapman and at Exeter, 126 Squadron (Spitfire IXB), Squadron Leader W W Swindon. 263 Squadron (Typhoons), Squadron Leader Henri Gonay CdeG—a Belgian, was at Harrowbeer.

"This was too scattered to control, so I moved 126 to Culmhead and later persuaded Tom Morgan to rename us Culmhead Wing and form a Harrowbeer Wing using 126, who had less range than our Spit XIVs and VIIs, and 'Birdy' came and took over."

Either Wing might be required for escort duties either to our own medium daylight bombers, or fighter bombers, or the American heavies. They might also be required to support an 11 Group show, but if nothing of that nature developed, then we would plan our own fighter sweeps. My few months in this job were most enjoyable. I even managed to get in one operational sortie, which was practically one tour in itself.

CHAPTER IX

RODEO 194

Following the invasion of France the Germans had started to pull away from Brittany and move eastwards. This for us in 10 Group meant that our fighter sorties, even with drop tanks, were taking us further and further east, and inland, from our west country bases.

We had a meeting at our Headquarters with both Wing Leaders and both, in their friendly, bantering, way said to us, "It's all very well for you buggers sitting on your arses and sending us further and further into France, but we've got to fly these Ops!" The long and short of this was that on August 7th, 1944, I planned a fighter Sweep for the Culmhead Wing—one squadron only—to fly in over Cherbourg which was still in German hands. The Squadron would then head towards Chartres and Orleans, back along the Loire Valley then out again past Cherbourg.

The whole show would cover an estimated 760 miles, so the Spitfires would have to carry 90-gallon slipper tanks under their bellies. As was normal, I had to get the plan approved by the AOC, Air Vice-Marshal J B Cole-Hamilton—very much the martinet and a stickler for time keeping.

It so happened that he was off duty and the SASO, Air Commodore Vere Harvey (now Lord Harvey of Prestbury) was in charge. I told him about the bantering that the two Wing Leaders had given us, and that this Op would be the deepest penetration to date. I suggested that to show there was no ill-feeling, I should offer to accompany the squadron selected, and he agreed. I immediately telephoned Pete Brothers to tell him, and he responded, "Good show, you can fly as my number two."

Take-off time from RAF Culmhead was planned for 2 pm, so after an early lunch I borrowed Vere Harvey's personal Hurricane which he kept at nearby RAF Colerne, and arrived at 1.15. Here I found that it was my old 131 Squadron who had been selected by Pete to fly the sortie, and the present CO, Squadron Leader I N MacDougall DFC, told me I could use his Spitfire VII, coded NX-M (MD165).

I have to admit though, that I nearly didn't make Culmhead in that old Hurricane, which must have been a Mark 'Nothing', just used by Harvey as part of the Com. Flight. I had taxied it to the end of the runway, began to open the throttle when one of the bad habits I'd picked up in the Spitfire, caught up with me. I was used to trundling down the runway and just before pushing the throttle right forward would push the pitch lever forward to put the propeller into fully fine. So now, in the Hurricane, I did the same thing, began to open up the throttle but discovered I couldn't find the pitch lever! The aircraft was gaining speed rapidly with the prop still in fully course pitch.

It was too late now as I was over a third the way down the runway, the throttle right forward with me fiddling about trying to locate this pitch lever. Fortunately the runway was some 2,000 yards long, so I was able to get off in course pitch, but if it had been a smaller runway I'd have had a hell of a problem; probably ending up in a heap at the end of it with my wheels up. It was a bad mistake in assuming the Hurricane was the same as the Spitfire, but I'd got away with it.

When I landed at Culmhead I taxied up to dispersal and asked MacDougall about it, saying. "This is a first class admission for you. I've just flown down from Colerne and I can't find the bloody pitch control lever; can you show me where it is?" In fact it was in the normal place but unlike the Spitfire it wasn't so obvious, being straight up without a knob, whereas the Spitfire had a knob sticking out slightly so one couldn't miss it.

After briefing during which Pete introduced me, pointedly, as the 'Planner of the Operation', he told the pilots, good humouredly, that in order to show no ill-feeling I was flying as his wingman! (Smiles all round.) He asked if I wanted to say anything, but all I said was that being some few months Ops-rusty, what was the form if we ran into enemy fighters? Pete's answer was that the Germans now seldom if ever, indulged in combat, and unless they got the Jump or Bounce, usually opened the taps and went for home at zero feet. "For our part," he remarked, "it's a free for all."

We took off and headed out across the Channel at zero feet so as not to alert the German radar, and then climbed when nearing the hostile coast to fly into France at Cherbourg, at 10,000 feet. Once over the German pocket of resistance, we dropped down to 4,000 feet. With about 10 minutes to the return point, we saw two Me109s flying northwards. Pete was just ahead, his Spitfire VII easily distinguishable with his personal initials 'PB' painted on the fuselage. At a signal from him, we jettisoned our drop tanks and gave chase but although we had a slight edge over the 109s, they had just that much start on us, so Pete had to call off the chase.

Because of this diversion we had cut the corner by quite a distance to get on to the Loire valley. I remember flying over Chateau Blois in a westerly direction when suddenly we all saw about a dozen fighter aircraft with cigar-shaped underslung petrol tanks. My first thought was that we were seeing American P47 Thunderbolts, but when they saw us we clearly identified them as FW190s.

As we were overhauling them they immediately half rolled and came towards us but diving beneath us so as to avoid combat and presumably to make for their home base near Paris. We, on Pete's command, dived after them which was followed by his instructions to, "Hack them down," and "Everyman for himself." Whether we dived better than them I am not sure but with my throttle wide open I could see I was gaining on two of them. Because of the sharp turn Pete was slightly behind me at this point, also chasing the two 190s. As I slowly closed on them I gave a two-second burst at 550 yards at one of them to see what reaction I might get. To my very pleasant surprise, the FW190 on the right started turning right and the other to the left. My instant reaction was, "Boy, you've had it now."

The Spitfire VII can easily out-turn a 190 and easier still if the 190 pilot opens his throttle. He started to climb off the deck and began to weave about. When I was about 250 yards away I gave two more bursts of three seconds each and the Focke Wulf went over and straight into the deck where it exploded. I looked around for Pete, seeing a large column of black smoke about two miles or so away from where I was, and could hear his voice answering Flight Lieutenant J C R 'Closet' Waterhouse, who was himself in the middle of a successful combat.

On the way home, I formated with Peter Bearman, one of the flight commanders. As it turned out, he flew over the German lines at 4,000 feet instead of the required 8,000, so we were subjected to some 'hate' from German ground fire. The flak started to explode about us and I sustained a direct hit from an 88 mm anti-aircraft shell, which made a very large hole in my port wing. Fortunately it did not hit anything vital, such as aileron or flap controls, but it gave me a jolt.

Heading out over the sea once more, the Spitfire performed perfectly despite the hole in its wing, and when we finally arrived over Culmhead I first advised the Control Tower of my situation and received the information that both the Fire and Blood Waggons had been alerted. I then selected 'wheels down' and asked Pete Bearman to fly under me to confirm both wheels were in fact down. Then I selected flaps down and they too seemed to be working satisfactorily. I came in and put NX-M onto the runway without any trouble and let out a sigh of relief.

We landed back at Culmhead just three hours, 20 minutes after take-off, well satisfied with our mission in which we had netted three FW190s for no loss. When I taxied up to 131's dispersal, MacDougall and the rest of the boys were all waiting and all looked slightly anxious, with the exception of the Engineering Officer, who took one look at the wing damage and commented, "Oh, for Christ's sake, that's going to take some repairing."

The Station Commander at Culmhead was Wing Commander I R Campbell-Orde (known as the General). He attended our de-briefing and was most pleased with the success of the Op and genuinely pleased with my success. For my part, I was privately annoyed with Pete Bearman for his error in leading me over the Hun positions.

As a matter of interest, I wrote the following combat report:

Personal Combat Report—S/Ldr R W F Sampson DFC.

(a) 7th August, 1944	(f) 3/10 cumulus at 8,000 ft -
(b) 131 Squadron	visibility good.
(c) Spitfire VII LR 90 Gall tank	(g) and (h) Nil.
(d) 1520	(j) 1 FW190 destroyed
(e) W of Le Mans	(k)

General Report.

"I was flying No.2 to W/Cdr Brothers on Rodeo 194. We were on the way back at 5,000 ft when we saw 2 Me109s N.W. of Alencon flying south. We gave chase as far as a point west of Le Mans, but could not catch them. We then saw a formation of about 12 a/c at 7,000 ft flying west; they had long-range cigar-shape tanks slung to their bellies which they jettisoned as we approached. The W/Cdr drew ahead and the aircraft broke and were promptly recognised by all as FW190s.

"I was about 1,000 yds away when the two e/a on the extreme left broke to port and came towards me head-on. I climbed slightly to avoid a head-on attack and they rolled on their backs and went down, both firing at nothing. I half rolled after them and they seemed to have to throttle back to pull out. I had no difficulty in quickly closing the distance from 1200 yds to 600 yds. We were now at 0 ft and I was only closing very slightly travelling in a N easterly direction at 350 indicated. I gave a short burst at 600 yds to make them weave and they broke in opposite directions. I selected the starboard a/c. I gave a 1½ sec. burst all armament at 450 yards angle off 40", 1½ ring deflection with no result. The e/a then broke starboard and I gave a 2 sec. burst at 300 yds, one ring deflection, speed 240, with no result. The Hun then started breaking both ways alternatively, and I was enabled to get in three more short bursts with small angles, speed about 180 mph. I observed strikes on the cockpit and the e/a pulled up vertically to about 600 feet, rolled over and went straight in, the pilot being killed.

F/Lt Bearman (Blue 1) and W/O Crayford (Yellow 3) witnessed this. I heard W/Cdr Brothers say he had shot one down, and noticed a large column of smoke about two miles to the west of my combat which was in the region of Beaumont sur Sarthe.

"I then set course for Cap de la Hague and whilst at 4,000 ft with Blue 1, F/Lt Bearman, I received a direct hit by Hun Bofors type flak in the port wing in the Argentan area. We both went down to 0 ft and I was able to get back to Culmhead without further incident.

"I claim one FW190 destroyed.

"Cine gun exposed."

I also managed to see Pete Brothers' combat report, or at least the report the I/O put in, which was somewhat shorter than mine, I noticed. It read:

"Wing Commander Brothers selected one and opened fire on it from the port quarter, 20 degrees angle off, 150 yards. Strikes seen on cockpit and port aileron. The aircraft immediately rolled over to the right, the nose dropped and as the aircraft dived down it did two more complete rolls to starboard, going into the ground vertically and exploding, 20 miles north west of La Fleche."

Pete himself recalls Rodeo 194:

"I remember 7th August 1944 as a 'good day' as for several days either side of it I spent leading my Wing as escort to long-range columns of 250 to 500 Lancasters attacking targets such as Bordeaux, darting up and down their line like demented sheep-dogs, no doubt good for their morale but with little enemy fighter reaction, total boredom for us. But that day Sammy and good luck arrived together.

"Leading twelve Spitfires of 131 Squadron with Sammy as my No.2, we crossed the Channel at low level as usual, climbing to the coast to clear the coastal flak belt then dropping to around 4,000 feet once inland of Cherbourg. Our route then was southerly to Vire, Le Mans, Tours and Bourges, some 400 miles from our Culmhead base, where we were to swing round north-westerly to Blois, Vire, Cherbourg and home.

"Eight weeks previously I had led 131 and 616 Squadrons of the Culmhead Wing in low level attacks on the airfields at Le Mans and Laval where we were lucky enough to catch the Luftwaffe taking off and destroyed six FW190s and damaged a further five for the loss of two Spitfires, much to our satisfaction and that of Air Marshal Sir Roderick Hill, our Commander-in-Chief, who wrote to express his congratulations. So we were in high hopes of again stirring up activity from these airfields and repeating our success.

"Approaching Bourges we saw in the distance two Me109s which we chased briefly but failed to catch so gave up as they were drawing us far off our route. Our action was to be rewarded however, for nearing Blois we ran into fifteen FW190s which dived away with us in hot pursuit. Sammy and I chased a pair which separated, mine to the left, his to the right. By now down to ground level, as I closed the range I was surprised to see my 190 start a gentle climb and weave equally gently to left and right, offering a perfect target. 'Oh, my God, you poor sucker. You must be straight out of training school,' I thought. It seemed so unfair and spoilt the exhilaration of the chase. This was not to be an exciting duel but a massacre. Worse was to follow.

"I think I am not alone in regarding air combat as tremendously stimulating fun as one shoots in an attempt to knock down an aircraft. There is nothing personal in it and one is usually spared the thought or sight of bodily injury. It can be wholly impersonal, unless one had the misfortune to have suffered like the Poles, Czechs and others who had left loved ones behind in the hands of a brutal enemy. I opened fire and was horrified and sickened to see my cannon shells not knock off a wing or tail of the aircraft, but blast straight into the cockpit instantly killing the pilot. The aircraft flipped over and hit the ground. 'I am sorry, I didn't mean that,' I said out loud. Then I thought at least it was quick—and you chaps nearly killed my wife in 1940.

"My thoughts came back to reality as I answered a radio call from 'Closet' Waterhouse, one of the flight commanders who had shot down another FW190. Gathering together as many of the squadron as were not too widely scattered by the combat, I set course for Vire and home. It had been another good day. Sammy had planned well."

The next morning I was sent for by Air Vice-Marshal Cole-Hamilton—who had returned—and he asked me to describe the events of the previous day. He listened without showing any emotion and when finally he spoke, said, "That's it. You are a staff officer so no more operational sorties." Vere Harvey, on the other hand, was highly delighted about the whole affair.

I imagine the AOC was even less enchanted when the press got hold of the story and the following appeared later that day in *The Evening News*.

DAY OFF, SO HE GOT A 190.

Spits and 'Skitoes Range France.

Squadron Leader R W Sampson DFC, took a day off yesterday—and shot down an FW190.

He comes from Cheam, Surrey, and is on the staff at his group HQ. When he can, he flies a Spitfire.

An "on-duty" Spitfire man, Wing Commander P M Brothers DFC & bar, of Westerham, Kent, led the County of Kent Spitfires over France, and found them a bunch of 190s north of Alencon, 10,000 ft above the Allied tank columns racing for Le Mans.

Sent Scuttling

He personally shot down one—hitting the pilot—and led an attack which sent the others scuttling.

Mosquitoes carried out a big programme of harrassing patrols, from points near the front line to 100 miles to the east and south east of Paris during the night.

Lieutenant-General Brereton, C-in-C Ninth Bomber Command said today, "The present critical state of the German armies in Normandy - slowly strangling for want of supplies—is attributable to the work of our Air Forces."

The reference to Cheam was due to the fact that my registered next of kin was at an address in that town on the edge of Surrey, just south of London. This was my sister-in-law, Victor's wife, my parents being in South America.

So much for showing the Group flag, and showing the Wing Leaders that we staff types could also fly as well as plan their shows. That I managed to bag a 190 was an added bonus.

As directed, I got on with my Staff job, but still managed to fly about in various Spitfires, visiting various units in the Group, or make the occasional trip in an Oxford. I also flew Vere Harvey's new Spitfire V, which had his initials on the side 'AVH' and I also had a trip in Pete's Spitfire VII with his 'PB' on the fuselage. Although not a wing commander, I did have access to my own Spitfire, another Mark VII, and rather cheekily I had 'SS' painted on the side to denote its owner.

During October the Group was gradually reducing as the war had really got out of reach of the two Wings and Vere Harvey was now in charge and slowly folding things up. I reminded him that when I had been rested, I'd been promised an operational job after six months, which Smallwood had agreed to also. Now that my time was up and things at 10 Group were ending, I asked Harvey if I could now resume operational flying. He said he would write a letter to Air Commodore Theodore McEvoy—later Air Chief Marshal Sir Theodore, KCB CBE—the SASO of 84 Group, 2nd Tactical Air Force, which were then near Ghent. This he did in mid-October and he sent me out to see the Air Commodore, taking the letter with me. The flight was made from Thruxton to Antwerp in an Anson. I was duly interviewed and McEvoy said I would get a squadron as soon as one became vacant, and meantime, I could go the Group Support Unit at RAF Thruxton. McEvoy said, "You'll enjoy that because you will have two separate tasks. First to test all new Spitfires, Typhoons, Tempests and Mustangs which are delivered from the factories, and second, to deliver such aeroplanes required by various Wings in the Group, to their airfields." Later Vere Harvey showed me the letter he received from McEvoy, the first part of which, read:

> My Dear Vere,   19th October 1944
>   Thank you for your letter of 16th October which you sent with Squadron Leader Sampson. We shall be very pleased to take him into our GSU until a squadron falls vacant for him. He seems a very good type.
>   We are having a very good time here and I hope you will get a chance to come out and see us before we finally disappear under the mud for the winter.

When I arrived at Thruxton, which is near Andover, I found that the Commanding Officer was none other than Wing Commander Douglas

Watkins DFC, who had commanded 611 Squadron at Kenley when I first went to 602. The Station Intelligence Officer was my old friend Duncan Brown, who was a keen Bridge player, as was Douglas, so we played a lot over the next few weeks.

Soon after arriving, I asked Douglas what his movements had been after leaving Kenley on a rest from Ops. He told me that he had been promoted to Wing Commander and placed in charge of the flying side of No 61 OTU at RAF Rednal. The Station Commander had been Group Captain H W Pearson-Rogers OBE, and he and Douglas got on very well together. So much so that the OTU was soon in popular odour as the number of trainees turned out were always better than other OTUs.

About four months after Douglas had been on the job, the Groupie was posted, to be replaced by Group Captain D O Finlay DFC, who had been the British Olympic Hurdles Champion before the war. Douglas told me that on the first day, Don Finlay sent for him, informing him that he required a Spitfire with his initials painted on it, for his personal use, which was to be parked in the nearest dispersal point to his office. Douglas said that it was not possible because every Spitfire was a working machine, required for pupil flying, but, of course, Finlay if he needed a Spitfire, could have one made available without delay. Finlay's response to this was that it was not good enough—"You have had my orders, now get on with it at once."

The result of this, of course, was that with one aircraft short, the next three monthly flying times for pupils dropped in comparison to other OTUs, which affected their overall output. Finlay then drew this state of affairs to Douglas, whose response was—"Well, as you know, we are one Spitfire short of our complement—the one you retain for your private use."

Soon after that episode Finlay again sent for Douglas and the conversation, I gather, went something like this. "Watkins, I am presently writing officer's confidential reports which go to Group HQ. I am giving you an Adverse Report which you have to sign." Douglas replied—"I refuse to sign it." "But you have got to sign it," said Finlay, "It is a Royal Air Force regulation." To this Douglas retorted, "Well I'm not bloody well signing it. I'm not in your bloody Air Force, I'm in the Auxiliary Air Force."

The next day, as so often happens over what really is a 'storm in a tea cup', an officer from Group telephoned Douglas and said, "I hear you are in a clash of personalities with your CO. Well, there are three possible wing commander postings for you, which would you like?"

Don Finlay had commanded 41 Squadron during the Battle of

Britain and into 1941, where he won his DFC. He later served in the
Far East. Some years later—after the war—I was talking to Air
Marshal Sir Anthony Selway and told him of this particular story about
Finlay and Douglas. Selway replied that he wasn't at all surprised
because when he was a member of the Air Force Board and was
attending one of the periodical meetings, an item on the Agenda was
'Adverse Reports'. The Chairman asked the Secretary who had raised
it, and was told it was Group Captain D O Finlay. The Chairman
remarked, "Oh, good Lord, why can't this chap get on with his
fellow citizens!"

I spent exactly four weeks at the GSU and flew most days, either
testing or delivering to the various airfields on the Continent. There
was a range of Spitfires, including a Mark XIV which I flew for the
first time on October 30th, but mostly I flew the Mark IXs.

Sometimes at Thruxton and Lasham we had more aeroplanes to be
tested and delivered than there were available RAF pilots. On those
occasions we called on the Air Transport Auxiliary pilots and I
remember the famous Jim Mollison appearing at the Station, as well
as some of the delectable lady ATA pilots. I helped out too.

The second time I flew a Spit XIV (MR807) was on 14th November
when I was down to fly it to B.70 at Antwerp. Because the Spit was
not fitted with a disposable 45-gallon tank and the Griffin engine was
very thirsty, it was necessary to land at Manston to refuel. This I did
but when I took off from there, the engine was decidedly rough and
at fine pitch control, flames poured out of the exhaust manifolds. My
first thought was that the plugs were oiled up and that if I flew round
the circuit it would clear. However, it didn't and the only way I could
damp down the flames was to alter the pitch control to fully course,
which was only ever used when flying on full economy of petrol.

I decided to land. When I reached the Control Tower and got out,
I went to the front of the Spitfire and saw that one blade of the five-
bladed prop was shattered from the tip up about six to eight inches.
All the other blades were alright.

The Squadron Leader Engineering Officer arrived and took a look,
saying to me, "It looks as if you touched the runway as you took off."
"Don't be stupid," I retorted, being most afronted. "If I had touched
the runway, all five blades would have been damaged." He thought
for a moment, then suggested, "Do you think you might have hit a
flock of birds?" "Definitely not," I said, "the same would apply with
more than one damaged, not to mention some other evidence such as
blood and feathers."

However, he was not convinced and spent at least an hour in a jeep with three other chaps going up and down the runway looking for bits of shattered prop (or damaged runway) but all to no avail. He finally returned and asked, "Will you please fill in this form and give your opinion as to the cause of the damage." I was rather angry by all this not to mention my enforced delay. I had already called Lasham, the 84 Group Support Unit, who had sent an Anson to pick me up. So I filled in the form to which I wrote, short and sharp—"Rotol prop failure."

This didn't go down well at all. "This has never happened before, you know; how many hours have you got on Spitfires?" My equally short reply to this was, "Nearly a thousand to what I think is a cheeky question," and stomped off indignantly to my waiting Anson.

Sometime later two civilian boffins arrived at Lasham from the Rotol Company. They could not understand the alleged failure and we went all through the episode once again. They had, they said, subjected the propeller to all sorts of tests and could find no weakness in the blade. I said I was very sorry from their point of view but very glad from the operational squadrons' point of view, as it wouldn't have been funny if the failure had occured whilst deep over enemy territory.

Finally, at the end of November, Douglas sent for me to tell me that I had been posted as a Supernumerry Squadron Leader to No. 135 Spitfire Wing, stationed at Maldegem in Belgium. This was in order for me to get some operational flying experience until a squadron appointment came up. So after nearly nine months I was finally to return for another tour of Ops. I couldn't wait.

CHAPTER X

SQUADRON COMMANDER, 2ND TAF

Immediately I heard of my posting to 135 Wing I was packed and on my way. The Wing, I discovered, was commanded by Group Captain P R Walker DSO DFC, known inevitably as Johnnie. I was told I should like him, as everyone did.

Johnnie Walker had joined the RAF in 1935 and had gone to France when war was declared as a flight commander in the famous No.1 Squadron. He had won his DFC during the Battle of France, and later in the war led the Tangmere Wing at the time of Dieppe, winning the DSO.

The Wing Commander Flying was Ray Harries DSO DFC & two bars, the brilliant Welsh air fighter with something like 20 victories. He had, of course, been a flight commander with 131 Squadron, and I had taken his place in December 1942. Despite his record, I heard that he was not liked much in certain circles, but personally I didn't have long enough with him to get to know him. Sadly he only survived the war by five years, being killed in a flying accident in 1950. There was a rumour that he was flying with his golf clubs in the cockpit and whilst in cloud the irons affected his compass which gave him a wrong heading.

As I was beginning to discover, 84 Group, 2nd TAF, had a good deal of talent from the top down. The AOC was Air Vice-Marshal Edmund Hudleston, his SASO being Theodore McEvoy whom I had already met. Group Captain Fred Rosier DSO, a distinguished fighter pilot, was in charge of Admin, while other equally fine fighter pilots on the Staff were Group Captain Johnny Baldwin DSO DFC & bar (i/c Ops), Wing Commanders Al Deere DSO DFC & bar (Wingco Plans), Bob Deacon Elliott DFC, in addition to my old pal Doug Watkins.

As I climbed out of an Anson next to the Control Tower, I was met by Johnnie Walker himself, who then drove me to the Mess.

He arranged for a batman to show me my sleeping quarters, said that Ray Harries was flying, so I should get myself some tea once I'd dumped my belongings.

Over tea I was delighted to meet Bill Bower, the South African who had been in my Flight with 131. News of my coming had preceded me so he had made sure he was there to see me. I asked him what Ray Harries was like. "Well, you will see he is not exactly a tall chap and his main preoccupation seems to be knocking down officers junior to him but taller, so I'd watch out if I were you!"

However, my time with the Wing was brief, so I never had to test Bill's theory. However, in that brief time I didn't like Harries, finding him pompous and if all his boasts and conquests were true, a prodigious womaniser too. Laurie Kelly, who was in the Wing, told me that on one occasion when the weather had clamped, Harries had all the pilots in the Intelligence Hut on what he described as an intelligence quiz. Putting his hand over his left breast so as to cover his medal ribbons, he asked one pilot, "What are the colours of the DSO ribbon?"

I only got in a couple of shows before a squadron came up. It is strange how paths cross in Fighter Command, or nearly cross on some occasions. Apart from Bill Bower, Otto Smik had been in my 131 Flight and he had gone on to fly with 312 Czech Squadron, winning the DFC & bar before taking command of 127 Squadron in November 1944, having been at 84 GSU with me too.

Smik I knew to be a very affable chap, spoke German, some Dutch, French, his native Czech of course, and pretty good English. He had gone out to take charge of 127 on November 14th and lasted just two weeks. On the 28th he had led an armed reconnaissance mission between Arnhem-Hengelo and Zwolle, carrying 250 lb bombs. They found little to attack so Smik had led them in a dive-bombing attack on a goods yard at Zwolle. Both he and another pilot were brought down by some murderous ground fire.

All this I learnt as soon as I was told that 127 Squadron needed a new CO. I was pleased finally to have my command, but apprehensive as to the missions the Squadron was engaged in. It was stationed at a Brussels airfield called Grimbergen, being part of the three-squadron, No.132 Norwegian Wing, there being only two Norwegian fighter squadrons in being, 331 and 332. The Airfield Commander was Group Captain Douglas Morris DFC, nicknamed 'Zulu' because he was a South African.

I had to see Morris, and he told me that 127 Squadron's morale was in a pretty low state because Otto had been rather foolhardy in attacking heavily defended targets and flak positions which is why he and his No.2 had bought it. I asked about the other pilots, and was told that on that mission they made no bones about it, and had quickly broken away when the withering flak commenced. The message, although not spelled out, was that I had a job on my hands to prove to the pilots that I would not attack heavily defended flak positions just for the sake of it. Otto, he said, had really overdone it. Morris advised: "The object in attacking a definite strategic but heavily defended target, is to try and avoid the flak or, at least, the worst of it with skill and speed."

I liked Zulu Morris. Later, when he was a Staff Officer in 84 Group, he told me that during the build up for D-Day, the various Wings were operating from new strips in Kent, Surrey, Sussex, etc, under the control of Wing Leaders. Leigh-Mallory instructed Zulu to produce a feasibility study as to how these Wings should operate once the invasion started. Zulu's suggestion was that each Wing should have an Airfield Commander of Group Captain rank and that these should be operationally experienced officers, capable and expected to take part in certain operations along with the various Wing Leaders. He made a number of suggestions—P R Walker, Johnny Baldwin, Denis Gillam, Sailor Malan as well as Polish and Czech senior officers.

Morris himself had commanded 406 Canadian Squadron during 1941-42, on night-fighter sorties. He was later to become an Air Commodore and receive the DSO, rising to Air Vice-Marshal in the 1950s, then Air Marshal Sir Douglas, KCB CBE DSO DFC. He was the boss of Fighter Command between 1962-66.

Now back in harness, I quickly discovered that the old-fashioned fighter sweep used so frequently between 1942-43, was a thing of the past as the Luftwaffe were so thin on the ground and so short of petrol, that their fighters only very occasionally reacted to our medium bombers. As these were closely escorted by Spitfires, they seldom pressed home an attack unless (which was very rare) they had a superior number in comparison to the escort, or the opportunity to pick-off stragglers.

This, from my point of view, was a pity because the Spitfire IXB was now fitted with a gyroscopic gunsight—a very sophisticated piece of machinery. When the sight was switched on there were some twelve small graticules which could be moved by turning the grip on the throttle, which could be twisted. At 800 yards the graticules sat on the inside edge of the sight and by twisting the grip these could be moved away from the centre where they stopped at 100 yards range. In the centre of the sight was a fixed + and in addition there was a movable dot. The object, when entering a combat with the enemy, was to get the movable dot on the fixed cross and, of course, that would obviously occur if you were approaching the enemy in line astern. However, by out-turning the enemy aircraft, it was possible to move the dot on the + and then you simply could not miss, because the sight also took into account the speed, the slip and the skid, if the enemy was to employ these manoeuvres.

The Wing Commander Flying was a Norwegian, Rolf Berg, who held the equivalent rank of Lieutenant Colonel. He had escaped from Norway in 1940 and following his training he had joined 331 Norwegian Squadron in 1942, seeing action for the first time over the Dieppe show. He later became a flight commander and won the DFC. In April 1944 he was promoted to lead No.132 Norwegian Wing with whom he won a bar to his DFC and was soon to receive the DSO.

My immediate impression of him was that he was most friendly, very charming and his general attitude to me (unspoken) was, you know the score and you will soon settle into my methods. Our main operations, Berg told me, were called Armed Recce sorties. These were undertaken to search for armoured vehicles, tanks, gun posts, trains or any form of motor (or even horse-drawn) transport. From time to time we would carry out dive-bombing missions with three bombs slung under the belly and wings, adding up to 1,000 lbs. In low level Ops, we would use delay-action bombs to give us time to get out of the way, although one had to ensure not to follow another dive-bomber in and end up in the delayed explosion of his bombs.

These dive-bombing sorties usually commenced at 10,000 feet and the bombs released at 4,000, the aircraft pulling away to either side as quickly as possible. As bombing operations attracted flak there were differing opinions as to the best way to avoid flak if possible. Peter Hillwood, my senior flight commander,came up with what seemed to me a sensible solution. He said that the Huns, being short of shells, were conserving them so would only open fire when Spitfires approached in a straight line to the target. It therefore seemed more sensible to fly some 100 to 200 yards either to left or right of the target as if we were on our way elsewhere, and then at the very last moment, scream down. There were then, two alternatives; the target could either be attacked from the side or the Squadron could proceed further and then turn and attack on a reciprocal course. It made only a slight difference if the target was to be dive-bombed with instantaneous explosive bombs or delay-fused bombs. With instantaneous bombs the dive commenced almost directly over the target, pulling out as the bombs were released at approximately 4,000 feet. With delay bombs, the leader had to arrive at ground level about 100 yards from the target. In either case the leader would be spraying the target area from side to side with cannon and machine-gun fire, hopefully to nullify some of the Ack-Ack, or at least to encourage the gunners to keep their heads down.

I said I thought all this seemed sensible and that when the first bombing trip came up I would get him to lead and I would fly as his No.2. I also discovered that at this stage of the war, rather than fly in squadron strength of twelve as we had done earlier, two sections of four was the norm and that to fly at a lower altitude where targets could be fleeting with a corresponding need for quick reactions, eight Spitfires in two sections of four was much more manageable, and didn't get in each other's way.

Without being asked I laid down quite firmly that on all formations we use what was described as the finger-four. This means that the sections are more or less in a slightly jagged straight line with no 'arse-end charlie' as in the line astern formations.

Another of our jobs was called 'Cab Rank'. This involved the Squadron patrolling an area requested by the Army. If they wished for a strongpoint holding them up to be strafed or bombed, we would be given the appropriate map reference and then attack. Our cannon and machine-gun attacks could be quite effective and if the Squadron had been fitted with bombs, so much the better. The three Wing squadrons usually took it in turn to be bombed up, so that the various tasks were evenly spread.

My Squadron was equipped with Spitfire XVIs, coded 9N, and again I selected the letter 'K' as my personal aircraft letter. My first operation leading 127 came on December 15th, an escort to B25 Mitchells to the same Zwolle marshalling yards that had claimed by predecessor. The flak was indeed heavy, but thankfully the Mitchells were doing their medium-height bombing and we Spit boys were not dive-bombing. As we left we sighted a white trail high up in the sky, but whether it was from a V2 rocket or a German jet aircraft, we couldn't tell for sure.

Following two more shows to the Aachen-Munchen areas, we moved base to a newly captured airfield some 20 miles north of Antwerp by the name of Woensdrecht, although we called it 'Wormshit'! Ops came thick and fast around Christmas time, for the Ardennes battle was in full swing—the famed Battle of the Bulge. Armed Recces and, despite my earlier briefing, fighter sweeps, were flown, aimed at winkling out any ground transport that might be bringing up men and supplies to the battle front. On Christmas Day we went to the Rheine-Hengelo-Appledorn region and found three locomotives, waggons and a flak waggon.

Rolf briefed us that most of 2nd TAF were concentrating as many Armed Recces as possible, thinking the Huns might be having a holiday. He also told us that there was a report of a large goods train halted not far from the airfield at Twente and would no doubt remain there during daylight and move off again in the night. Sure enough, as we reached the airfield we could see the train and he decided to attack, with the airfield literally about 100 yards on our left.

I was flying No.2 to him and just before commencing his attack he warned us of potential flak from our left. As we started our run in I could see shell bursts behind his Spitfire and just in front of mine. Apart from being very frightened indeed, my thoughts were that I wouldn't survive to enjoy the Christmas dinner which I knew had been promised us. In the event I was lucky and only received some light flak near the tail of my Spit, causing small damage.

However, we severely damaged this train and then two others we found elsewhere, one of which was seen to blow up. When we found the one with the flak wagon Berg, as was to be expected, attacked it while we concentrated on the train itself. It was a sweaty business but we did get back for our dinner.

That afternoon, Rolf Berg led us out again in company with 66 Squadron which had joined the Wing. We carried 1,000 lbs of bombs, this being my first experience of dive-bombing. Our target was a wood to the north of Emmerich in which a number of FW190s had been seen dispersed and Zulu Morris accompanied us. Berg headed down and dropped his bombs but thought the 190s he saw were dummies, so as the rest of us attacked he told us to bomb the surrounding woods in case the real aircraft were there. As we flew off it looked as if we had destroyed or damaged at least six aircraft.

Amidst the Ardennes battle we were warned that the way the Germans were making rapid progress—at least initially—we might have to abandon the airfield because it was also on the cards that the various German units on Walcheren Island could pull the plug and flood the whole area whilst moving inland towards us. However, we were then told that Field Marshal Montgomery had been moved by Eisenhower to assist General Omar Bradley and the picture soon changed.

On Boxing day we saw some Hun aircraft during a sortie into the Enschede area. There were some jet jobs reported and then we saw four Me262s but we had no hope of catching them. I had a long-range squirt from 1,500 yards but more out of desperation than with any sense of hitting one. Two of my pilots also spotted a Me109 and a FW190 and went for them, but these two Huns had their fingers well out and got away. On the 28th I actually led the Wing on another show to Enschede but we saw nothing. The year of 1944 ended for us with a Ramrod to Mitchells and Bostons bombing targets in the Ardennes.

I always made a point of discussing each potential operation with my two flight commanders, the very experienced Peter Hillwood DFC, who had flown in the Battle of Britain, and Harry Lea DFC, who had previously served with 43 Squadron.[1] This not only got them involved but it helped allay any worries they might have. Bombing operations were, of course, pretty hazardous and I made sure we were in full agreement as to how we would make the attack.

The new year of 1945 dawned bright and clear after several days of poor weather. With the Ardennes battle in full swing, the German ground forces had managed to push deep into the Allied line, helped by the fact that RAF and American aircraft had been handicapped by the weather to give support to their own troops.

The Luftwaffe too, of course, had also been affected by the weather, but they had been planning a strike on Allied air bases in Belgium and Holland in an effort to knock out 2nd TAF on the ground. It just so happened that 1st January 1945 gave them the first chance to make this mammoth strike when the weather forecast indicated clear flying weather. The fact that many 2nd TAF people would be waking up with thick heads after the New Year celebrations of the previous night, would be a bonus.

In the event there were some sore heads, but 2nd TAF had also read the weather signs and knew that they could at last, give some desperately needed support to the battle front soon after first light. Thus, when the Luftwaffe struck soon after dawn, they did catch a number of squadrons on the ground, but just as many had been alerted for a dawn show and were in the air and away from their airfields.

We at Woensdrecht were fortunately in the latter category. We had been briefed for a Ramrod operation—close escort to RAF Bostons and Mitchells bombing a road junction at Dasburg. I led the Squadron off at ten minutes past nine and carried out an uneventful sweep in the target area. Just 30 minutes after we had left, came the first reports

---

[1] After the war, Harry Lea became a pilot for BEA. He gained a lot of publicity in the late 1950s when flying a Viscount from Glasgow to Heathrow, for some madman threatened to take over the aeroplane but somehow he was over-powered.

of the German attack on 2nd TAF. As it happened, the enemy fighters totally missed our airfield, although Flight Lieutenant Covington and two other 127 pilots were Scrambled to Antwerp, but they saw nothing. We heard over the radio of some excitement to our rear, but by the time we arrived back, it was all over. It was the Luftwaffe's last throw which cost them dear not only in aircraft but in pilots whom they could ill afford to lose. The attack did inflict losses on 2nd TAF and some American units, but few pilots were lost. Of course, by this stage of the war the Allies could easily replace aircraft and equipment, and within days 2nd TAF was up to full strength again. The Luftwaffe never recovered.

Expecting more activity that afternoon, the Wing was airborne after lunch to fly a Sweep in the Enschede-Rheine area but this too proved uneventful.

We now commenced flying Armed Recces and dive-bombing sorties over the front. One day I spotted a German Mercedes-Benz staff car which I shot up in no uncertain fashion and got another the next day which did every known form of 'roadabatics' when I hit it. We were still supporting the US forces in the Ardennes, although by now the German attack was losing its drive.

On January 6th the Wing escorted Marauders to St Vith, meeting plenty of flak, although because of 10/10ths cloud we did not see any sign of the ground all during the raid. Bad weather then curtailed our operations so we did not get off the ground again until the 14th. On this day we took bombs to some railway sidings at Wierden, near Zwolle, right next to a V1 and a V2 launching site. We met flak during the journey which made navigation a bit tricky, but our bombs certainly pranged the target.

Later that same day I led the Squadron to dive-bomb a concentration of barges in Hellevotesluis. The target was partly obscured by cloud so results were difficult to assess, but a big explosion to the west gave us some hope that damage had been inflicted, and an oil tank went up in flames. Two more sorties, on the 16th and 17th, netted us some MT and saw us taking part in a Wing show to attack Midget Submarine pens near Rotterdam, with good results, but then something of a shock awaited me.

A couple of days earlier, on the 15th, Zulu Morris had quizzed me as to whether I knew Group Captain Loel Guiness who was coming to lunch that day. When I said yes I was invited to join them. Later that same evening I had a call in complete confidence from Wing Commander Bill Crawford-Compton DSO DFC & bar, the New Zealand Wing Leader of No.145 Free French Fighter Wing. "Keep this under your hat," he told me, "but I am being rested and you are going to succeed me."

Next day I had a call from Loel Guiness telling me to put up the necessary stripe and come over to Antwerp immediately to take over. I was sad to leave 127 after so short a time, but I was obviously very pleased to have been given my own Fighter Wing. Before I left, I said goodbye to the boys, and to Rolf Berg. He wished me luck and warned, "Don't forget that the French wrote off Wing Commander Roy Marples when he was leading them through thick cloud!" So with this salutary warning still ringing in my ears, which I could have done without, I headed for Antwerp.[1]

I didn't see Rolf again; he was killed just a couple of weeks later.

---

[1] Roy Marples DFC & bar, had been a Battle of Britain pilot and later, in the Middle East, had commanded 127 Squadron. In April 1944, while leading the Merston Wing, he had collided with an aircraft while flying through cloud and was killed.

CHAPTER XI

THE FREE FRENCH IN THE RAF

I knew very little of the gallant Free Frenchmen with whom I was to spend the final months of the war. Of course I knew that there were several Free French squadrons within the RAF, heavy and light bombers as well as fighters. I suppose I knew also that these men, like the Poles, Czechs, Belgians, Norwegians and so on, had all needed to escape to England in order to continue the fight against the common enemy—Germany.

Very little has been published in English about the Free French airmen who flew with the RAF between 1940 and 1945. I believe it is appropriate here to add some background as to how some of these men, and those whom I was to lead in 145 Wing, had found life in the RAF during the war years. To fight one's enemies is one thing, to fight him from a foreign country, with the difficulty of different language and culture, are added problems which must be faced and overcome. That most did overcome them and fight with courage and success, should not be forgotten.

I had already met a number of Free French since 1942. We had a couple in 131 Squadron, and I recall meeting the dark, small, compact figure of Jean Maridor during one of our excursions into 11 Group from Exeter. One of our Frenchmen in 131 introduced me to his friend Jean, who everyone called 'Mari'. Jean Maridor was what the RAF would call, 'a very press-on type'. That is to say he was always to be found at the forefront of any action and always keen to get to grips with the men who were occupying his country.

I met Jean only a few times but strangely I was, long after the war, to live in the Kent village close to where he was killed. He made his name flying with the RAF's No.91 Squadron, known as the 'Jim Crow' outfit for they were tasked mainly with seeking out German naval activity in the Channel, along the French coast, or in French harbours.

By 1944 Jean had won the DFC and several French decorations, and that summer they were flying sorties to combat the V1 flying-bomb menace.

Jean shot down a number of these highly lethal and dangerous robot bombs. He had also become engaged to a WAAF officer and was due to be married on 10 August. Just a week before that event was to take place, on 3 August, Jean attacked a flying-bomb, his fire damaging it but not destroying it. Instead he saw it go into a glide, heading for a large building which was Benenden School. The teachers and pupils had been evacuated to Torquay, but the building was now being used as a military hospital.

Exactly what happened next is still not totally clear, despite a number of witnesses. Of course, these were all civilians and a flying man might have seen something that would have shown more accurately Jean's last moments. From what I have been able to establish however, it would seem that Jean was quickly aware that the bomb was heading for the hospital and knew too that he had little time in which to act. By this time witnesses saw that he was very close to the bomb, too close to destroy the V1 with his cannon armament and not be effected by the blast if it exploded. As he was so close he may also, having fired already and only damaged its directional components, have decided to try and tip the bomb over into a field with his wing-tip. This had already been done before by RAF pilots, which took quite a bit of flying skill and courage.

The result, whatever this gallant Frenchman tried—whether he fired at close range or attempted to tip it into the ground—was that the bomb exploded and Jean's Spitfire was engulfed and disintigrated. Several people recall distinctly seeing one wing of his Spitfire spiral down. We now know that the Germans had become aware of the tipping method through the British press and some bombs were fitted with a trip-wire, placed from the V1's wing-tips to the explosive warhead. Whether Jean did attempt to tip this bomb and whether is was booby-trapped in this way we shall never know.

Today, however, I live just a short distance from the spot where he died, so my few brief meetings with Jean Maridor have turned full circle in this unusual way. The school is still there, and Jean's wartime fiancee (her name also is Jean, and whom I have had the pleasure of meeting), long since happily married, has never forgotten him, and hopes to have a memorial plaque erected at Benenden to his memory. I, too, hope she succeeds.

Pierre Laurent is another Frenchman who had a distinguished career as a fighter pilot, winning not only the French Legion d'Honneur and Croix de Guerre, but also the British DFC. When I joined 145 Wing, Pierre was a flight commander in 341 Squadron, under Jacques Andrieux. By that time he had been with 341 for two years. He would later become a French Air Force General. Pierre remembers how some of the French pilots who would serve with the French Wing, came to England:

"The qualification—or should I say quality—of 'Free French' officers who joined General de Gaulle's forces before the liberation of North Africa by the Allies in November 1942 was good. From then on, a good number of French pilots became available from Algiers, Oran and Casablanca. Some squadrons of the French Air Force since the beginning of the war, were reactivated. Two of those were sent to England, 329 'Cigognes' and 345 'Berry', which became part of 145 Wing.

"There were also some individual pilots who after some training in RAF OTUs, were sent to make up for the losses sustained by the old Free French Squadrons, 341 'Alsace' and 340 'Ile de France'. We were extremely happy to receive them and we mingled beautifully, as we did with the British pilots.

"During action one has to harden inner feelings to keep going in the face of events but when all has become quiet, memories and feelings are permitted to come to the surface and be expressed. I recall specially Michel Brunschwig, Georges Lentz, Jean Maridor, Maurice Mailfert, Michel Boudier, Georges Girard, Roger Borne..... among so many more, they were my friends. From Angers and Etampes flying schools, promotions of 1939-40, I was close to Boudier, Mailfert and Maridor.

"Michel Brunschwig was imprisoned in Morocco for activities in the Resistance there. He escaped and joined us in England. In September 1944, hit by flak over Belgium, he managed to glide over the lines and parachuted *in extremis*. He got out with only a broken arm but was flying again in no time. He did not have such luck a few years later in Indochina when, still on Spitfires, he was hit in action by a Vietnam machine gun and went straight into the ground with a desperate cry over the radio. We had kept in close friendship and he was a gifted pianist, a wonderful man. Full of kindness, delicately witted and generous. May his children inherit all this. He had lost a brother in RAF Coastal Command.

"Borne and Girard... in 1942 we went to SFTS together in

Canada. Roger Borne was one of the very last losses of 341 Alsace Squadron. On a ground attack sortie over Germany he was shot down by light flak. He had taken over my Flight (Escadrille Mulhouse) when I left the Squadron the month before. Georges Girard was one of the hundreds of victims of the V2 that fell on a cinema in Antwerp on 14 December 1944. His mark, a smiling and indefatigable humour. Four days later another V2 fell on 341's dispersal and killed Georges Lentz. The Squadron had just been released and I had asked everyone to go and relax. Off we went, except 'Tojo'—as we called him—whose extra duty as 'officier d'Etat Civil' of the Squadron meant that had to write the administrative papers concerning Girard's death.

"We shared the same room or tent for a long time. He was my No.2 on a squadron mission near Paris on 3rd October, 1943. Over the Bay of the Somme, we had a dog-fight with too many FW190s and he was hit and crash landed. Through French Resistance and then across Spain, he was back with the Squadron within three or four weeks and flying again and fighting to liberate his country. What a loss. That night I think I did cry.

"Yes, they were my friends! Along with those already well known fighter pilots, their names, what they did for their country and liberty in the world should never be forgotten. They should be glorified in any literature on the French Air Force during the Second World War.

"I recall too that first day of January 1945 when we were at Antwerp/Deurne. I was in charge of the Squadron that early morning and had been briefed and ready for a bomber escort. As in most parts of the region, the runway was iced-up and we were waiting for it to melt. We waited. All at once hell broke loose and it seemed that all the remains of the Luftwaffe flew over, strafing the field as they were heading south. When permission to Scramble arrived they had flown back over again. We took off as best we could but did not catch them. All I caught that day was a hit from our flak, north of the town, which forced me to land in a hurry with my No.2, Lois Le Flecher, on B.79, near Bergon-op-Zoom. Even today I feel frustrated and mad when I think of the number we could had scored on those Jerries, out of ammo and short of fuel, had we taken off a few minutes sooner. C'est la vie!!"

Marcel Boisot was one of those few airmen to actually fly to freedom and eventually ended up with the Wing in 1944. He recalls:

"My landing at Gibraltar on 28th June 1940, after escaping from jail in Meknes, Morocco in a little trainer having only amassed a total of 25 flying hours, felt great. Having landed on a race-track and later learned there was a certain French General in London whose name was De Gaulle, ready to fight on, I decided that this was for me."

Marcel completed his training, and by 1944 was operating over France with the Wing:

"I was nearly shot down on D-Day by two squadrons of Spitfires, even though I was in a Spitfire myself. I have also to admit that once I was nearly kicked out of the RAF by none other than Sailor Malan!

"My first landing in France was on B.8 near Bayeux, pretending to have a glycol leak which was, of course, purely imaginary. Thanks to some over-enthusiastic villagers, I soon became stinking drunk with Calvados but this did not prevent me from taking off an hour later. I then made a slow roll to thank them for their welcome which nearly put a final point to my terrestrial life."

There were others who came early, via Gibraltar, several of whom would fly and die with 340 or 341 Squadrons, as well as other units, long before the French Wing was formed. Sixteen came from the l'Ecole de Chasse III and got on a Swedish ship from Bayonne to Casablanca and then, mixing with some Poles, reached Gibraltar on a British cargo ship. That list of 16 is impressive:

Henri Daoulas	Served with 232 Squadron RAF	
Victor Dubourgel	340 Squadron:	Killed Sept 1944
Robert Gouby	340 Squadron:	Killed Aug 1944
Claude Helies	340 Squadron:	Killed Oct 1942
Rene Huin	340 Squadron:	Died Aug 1944
Paul Hubidos	340 Squadron:	Killed Mar 1943
Francois de Labouchere	340 Squadron:	Killed Sep 1942
Pierre Magrot	341 Squadron:	Killed Aug 1943
Jacques Mallet	5 SFTS:	Killed Mar 1941
Pierre Mathillon-Croizet	222 Sqdn RAF:	Killed Apr 1942
Oliver Massart	340 Squadron:	POW Mar 1945
Hubert Michelin	340 Squadron:	
Monnier		
Xavier de Montbron	64 & 92 Sqdns RAF:	POW Jul 1941
Raymond van Wymeersch	174 Sqdn RAF:	POW Aug 1942
Reynaud de Honington		

I was to fly with Oliver Massart in 1945. Another future Air Force General I knew in 145 Wing was Victor Tanguy, who flew with 341 Squadron after being with 329 Squadron earlier. He writes:

"Group Captain Malan was our first boss when we came to the RAF in February 1944. I was still only a young flight lieutenant in the 'Storks' (Cigognes) and relations between base commanders and young officers were too often limited to precious little. However, the fame of Sailor Malan was extraordinary. Right from the word go, he became our model and 'guide'. He helped enormously to integrate the Storks with other squadrons which made up 145 Wing.

"Our use of English aeronautical terms was very, very inadequate. We often ran into great difficulties at that time, both on the ground and in the air. It was due to a lack of understanding of the signals which were being transmitted in flight through our radio headphones; we often quite failed to grasp their meaning. Group Captain Malan forgave us much. Unfortunately he was summoned to greater things and left us too soon.

"I maintain an image of Group Captain Loel Guiness as the perfect gentleman. There had to be a man like him to run 145 Wing from Tangmere to Fassberg and please everybody. I do not remember one single problem between him and the French forces, pilots or mechanics alike. His courtesy was remarkable, as was his respect for the active pilot.

"Bill Crawford-Compton was our Wing Leader. After flying side by side with him on numerous sorties over Normandy during those difficult days of June 1944, I was able to appreciate his calmness, his sense of observation, his speed of reaction, skill and courage.

"I recall one particular sortie at the end of the afternoon of D-Day during which we had to protect a huge flight of gliders towed by Dakotas, full of elite paratroops. In the sky there was no sign of German fighters, but below us was carnage. As the gliders prepared to land we saw them crippled by flak; wings came off, others nose-diving into the ground.

"The sight was too much to bear. All of a sudden on a command that was so clipped that none of the pilots understood it, our leader, Bill Compton, dived vertically towards a target that we could not identify but which he had recognised. The other 11 Spitfires in the formation followed him as if we were one in this vertiginous dive from 2,000-2,500 metres. At 3-400 metres from the ground our Wing Leader opened fire. His aim was perfect and highlighted our target—a German barge full of anti-aircraft guns, moored on the River Orne in a suburb of Caen.

"Our twelve planes made several attacks until we ran out of ammunition. During all this the formation flew through a curtain of gliders and their Dakota 'tractors'. God was with us and there were no collisions.

"The results were excellent: no more gliders were knocked out by flak before landing. We had silenced the guns on the hellish barge which had wreaked such havoc and caused so many deaths before our attack. In the debriefing on our return to Merston, we were able to spot accurately the point of our attack. It was at Comolbelles-sur-L'Orne, by Caen, close to Benouville, famous for its Pegasas bridge which the 7th Airborne Division had to capture during one of its first D-Day missions."

I was to meet Jacques Souviat as a flight commander in 329 Squadron, under Jacques Marchelidon. The other flight commander was Capitaine Maurice Avon. That both Souviat and Avon were to become French Air Force Generals must reflect on their wartime achievements. Souviat has recorded for me some of his recollections on coming to England in early 1944 via Gibraltar:

"Our take over by the RAF was done gently, and we arrived on 10th January 1944, at No.61 OTU, Rednal, in Shropshire. In the first week we learnt the RAF codes which were indispensible for flying. I was prepared for my first flight by an OTU instructor, in a Miles Master. I was impressed by the quality of the controls of the wings and by the clarity of the radio. The release of a Spitfire Mark 1 the following day, showed the confidence the British had in our qualities of pilotage.

"In spite of our Engish lessons, we had great difficulty in understanding what was said on the radio. Perhaps the Controllers articulated excessively in order to overcome our problems, which were made worse by the various bits of RAF slang which were used. I recall the experience of one of our pilots one dark night. The radio conversation between the Controller and the French pilot went: 'Transmit 105 over Pundit,' said the pilot. Pundit being the flashing red beacon which indicated one's position accurately. '105, this is Rednal Tower—clear to land. Rotate 105 downwind.' '105 to Tower, I don't see your lights; flash please.' Then the pilot, after a few minutes said, 'Rotate 105—instructions for taxying.' 'Rednal Tower to 105, receiving you strength five; I don't see your lights, where are you?' The Controller had good reason not to see Pundit 105, nor to understand, as 105 had already landed on another airfield 15 miles away!

"We were soon on Spitfire Vs, under the control of Jean Maridor, an excellent French fighter pilot who spoke to us about his recent battles and the superb manoeuvres of the Me109 and FW190. Maridor was killed a few months later by an exploding V1 over Kent. He could see it was falling towards a hospital and closed in too close in order to destroy it.

"We got used to life in the RAF; we rode about on bicycles because the various installations were spread all over the camp. We found an English breakfast delicious and we were able to enjoy the luxury of having a bath in the evenings, before going to the Mess, clothed in our Armee de l'Air uniforms, having spent the day in battle-dress.

"In the enormous organisation that was the RAF, many things seemed illogical and shocked our French backgrounds. Each time we received the same explanation: 'Yes, but it works!' and it was true. Everything was based on pragmatism and the confidence reciprocated in general, called the 'team spirit'.

"Our second impression was that while the vast RAF 'machine' turned without any apparent effort, its wheels having been perfectly oiled, there was no panic or nervousness among any of the 'high-ups'. The cool British temperament was very much to the fore. Our third, and very strong impression, concerned the WAAFs. This base, at which we were training was a school for personnel and the majority were female, particularly the drivers of the lorries, the flight controllers and the mechanics for the aircraft. The courage of these young ladies gained our admiration, for to see them sitting on the wings of our aircraft at dispersal, with the huge pipes of pouring petrol under their arms in order to refuel the aircraft, was remendous. Also to see two or three holding onto the tail of a Spitfire in the freezing back-blast caused by the propeller, impressed us all. You only had to see their hands, blackened with oil and often bloodied, turning a screwdriver or spanner, and all with a smile, to warm to them.

"On 10th February we left Rednal, our Ops training having been completed and we arrived at Perranporth where our Group was integrated into the RAF to form No.329 (FF) Squadron. With 340 (Ile de France) Squadron and 341 (Alsace) Squadron, plus No.74 Squadron RAF, we became No.145 Fighter Wing in 10 Group.

"Perranporth was a little station, pitched on the rocks in the west of Cornwall. Our Station HQ and aerial base was situated on a little plateau which was about 200 metres above the sea; it really felt like an aircraft carrier. We made our acquaintance with the other Free French Squadrons' pilots, some of whom had been at Biggin Hill until recently, where they had flown Spitfire IXs, the excellent aircraft of the moment. They told us all about their battles, asserting that the Jerries were tough adversaries. The CO of 341, Chris Martel[1], who had several victories, but who was killed just after the war at a French OTU, which was to bear his name and become a fighter school, made a great impression on us.

"We made a tour of the pubs and the main night spot in Perranporth, the Stork Club. The first time we were able to go there, we stuck out our chests, showing our 'Stork' emblem of the old Spa3 which we wore on our uniforms. We noticed the young ladies, who looked at us, and at the insignia, then cried out, 'We don't want a baby!' We did not understand the relationship between storks and babies—then—but we certainly understood the effect!

"On 1st March we gave up our Spitfire Vs and received the Spitfire IX. I flew my first operation on the 6th, a Scramble from Readiness, but without success. We also flew some convoy patrols and sometimes went as far as Brest, heading out just above the waves in order to avoid detection by German radar. Our windscreens would be covered in spray and pretty quickly, with a layer of salt. We learnt to change formation without gaining height and to read our compass, situated between our feet, without hitting the water. One day, however, we lost a lieutenant from 340 Squadron.

"The Spitfire is an aircraft that doesn't ditch well. It doesn't know how to sit on the water after first contact with the waves. It dives and disappears. It was in this way we lost two friends, right in front of my eyes. One had an air-lock and his engine just stopped; another lost his engine when he changed fuel tanks at low level on a convoy patrol. Both had plunged into the sea like a stone.

"Two weeks after receiving our Mark IXs the order came to move to Merston, opposite the Isle of Wight. Our Wing was about to join the 2nd TAF, attached to the British Army. We were to

---

[1] Christian Martel's real name was Pierre Montet. Flying with 341 he destroyed seven enemy aircraft. He escaped across the Pyrenees to join the Free French but before flying on Ops he returned to France to help set up an escape route into Spain. He returned to the UK in 1942 and became operational the following year. He died following a crash in August 1945.

leave on 17th April and a big briefing was held, assembled by our new Wing Leader. His name was Roy Marples, 24 years old and something of a cunning type. He had recently returned from North Africa and was a distinguished fighter pilot. During his briefing he had said, 'During our flight to Merston we won't fly straight like our bloody bombers, we'll train instead and practise manoeuvres. I will lead the four squadrons as Freehold Leader; please keep in mind that flying east at noon, the sun will be on your right shoulder. Check—there is no need to look at your damn compass!' This interjection was accompanied by great gestures of his left hand on his right shoulder.

"We left the Ops Room, thinking hard and rocking with laughter, going out to our aircraft, mimicking the scene with a certain lack of respect for our chief who hadn't yet really established his place with the Wing. After an impeccable take-off, 48 Spitfires found themselves in combat formation at 30,000 ft above the sea, with cloud at 10/10ths below, and started to carry out the orders of Freehold Leader. We turned 180″, then 90″ left, 90″ right, while the formation stayed solid. I felt the resulting course was a little south and I instinctively approached my section leader, Marchelidon, who was flying Yellow One—I being Yellow Three—who nodded that he was aware of the situation. Then over the radio came: 'Freehold Leader, this is Elflike calling;' (this was the Ops Room of 10 Group) 'Do you know your position? Over.' It was the delightful female voice, a little nervous perhaps, of the WAAF Controller. 'Of course I do,' replied our Wing Leader, somewhat dryly. Five minutes went by. 'Freehold Leader, this is Elflike....' This time is was a male voice, the Senior Controller at 10 Group. 'For your information, you're over Cherbourg and you have bandits at 3 o'clock above, heading towards you!' There followed some swearing by our Wing Leader who thought he was over the English coast and we changed our course rapidly to the north. Short of petrol, we had to make a landing at Bolt Head, between Plymouth and Dartmouth. We finally arrived at night that Merston in frightful visibility.

"On 25th April I carried out my first sweep over France, towards Bethune. We were burning with desire to have a fight and my eyes felt tired after looking at the sun and sky, but alas, we saw no enemy aircraft. Between more sweeps we flew convoy patrols.

"Our Spitfires were now loaded with bombs and we started dive-bombing practise. Action, principally against railway lines in the valley of the Seine. We also got to know that German AA fire was pretty intense and effective. One day we received orders to bomb a somewhat extraordinary target. The photographs showed us a little stretch of railway, the end of which seemed to disappear into a tunnel. The Intelligence Officer explained to us that this was a ramp for sending off missiles against London. These ramps would soon be sending off the infamous V1 flying bombs. We did our best to destroy these nests but they were not easy to hit.

"Since the end of May, the number of convoys in the Channel increased and whatever the weather, we left our base and covered them. Then on 3rd June, in the evening, we found pots of black and white paint near our aeroplanes together with a brush. Soon, all the pilots were asked to paint their aircraft with great black and white stripes on the fuselage and wings. It was explained to us that this would facilitate our identification among the Navy and Army gunners, a measure which proved to be a good precaution.

"The weather was quite revolting which upset us because we felt we were approaching a vital period. On the evening of the 5th, still in terrible weather, we again flew over the Channel and just off the Isle of Wight found ourselves between clouds at 100 metres and a very unruly sea. Suddenly we flew over hundreds and hundreds of ships and landing craft. Their number and course left us in no doubt—the great invasion had started.

"We had to keep absolute radio silence and were very much concerned we should do so, because we were far from being alone in the air. It was already beginning to get dark and we were all in a pretty excited state. After landing we rushed towards the Ops Tent where drinks were available. Our new Wing Leader was there—Crawford Compton—a delightful New Zealander, who had replaced poor Marples who'd been killed in a collision on 26th April with one of our pilots, together with Sailor Malan, who commanded the base. Willie Compton, in absolute silence, unfolded a map of operations and explained to us the enormous combined movements of thousands of ships, aircraft and soldiers. Then we were off to our tents, to try and sleep, for tomorrow was The Longest Day.

"We took off at dawn on D-Day 6th June with some slightly improved weather. From the Isle of Wight we could see lines without end of ships of all sizes. Several of these lines went uninterrupted to the beaches of Normandy, where we could see landing craft disembarking troops. The whole spectacle was magnificent. On the ground we could see smoke and explosions.

In the afternoon we were called to the Ops Tent for another briefing, being told all had gone well so far, although there were some difficulties. Progress in front of Caen was being blocked and progress by some parts of the American front was also being hindered. But I had to admire the confidence and phlegm of our chiefs who behaved as if it was all a game of rugby.

"That evening we escorted aircraft and gliders which were to drop airborne troops into the battle area to help unblock the situation. The huge armada began to over-fly our base and by the time we had taken off, the tail of the stream was still over England while the head, we could see, had attained the beach-head. Night fell and the ground took on a violet tint as we arrived at the drop-zone. Near Caen, in an area supposed to be controlled by our troops, or at least empty of the enemy, the gliders and paratroops went in. I could see a field of corn changing colour, becoming a sombre red. The cause, the cavalcade of fire of all calibres from a German Division which was supposed to be elsewhere and which was firing at the great birds as if they were on exercise. The carnage was such that we were nauseated.

"The wretched gliders were in flames before touching the ground and the paratroops killed, sometimes before having jumped. We looked on powerless at this terrible disaster, not even able to machine-gun the field because we didn't want to kill any of our own men. We found out later that the Division carried in the air, lost some 85% of its strength.

"The following days came and went, while we carried out protection missions over the beaches. I came across a single Me109 which unfortunately disappeared into cloud before I was able to open fire. From time to time we protected bomber formations and these forces hold my admiration as they always flew in impeccable formations into the German flak.

"Then we started ground strafing, these sorties paying dividends because, despite good camouflage by the Germans we were still able to see them. These operations were not without loss to ourselves, and some of my close friends were hit and wounded. Then at the beginning of July, short of petrol, I landed on a forward landing strip near Bayeux. It had been two years since I had last stood on my native soil.

"At the end of the landing strip we were taken across to two local people who, seeing we were French, gave us some camembert cheese in exchange for two half-crowns. I stuck them in my Mae West and took them back to England after we'd been refuelled. When I landed my mechanic came to help me out and nearly fell backwards when he smelt the inside of my cockpit. I should mention that it was high summer and about 100 degrees in the aircraft!

"Finally we moved to France and continued our strafing attacks from there as the Germans retreated towards Belgium. We continually changed bases as we supported Canadian troops during the advance. We moved to Lille which I recall because the local inhabitants and especially the ladies, were in a great state of excitement, having just been liberated by the Anglo-Canadian forces.

"By the end of November we were on an airfield at Antwerp and everything changed. It became cold and wet and we had to live in cellars because of the attacks by V1s and V2 rockets. One fell on the Alsace Squadron, killing one of our pilots and destroying 12 Spitfires.

"We continued offensive operations into early 1945, even though through casualties we could hardly put up 12 aircraft. Then in early March, despite our desire to continue, we were sent on rest to Turnhouse, near Edinburgh, Scotland, then to Skaebrae in the Orkneys to help protect Scapa Flow. By that time I was a flight commander and had flown well over 100 missions with 'The Storks'."

Felix Boyer de Bouillane was another Frenchman who arrived in England in early 1944, destined to join 345 Squadron. Felix had been a cadet at the l'Ecole de l'Air and was a regular Air Force officer. By 1945 he was a Capitaine and he later rose to the rank of Colonel in the French Air Force. He remembers:

"Having arrived in England after a voyage of some three weeks on the SS *Strathmore*, we thought we would be quickly put through a short and symbolic conversion onto Spitfires and integrated with the RAF. But we didn't realise then the strictness with which our hosts had organised all their operational efforts, taking four years of wartime experience into account.

"Integration, therefore, was preceded by certain formalities and tests, well organised, to bring us into the mould of wartime pilots and also to be efficiently part of the total war machine, whose operations more or less concentrated the activity of the country.

"One of the tests we were given was to learn how to survive in hostile territory. It was during this exercise that we pilots thought of ourselves as the equivalent of James Bond! It was designed to make us familiar with the crude process of disappearing into the environment and then rejoining our own lines, in case we had to make a forced landing inside enemy territory.

"The pilots, in battle-dress, were deposited in the countryside in batches of two at about 40 kilometres from the base. We had two pennies in our pockets in order to telephone in cases of emergency, a compass and a few sandwiches. The British Home Guard was alerted and it was necessary to evade them and return to base. As for me, I was coupled with Joubert de Ouches, an old friend who was on in his second tour.

"We two were dropped outside a village and we stayed there for about half an hour, paying great attention to everything around us. Checking into every nook and cranny to try and discover an unattended vehicle which would allow us to rejoin our base. No corner escaped our attention and at the end of a courtyard, we found an enormous grey lorry. After a few moments of thought, we came to the conclusion that this might be our method of getting home.

"We crept carefully and discreetly under the gateway where the lorry stood, its doors unlocked. What person or idiot left such a vehicle unlocked and unattended? We climbed into the cab and Joubert allowed me to drive. We carefully examined the dashboard and controls for a few minutes before leaving as prudently as possible. At first we had no problems and we took to the road after a wink or two of satisfaction from my companion who was now my navigator. His perfect knowledge of English and English customs, helped us in our task and we were soon overcome with optimism.

"We drove at a reasonable speed although I wasn't really at ease driving such a heavy vehicle and we couldn't risk the least lack of concentration. Then, about 20 kilometres, the motor missed and began to lose all power, leaving me little time to find a parking place where we could stop without causing a jam on the road.

"Panic! We stopped and opened the bonnet, although neither of us were mechanics and the sight of the engine only accentuated our sense of powerlessness. Then, closing the bonnet, and thinking of possible plans and what might have gone wrong, we wondered if it was simply a lack of petrol. This idea wasn't quite as stupid as we thought. While searching the lorry we found a jerry can and we went to all the metal caps which all resisted our unorganised attacks. Very upset by this final obstacle, we got back into our

Lieutenant Freddy Hardi, 340 Squadron.

Commandant Aubertin, CO of 340 (Ile de France) Squadron.

Lieutenant Albert Cavet, 340 Squadron, missing 1 April 1945.

Lieutenant Jacques Carre, 340 Squadron, missing 23 April 1945.

Sergent Chef E Graillot, 340 Squadron, crash landed in a minefield and seriously injured, 1 April 1945.

Sous Lieutenant A de Reynel de St Michel DFM, 340 Squadron.

Sergent Chef R Pottier, 341 Squadron, shot down 17 April 1945.

Capitaine Victor Tanguy, 341 (Alsace) Squadron.

Sous Lieutenant Lucien Foissac, 341 Squadron, killed in action 1 April 1945.

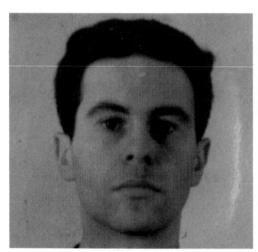

Capitaine Henri de Bordas, 329 (Cigognes) Squadron.

Warrant Officer Gabriel Wolloshing, 341 Squadron, killed in action 1 April 1945.

Commandant Jean Ozanne, CO 329 Squadron.

Capitaine B de Larminat, 341 Squadron. Shot
down 1 April 1945 he evaded capture and
returned on the 7th.

Commandant Gaston Guizard, CO 345 (Berry)
Squadron.

Lieutenant Michel Fleischel, 345 Squadron,
killed in action 14 February 1945.

Lieutenant Pierre Decroo DFC, shot down
three times; killed as a test pilot in 1950.

Capitaine Felix Jaquemet, killed flying my
Spitfire just after the war.

Lieutenant Robert Etlin, 341 Squadron, killed in
action 21 March 1945.

Top: My Spitfire LF XVIE as Wing Leader with 'SS' on the fuselage.

Middle: Lieutenant L Le Flecher, 341 Squadron, POW 25 April 1945.

Bottom left: Capitaine Jacques Marchelidon DSO, 329 Squadron, badly wounded 28 February 1945.

Bottom right: Commandant Maurice Perdrizet, 345 Squadron.

Top left: Lts Pierre Laurent DFC (left) and Roger Borne, 341 Squadron.

Top right: Spitfire fighter-bomber, 145 French Wing

Middle left: Capitaine Oliver Massart, 340 Squadron, POW 13 March 1945. I shot down the Me109 that got him.

Above: Capitaine Jacques Souviat, 329 Squadron.

Above right: Lt Michel Brunschwig, 341 Squadron – in the wars, Anvers 1944.

Top left: Lt Jean Maridor, who crashed near my present home in August 1944.

Middle: Sgt P Lavergne, 340 Squadron. POW 9 April 1945.

Above right: Roger Borne, 341 Squadron, killed in action 20 April 1945.

Bottom: Seated in my Spitfire - note wing leader's pennant.

Top left: Arnaud 'Fifi' de Saxce (left) and Michel Brunschwig, 341 Squadron. Fifi was shot down 10 April 1945 but his parachute failed to deploy.

Top right: Valin presenting me with the Croix de Guerre - but without a kiss!

Middle: General Valin during his inspection of the Wing, 5 June 1945 at Drope.

Bottom: With Air Marshal Sir Sholto Douglas. Left to right: GC Walker, self, S-D, AVM E C Hudleston.

Top: Me and my Spitfire.

Middle: Captaining the Barbarians v Penarth 1948. Rear left to right: C W R Andrews, L E Grose, D D Mackenzie, W P Black, W R Hamp, H H Campbell, T B M Norman, Goldsworthy (Ref); Middle: B O'Hanlon, J E Nelson, C R Bruce, R W F Sampson, V G Roberts, D P Hepburn; Front: A G Black and B J B Hazel.

Bottom left: Representing Scotland.....................

Bottom right: ....and the Air Training Corps.

seats for another conference. A miracle! We discovered at the bottom of the cab, another small cap—perhaps this was to be our saviour?

"We tried not to hope for too much and with hearts beating, we opened it up, poured in the contents of the can and tried the engine, which immediately restarted. We had lost little over half an hour but a lot of adrenoline. Despite all we had succeeded. After rejoining the road, we arrived back at the Mess at the tea hour, preceded by a few yards by the Station Commander's car. He was horrified to see us arrive in such a vehicle and I heard des Ouches say to the Commander, who he had known beforehand, 'But, Sir, this is my personal car!'

"The tea hour was among the many venerable English customs we discovered in our time with the RAF. This English institution was practised in a religious silence but at this particular base was upset by the noisy arrival of the French, who continuing their discussions, and forgetting the usual reserve in these places, threw themselves at the table, filled their plates—somewhat immoderately—with a selection of cakes, which they hastened to consume without interrupting their talk! They then returned to the table to refill their plates under the gaze of their English friends, who, with their usual good manners ignored what must to them have seemed most unusual behaviour.

"In September 1944 we were detailed to escort transport aircraft to supply Allied airborne forces in the redoubt at Arnhem. All the facts combined to make this operation difficult and effectively useless. Nevertheless, it was important to try and assist our troops who had been surrounded for several days, despite the appalling weather.

"The sky was overcast and visibility down to about 100 metres, with cloud base less than 200 feet. In short, it wasn't possible to get aircraft airborne but our troops couldn't wait. Seventeen squadrons—on paper—were assigned for the escort, a dangerous one into hostile skies, and I believe only about two squadrons actually took off, with little hope of an improvement in the conditions after passing the coast to make a rendezvous with the Dakotas and their gliders. We took off in a thick drizzle, flying in a very tight formation across the North Sea. The horizon continued to be obscured and each pilot had his eyes fixed on an imagined horizon or on the aircraft next to him.

"Progressively in this 'pea-soup' we came down low over the sea and as we flew some silhouettes, thought to be superstructures of battleships, appeared—so quickly it was impossible to escape them. We realised too late that we were heading over Ostend docks, but fortunately the defenders were so surprised they hadn't even had time to man their guns.

"There was now some discussion about the prudence of continuing our mission, as we were heading over the Belgian countryside in almost nil visibility. We finally had to give up and made a turn towards home and after some minutes once again saw strange silhouettes coming at us. Surely we hadn't flown back over Ostend? This time we were surrounded by vicious flak fire which exploded in a mass of tracer bullets. All the fire came towards us in a most indescribable disdorder. It wasn't Ostend—this time it was Dunkirk. It was everyone for himself and the formation broke up. Scattering over the sea we were followed by exploding 88 mm gunfire which erupted about us and churned up the sea all around. There were several moments of torment, knowing that we could not outrun immediately the 88 mm shells, but at last it abated and we were able to form up into sections of two or three as we headed for home. We all got back and were reunited by the end of the afternoon. The whisky was agreeable after these moments of excitement."

Felix operated with 345 Squadron for most of 1944, and was still with them when the unit was at Antwerp after I'd become Wing Leader. He continues:

"At Antwerp, where we had to put up, day and night, with disorganised attacks from flying bombs and V2s, we were housed in the cellars of modest buildings situated on the edge of the landing field. In peacetime it had been the city's airport.

"We weren't under any illusion about the lack of safety given by wooden buildings and knew these would give little actual protection. Unfortunately we were not protected from the noise either, especially that which came from the V1s. When they arrived above our heads we would hold our breath for long seconds, until the engines stopped, indicating that the flying bomb was starting its final dive. The explosions which resulted gave us relief; 'That one wasn't for us.' Remission lasted a very short time because often a new bomb announced itself and our nervous system was strained again. On some nights as many as 60 flying bombs would come in and explode around us and the city. This was not counting the V2 which fell in a vertical dive and gave no warning of its arrival, exploding in between those of the V1s.

"Still in our pathetic cellars, we were woken one night about 2 am by our squadron commander, who, like a bomb, arrived at the bottom of the steps to tell us the unbelievable news—German parachutists at large on the aerodrome and its surroundings. In the panic, everyone jumped into their battle-dress over their pyjamas—quite a usual way of dressing due to the terrible temperatures outside. Everyone seized a pistol or revolver, which they hardly knew how to operate, and rushed out to send the enemy fleeing. For some time we crept about, full of fear and apprehension, checking into the shadows and listening for the slightest noise or sign.

"As you might expect, our routes were not co-ordinated and we often found ourselves face to face with each other. We exchanged a few words and with a grin of resignation, started on our dangerous manoeuvres again. Just as we thought this form of fun had lasted long enough, and because we began to realise we ran greater risk in the darkness of killing one of our friends rather than the, so far, unseen parachutists, everything was called off. We never understood where the story of the parachutists came from. Either it was nerves or a collective hallucination caused by von Rundstedt's offensive in the nearby Ardennes.

"It isn't possible to forget certain moments of sadness after the loss of comrades with whom you have been living for several weeks or months of intense activity, in an atmosphere of friend-ship, sometimes in humour, but always genuine. So it is difficult to forget certain nights in the month of February 1945 when we returned to our quarters after days of particular danger.

"Our armies were involved in the final stages of the war and engaged in the assault against the Siegfried Line. In a few days we lost four pilots, brought down by flak which was very heavy as it was part of the defence line between the Meuse and the Rhine—a line of uninterrupted war-works.

"I remember the atmosphere and the depression which fell on us while sitting in our rooms which served as our private refuge, not far from the town of d'Hertogenbosch. In our room we originally had six pilots, camped between great piles of soil, covered in sheets of tarred material over planks of wood. Amidst this sad decor, in less than a week we lost three pilots, one each on the 8th, 13th and 14th February. These men had become friends—brothers. I remember two of them particularly, as I happened to be their personal representative; and what an appalling job. There were certain papers which seemed too intimate to send home to parents and loved ones. The last one to disappear had been my own No.2. After he carried out an attack on a train, he went down on a strong-point on the Siegfried Line, near Wesel, and didn't come back.

"Then some joy when three of our missing six comrades did return, but we continued to wonder between ourselves, who would be the next to go.

"To illustrate the strength of our friendship with our English friends and to underline their sporting spirit within the RAF, I don't want to forget to say that after the liberation of Paris, they allowed those of us who had relations in or near the city, the chance of making a visit. There was also, at the request of our chiefs, agreement by 2nd TAF to put a Spitfire at our disposal, which allowed dozens of us to pay a rapid return visit, via the airfield at Villacoublay.

"For a few hours we were able to enjoy the warmth of family life and carry items and souvenirs to them. Our people had been so severely rationed that many had practically forgotten the existence of anything of any luxury. To crown it all we were able to bring out from our cellar, an old bottle of champagne, or the more popular Mosel, with which to celebrate. These are moments we will always remember."

Maurice Perdrizet was a Capitaine in 345 'Berry' Squadron and when I joined the Wing he was about to leave to command a French P.47 Thunderbolt squadron. But he had flown with 345 during 1944, and was with it when it had joined 145 Wing in October. He recalls:

"No. 345 Squadron joined 145 Wing in Belgium at the end of October 1944. We moved to the Continent and our airfield was B.55—Wevelghem. At the beginning of our posting we were not very lucky with the weather, low cloud and very poor visibility hampering almost all operational flying. So after a few days, the Wingco and our CO, Gaston Guizard, made up their minds and replaced operational sorties by sports and especially football, to keep the pilots busy and fit.

"Two or three days later our CO, during a football match, had an unlucky fall which sent him to Brussels Hospital for a month. Being his deputy, I became acting CO and with the flight commanders, we decided to stop football and sports after reporting to the Wingco, naturally. The pilots then took up again their former main distraction, of playing 'Crapette Cards'. I wonder if, for fighter pilots, sports may be as dangerous as operational flying?!

"One of our first operations with the Wing, came on 19th November. Sous Lieutenants Porchon and Marchal were reported missing from a dive-bombing mission near Dunkirk. On the morning of that day, twelve Spitfires of 345 Squadron led by Bill Compton, each loaded with two bombs, were assigned to this sortie.

"The target was a German Headquarters housed in a bog farm in the east-south-east part, 15 miles from Dunkirk itself. Blue, Red and Yellow Sections were flying line astern and on this occasion I had chosen to fly as Yellow Four.

"Being the last one to go down I had not noticed any enemy flak since the beginning of the attack by the first two sections; however, after dropping the bombs I joined the tail of Yellow Section as fast as I could. Looking up at Blue and Red Sections, which seemed to be circling the target, my eyes were on Red Section when I was eyewitness to the loss of our two comrades.

"I can clearly remember Porchon's Spitfire to this day, as all of a sudden, it became stationary in space and the propeller of Marchal's aircraft began to slice the tail of his leader. Then, in a split second, their two Spitfires had been rubbed from the sky. Now only hundreds of pieces of aircraft could be seen fluttering down towards the ground. Presumably both of them had been hit by enemy flak, whose flash bursts could now be perceived around us.

"We returned to base in sad silence, thinking of our two friends and about the German flak which, on the Western Front, remained the main mortal enemy of pilots and crews, especially those engaged in air-to-ground operations. Life and death had become in the main a question of luck, the same as in a raffle."

CHAPTER XII

WING LEADER

When I joined the Wing it comprised only two French Squadrons, No.329 and 345, the other Squadron being 74. 329 was commanded by Commandant Jean Ozanne, 345 by Commandant Guizard. 74 was commanded by Squadron Leader A J Reeves DFC. 340 and 341 Squadrons were taking it in turn to re-equip with Spitfire XVIs at Turnhouse.

Later I was to have all four French squadrons in the Free French Fighter Wing, the original 340 and 341 Squadrons which had been formed from French personnel who had followed General de Gaulle to England in 1940; then 329 whose original personnel had been under General Giraud in North Africa, and finally 345. The original French Escadrille which became 345 in England had been disbanded by the Germans but allowed to use gliders in Vichy France.

One thing I noticed looking through the paper work was that earlier, when the Wing was known as No.145 Airfield, during the build up to the Invasion, it had been commanded by my old Wing Leader, Cam Malfroy.

Loel Guiness was the ideal person to command the Wing, not only because he spoke fluent French, but understood them, for he owned land and property in France. Loel informed me that he wished me to have breakfast with him each morning in his private caravan and also drinks with him each evening at 6 pm before going to our Mess. The object of this was firstly to discuss our operations for the day, and later to have an inquest before dinner.

Within a few days of my arrival I was presented with a small, gilt and enamelled 'wings' with the Cross of Lorraine in the centre. Because they were unofficial, they were only to be worn on the Battle Dress. However, I happened to be in my No.1 Blues when they were presented.

That evening four of the senior officers said they were going into Antwerp first to have a meal at the Officer's Club in the Century Hotel and then on to a drinking club, and would I care to join them. The answer of course was yes. The drinking club was very nice and not crowded and we were looked after by a very beautiful girl who in between taking orders, sat with us. I was concious that she kept looking at my new enamelled wings.

One of the French chaps had a long and earnest conversation with her and all the others listened. One of them said, "He has been asking her what the price is for bed and the answer was £30." To this they had said, what nowadays would be, 'You must be joking!' She then pointed to my new wings and said something to the Frenchman who turned to us and said, "For you, Sir, no money, just your new wings." To this I replied, "Tell her that regretfully I cannot accept, because the French honour to me is greater than her honour."

When I had been at Antwerp for a week I remarked to Loel that with all the V1s and V2s that were aimed at Antwerp Harbour but which sometimes fell short, doing damage to the airfield, as well as our Spitfires, we really ought to move. The danger too of loss of life in pilots and ground crew, quite apart from aircraft, was a serious consideration. Sure enough, within a week we were moved to Schijndel (B.85), a strip some 10-15 miles south of Nijmegen.

I only flew one sortie from Antwerp Deurne (B.70) in January— my first as Wing Leader—and that was on January 23rd. In my Spitfire IXB, with my personal letters 'SS' painted on the fuselage—a prerogative of a wing leader—I led 329 and 74 Squadrons on a Sweep and Armed Recce into the Osnabruck area. We found the sky clear of enemy aircraft but on the way back came across a train pulling 30 goods trucks. We severely damaged this and also left some lorries in various stages of disrepair, although we received plenty of flak when flying near Rheine airfield.

I flew two more Ops from Deurne, both on February 3rd, and both dive-bombing sorties. The first was a late morning show, leading 329, 345 and 74 Squadrons to V1 and V2 marshalling yards at Nijverdal where, despite clouds we achieved excellent results, and then leading 74, bombing and strafing targets on Goringhen Island in support of ground troops.

We moved to Schijndel on the 6th, which we found muddy, but safer that Deurne. It was here during February and March that 340 and 341 Squadrons joined us. These two units were commanded by Commandant Olivier Massart and Commandant Christian Martel.

When finally I had all four French squadrons together, Loel Guiness took me to one side and told me there was a problem which Bill Compton had pointed out earlier. It seems that the people in 345 Squadron looked 'sideways' at 340 and 341 while 329 looked 'sideways' at the other three! Some of the senior members of the squadrons were becoming tour expired and Loel asked me to consider promoting those pilots ready for promotion, from one squadron to another—in effect, mixing up the different identities. I suggested that I would have a word with the COs. The idea was not greeted with tremendous enthusiasm and I was glad I interviewed them individually, because it was easier to appeal to their loyalty to France. Later I was able to report to Loel that we would have no problem and in fact we didn't.

We were the first Allied personnel to occupy Schijndel and it was close to a Nunnery. Loel Guiness asked me to make our number with the Mother Superior. She spoke good English and hoped the boys would behave because all the girls were Novices who had not yet taken their celibacy vows and could fall for strong persuasion. My visit was on a Sunday and I noticed that whereas the hens were free range, the cocks—some dozen of them—were in an enclosure. I was prompted to ask why and was told, "Because they must not be allowed to indulge on Sunday. We pen them in on Saturday night and release them again on Monday morning."

Another bonus at Schijndel was the canteen. Air Chief Marshal Sir Arthur Tedder, Deputy to General Dwight Eisenhower, the Supreme Allied Commander in Europe, had married 'Toppy' Malcolm, the sister of Wing Commander Hugh Malcolm, a bomber pilot who had been killed in action and been awarded a posthumous Victoria Cross. Toppy had set up the Malcolm Clubs in his honour, at various airfields as the Allies advanced. These were glorified canteens (somewhat more high class than the NAAFI canteens) run by personal friends of Lady Tedder. At Schijndel, Miss A M 'Billie' Yorke, was in charge.

Billie was a pre-war Whiteman Cup tennis player and was great fun to be with, and she had tremendous personality and organising ability. We saw quite a lot of the Tedders as they made frequent visits to see how the Club was doing. My one abiding memory of him was that he was a tremendous critic of Montgomery and never ceased to voice that opinion.

In early February came the sad news that Rolf Berg had been killed in action. He had finally fallen victim to ground fire. The report I got was that he went in to see if an airfield was occupied before making a Wing attack and flak had opened up on him. The way he crash landed on the airfield as if he was making a belly landing suggested that he been hit himself, possibly a bullet in the head from the side—there was a gun firing from a water tower.

I remember Rolf with affection and admiration and I have a photograph of him in my den. I recollect vividly the show we did together on Christmas Day 1944 against that goods train by Twente airfield, when I flew as his No.2. I suppose I was no more than 75 yards behind as he started his run in, firing as he dived. I lined my sights on the train at the same time seeing Rolf's Spitfire in the top of my sight ring. The next day we were looking at the films produced from our camera guns and when mine was on the viewing screen, strikes on the loco were seen, as was Rolf's fighter at the top of my sight. Rolf ordered a re-run of the film, at the same time saying, "Did you know I was in your sight ring?" I said I did, but that as he was at the top of the ring and allowing for gravity, the bullets would fall well below his machine. Rolf accepted my explanation but was clearly not totally convinced. I also remember Zulu Morris telling me that he'd flown a number of times as Rolf's wingman, admitting that he was really shaken on many of them.

I think that the secret of Rolf's success was that once he had sighted a potential target, he opened the taps and his sheer speed placed him ahead of enemy Ack-Ack fire. I know this was the case on Christmas Day, because flak aimed at him was actually bursting behind his Spitfire and in front of mine! In my opinion, which is shared by Zulu, he was not only the bravest but without doubt the most brilliant exponent of the low level Armed Recce Ops.

At this stage of the war, the British and Canadian Armies were making an all out effort to push towards the River Rhine, the German's natural border in the west, by way of the Reichwald and Hochwald Forests, which lie west of the river and were heavily defended.

We spent every day either on Cab Rank sorties or escorting rocket firing Typhoons, from 8th February until 23rd March, when the Armies finally crossed the Rhine. On the first day we attacked some MT and I strafed four of them but was shaken rigid by the ground fire that came up to meet us.

We successfully introduced a tactic whereby half of the formation carried out the dive-bombing, followed almost immediately by the rest going in with 23-second delay bombs at zero feet. There were two basic rules to all our sorties. Very careful planning and briefing and then great speed in carrying out the attack. Because of the strain on the wings when pulling out of an attack dive, the wings of our Spitfire XVIs were clipped.

Mission followed mission. Strafing and bombing sorties, being so close to the front line, lasted sometimes only 30 to 40 minutes from take-off to landing. I remember the Wing dive-bombing the village of Hassum in Germany, south of Reichwald Forest, just 300 yards ahead of our troops. We were told the village held a battalion of German soldiers and we certainly saw many dashing all over the place during our attack. In the event it took two further sorties to Hassum before our boys could occupy it.

I had decided to lead this show myself and to make it strafing only. Soon after becoming airborne I suggested to the Ops Controller that as the area might be fairly wide it may require more than one strafing run and that as the village was only ten minutes flying time from our strip, this could be undertaken very rapidly.

When we arrived over the target I could see that it would require at least two if not three runs. The first strafe was fairly uneventful in that there was no obvious defensive reaction. We soon emptied all our ammunition and told the Controller to liaise with his Army counterpart to the effect that I reckoned it required two more attacks. I then called our own airfield control tower to have all ground crews on the top line for a quick re-arm and turn around. Ops gave me the all clear for two more runs.

On our second attack we noticed enemy soldiers and we received some light flak—Lieutenant Borne, my No.2, received a number of hits in his wings. When we carried out the third run the Hun soldiers realised the position was untenable and we could see them running in all directions. Later on, as was usual, we received the feed-back from the Army with praise and thanks as the Huns had finally surrendered.

When I took over the Free French Wing, Loel Guiness had told me that I was to confine myself to only one offensive operation per day. So he was not too pleased with me when he saw the Daily Routine Order, which showed him I had done more than one strafe on Hassum. He had not been on the airfield that day, but soon told me—"Don't do it again!!"

Towards the end of February, Loel suggested I take a weekend leave break, which for wing commanders usually involved flying their own Spitfire back to Lasham, situated to the south of Basingstoke, and then being loaned a service car for the few days.

Just before taking off after lunch, I asked Flight Lieutenant Scott, our Airfield Controller, to give me a weather report. The report indicated there was a low pressure area gradually building up from the west but I would be ahead of it, so it should be alright. My course from Schijndel took me via Breda-Tilburg, just east of Dunkirk—still held by the Germans—Cap Gris Nez, Manston and then Lasham.

I started off at 2,000 feet but when I was in the Dunkirk area I had to go down to the deck to be below the cloud base. I called up Calais Control and was told the weather had suddenly clamped and that the UK was out. He suggested Grimbergen, Brussels, where he could arrange for me to be talked down. I said, "No thanks, I'll go back to Antwerp." I took a course due north which would take me to the River Scheldt where I could turn to fly up the river to the airfield which was fairly near the north bank.

Visibility now was almost nil and as I was at zero feet I prayed that I would not run into overhead cables or tall trees. When I reached the Scheldt I got a very nasty shock because I found myself in the Balloon Barrage and could see the close-hauled balloons some 100 feet above. Again I was lucky and as the cables were on land, flew up above the river and landed at Antwerp airfield without further ado. Here there was a Care and Maintenance Flight under a flight lieutenant who lent me his jeep so that I could drive to the Century Hotel—an Officer's Club next to the main railway station. V1s and V2 rockets were still landing almost continually in the harbour area so one just hoped that they would not land near the centre of the town.

I met a number of old friends, had a few drinks, dinner and went to bed early. I suppose it was about 3.30 am or so that I heard the dreaded sound of a Buzz Bomb (V1). As I listened, its engine cut out and I knew it was going to fall nearby, if not on me! In the event it hit the railway station and the room I occupied was, I suppose, about 40 or 50 yards away. The windows were shattered and a bottle of whisky, which I had just purchased for two shillings, finished up on the floor. I immediately jumped out of bed, dressed, and drove off to the airfield. I jumped into my Spitfire as dawn was breaking and got the hell out of there.

I got to Lasham alright this time, then talked my way into being allowed to fly up to Northolt because of my now reduced time in England—which I don't think the people at Northolt appreciated very much—and after a couple of days, headed back to B.85, via Manston. Even now the weather was still on the deck, but Scotty got me back and down with some excellent controlling. Although it had been a break, I had begun to wonder if I wasn't safer staying in Holland and flying on Ops.

For a brief period I had 329 Squadron in the Wing at Schijndel, which was finally commanded by Commandant Henri de Bordas. One of the most outstanding bombing raids on a combined Via and

Aquaduct was carried out by this Squadron on 28th February, led by Capitaine Jacques Marchelidon. Jacques had taken over from Ozanne on 6th February.

He was leading eight bombed-up Spitfires to dive-bomb the target from 4,000 feet, having approached on the usually agreed format of 8,000 feet, before turning from one side to commence the dive. As he half rolled his Spitfire, his No.2 spotted that an anti-aircraft shell had entered his leader's aircraft while inverted, via the perspex canopy and called up to ask if everything was alright. He immediately got the response—"Follow me." Once he had completed his bombing run, Marchelidon, instead of gaining height as was normal, stayed on the deck, heading for home in a somewhat haphazard and uneven way.

"Are you alright?" asked his No.2 again, "Shall I take over?" A now very slurred voice replied, "Follow me." At that stage the No.2 advised the Airfield Controller that something was obviously wrong with his leader and the Controller called me. I went to the control tower and alerted the fire engine and ambulance, while the Controller made sure the landing strip was kept clear.

We watched anxiously as the Spitfires came into sight, and were slightly relieved to see the leader's wheels come down as he curved in to make his approach. Marchelidon made a safe, if somewhat bumpy landing, turning off at the first runway intersection. With the doctor in close attendance, I got to the Spitfire as its engine died and its prop jerked to a halt, slid back the cockpit hood and found the pilot slumped over the control column. The whole of the interior looked as if it had been sprayed red. Mercifully, Jacques had passed out.

We got him out and the ambulance raced off with the doctor to the nearest military hospital. We later heard he had been very lucky for a shell, presumably a 20 mm, had indeed come into the cockpit as he'd rolled over for the attack and hit him in the top of the leg near his groin—gratefully causing no permanent damage. The Army got in touch with 84 Group HQ to say that the operation had been 100% successful and the target obliterated.

We pieced together the facts of the sortie which left us in no doubt that Marchelidon's only thought after being hit was to carry out his attack and then lead his men home.

On the Group Captain's suggestion, Flight Lieutenant Craig, the Wing Intelligence Officer, and myself wrote out a citation and recommendation for the award of the Victoria Cross. What we hadn't realised at the time was that the Victoria Cross is an exclusive medal for British, Commonwealth and Ghurka troops only, not for foreign combatants fighting on the British side. So the recommendation went through but for the Immediate award of the Distinguished Service Order, which, I am pleased to say, was approved a few days later.

On the second day of March, I led all four squadrons on German mortar positions in the Hochwald Forest, again just a few hundred yards ahead of our troops. This time it was the Canadians who were being bogged down by the enemy mortars. We were again flying Cab Rank sorties whereby we would patrol an area with a map on our knees while a ground officer would call up, give us a map reference, define the target and request a strafe. Great care was needed as some of the targets were often a matter of yards ahead of our friends; also we usually got a lot of light flak. The Wing carried out many of these type of sorties and I can say with some pride and satisfaction, that we made no errors such as strafing our own troops.

After some successful Wing Operations, allowing the Canadians to move forward, I received requests from Flight Lieutenant Craig, our hard working IO, and Major Mitchell, the Army Liaison Officer attached to the Wing, to see targets in the battle area. For some reason I agreed to fly them in the Wing's Auster. On the 5th I flew Mitchell over the Xanton-Goch-Cleve areas for an hour, then on the 9th, took Crane out for a similar period. However, that same day another spotting Auster was shot down near Xanton by three marauding Me109s, so Group quickly put a stop to this joy-riding.

On the morning of March 13th we were scheduled to escort 54 Mitchell bombers who were to bomb the Lengerich marshalling yards. The bombers were in three boxes of 18, and 340 Squadron with me leading, was the only escort of the last group, themselves flying in three boxes of six.

After the Mitchells had dropped their bombs the first boxes opened their throttles and there was soon a gap of some three miles between the first two and last box. I instructed Commandant Massart and his Yellow Section to stay behind with his section to guard them, whilst I and the other two Sections stayed between the first and second box.

Massart then called up to say they were under attack by a dozen Me109Gs, so I told him I would turn to help them, leaving one Section with the leading 12 bombers. I could see a general melee in progress as I approached and, horror of horrors, I heard Massart say that he had been badly hit and was going to have to bale out. As I closed in I was able to see the 109 still firing at Massart and began to line up the Messerschmitt in my gyro gunsight at 800 yards.

When I was at 600 yards, the German pilot saw me, turning in my direction. I gave him a short burst of all my armament having got him with both the '+' and the movable 'dot' together. To my surprise I saw a strike on the front of his fighter which seemed to knock him off balance because he then turned hard towards me and my immediate reaction was once again, "You've had it, boy."

I easily out-turned him and got on his tail. I was still firing when the pilot baled out, but I had the feeling he was hit; then the 109 disintegrated. By this time I was so close that my Spitfire was hit and slightly damaged by Hun debris, but it caused no serious problems. Needless to say I was very impressed with the gyroscopic sight and I wished I could have had it at the time of the Dieppe Raid.

When I landed my rigger and fitter told me that there was blood on the leading edges of both wings which tended to confirm that I had indeed hit the German pilot as he was attempting to get out.

In addition to my kill, the boys chalked up a probable and two damaged, claimed by Sergent Chef de Reynel, who had been my No.3, the damaged by Lieutenant Carre and Sergent Chef Boudard, Massart's Yellow 2 and 3. It was with some relief when Massart, who had indeed baled out, got down safely and 'undamaged', rejoined us a few weeks after VE Day. Command of 340 Squadron passed to Capitaine Jacques (Jacko) Andrieux DFC, a flight commander from 341 Squadron, and future French Air Force General.

My combat report for this sortie read:

13th March 1945.   Time: 1126-1311.   10,000 ft.   Bocholt area.

"I was leading 340 Squadron escorting the third box of eighteen Mitchells bombing Lengerich marshalling yards. After bombing, six Mitchells straggled and I detailed Yellow Section to stay with them. When in the Bocholt area, Yellow Section, who were now well behind with their six bombers, were bounced by twelve Me109s. I detailed Blue Section to remain with the twelve bombers and went back with Red Section to help.

"After a few minutes I saw a general melee going on, and identified five 109s. I bounced one Hun at 10,000 ft, whom I noticed was firing his guns; he broke port at about 1,000 yards and came towards me head-on at 30″ angle off. I gave a one second burst at approximately 600 yards, and immediately saw strikes. The Hun continued turning port, and I slid in behind him at 250 yards and gave him a burst of about five seconds, closing to 150 yards.

"The Hun endeavoured to bale out but was hit; the aircraft disintegrated. My aircraft was covered in oil from the Hun and a piece of debris struck my port wing-tip causing slight damage.

"I claim one Me109 destroyed. (Confirmed by Red 2—2/Lt Rosa)"

'Stormy' Massart had been among the first of the Free French pilots to get to England and had been with 340 Squadron for over two years. In the early 1960s he was put in command of the air base at Djibouti, taking advantage of the presence of a detachment of F.100s to carry out ground attacks. During one attack at very low altitude, he was hit by an exploding rocket, plunged into the ground and was killed.

The morning after my 109 victory, the AOC's PA rang inviting me to come over for lunch as the Chief of Air Staff, Sir John Slessor was on a visit. Sir John had been told of my kill and asked me about it. I gave him a description of the air fight but didn't tell him about the blood. Slessor quite rightly observed that taking our closing airspeeds into account, the first strike was probably about 400 yards.

My 'SS' was obviously not seriously damaged, for I flew it again on the 14th during a similar operation, this time the Mitchells going for the marshalling yards at Haltern. We met bags of flak—more than I care to remember, and again Me109s came sniffing around. We chased three of them but they had their fingers well out and enough distance to escape.

Despite my Me109, I was far from happy about the event of the 13th and I asked Loel to put in a complaint to No.2 Group, stressing the impossibility for the escort to give 100% cover if the bombers got themselves strung out. He did and was told that I should visit to discuss this with the 2 Group Airfield Commander, Group Captain E L Colbeck-Welch (later Air Vice-Marshal CB OBE DFC). By coincidence he had been Group Captain Ops at 10 Group following Tom Dalton-Morgan, so I knew him. I got in touch and he invited me over to lunch, his base being only some 10-15 miles away.

We had a most amicable discussion plus lunch and he assured me that the necessary action with his command would forthwith take place. I always found him a first class chap and was pleased when he later made air rank.

I was able to get away for another break on 20th March, flying to Fairwood Common and then to Lasham. However, my leave was cut short when I received a signal, recalling me to Holland. There was obviously a flap on, or about to start. I hurriedly flew 'SS' back to B.85 to find that the next morning—24th March 1945—the ground troops were going to make an assault across the Rhine. If successful, we would soon be on German soil.

The most heavily defended areas by the German Army were around the forests of Reichwald and Hochwald, with a concentration of AA guns of all calibres. If any evidence of this was needed it was a few nights before the Rhine crossing when some 500 RAF Lancaster bombers in wave after wave, bombed the towns of Cleve and Goch. The flak had to be seen to be believed and at our strip below Nijmegen and some 15 miles or so from those two towns, we had a grandstand view.

The following days, 82, 83 and 84 Group's medium bombers, Typhoons, Tempests and bomb-carrying Spitfires, concentrated on an endeavour to eliminate as far as was possible, known flak positions. We were told that the airborne troops which were to be dropped on the Dutch and German side of the Rhine would be fairly free from flak. This in fact was not so as the Germans were good at moving mobile Ack-Ack units about quickly. Here again, we could see this from our airstrip.

Nevertheless, we were all very confident that the Operation would be a push-over, as the feed-back from Montgomery and the Canadian HQ was full of confidence, not only of success but of victory in a matter of weeks. We were anticipating an early move to an airfield either in east Holland or Germany itself, to get away from the daily routine of having to enter Germany via the Nijmegen Bridge at 10,000 feet, avoiding the flak from Arnhem and the two forests.

Thus on the morning of the 24th, we were flying a patrol from Zutphen to Enschede, with a spectacular view of Dakotas and gliders going into the assault. No Hun aircraft were about although we spotted five Me262 jets way, way above, and for once the flak was not too bad. The next day we were out on an Armed Recce but the roads were all clear of any transport.

Loel Guiness flew with us on the 26th, when we went to see a train with 30 or more trucks and waggons, including petrol tanks, which we stopped near Zutphen. Lieutenant Borne had found it on an early Armed Recce Op, moving east. It must have been delayed for it was unusual to find a train still moving in daylight—they usually tried to hide up as dawn approached. Borne had attacked it immediately and after he and his No.2 had thoroughly strafed it returned with the news. From then on the Wing sent out two-man sections to keep the train occupied and under fire before the Typhoons finally finished it off. It must have contained fuel and ammunition for the final explosion tore up some 1,000 yards of railway track.

After Loel and I took a look at the train, which by then was burning well, we then flew over the flooded areas north of Wesel, but the weather was pretty filthy so came back within an hour.

March ended with a dive-bombing sortie against a concentration of barges at Berm on the Maas. We achieved fair results followed up with two strafing runs. Flak on the second run really shook me and my No.2, Lieutenant Rigaud of 340. In fact this was one target we got wrong. Our original target was right under some low cloud with poor visibility, so we headed further along the river and found another batch.

We anticipated there would be flak near the target itself but were considerably shaken when we received a hot reception before commencing the approach at full speed. It came from Ack-Ack positions some distance from the target and for a moment or two I fully expected to be shot down. Luckily only one aircraft was damaged by ground fire, and another had to make a forced landing with mechanical trouble but Lieutenant H LePage got down safely. We scored three direct hits on the second group of barges.

The Royal Air Force was well served by any number of superb air leaders during the war, and I was privileged to meet and know several of them. There were also a handful of colourful individuals whose exploits became well known to the service.

Number 2 Bomber Group RAF, whose medium bombers we often escorted, (Bostons, Mitchells and laterly, Mosquitoes) was commanded by the legendary Basil Embry, who would end the war with the DSO and three bars, DFC and AFC, and retire from the RAF as Air Chief Marshal Sir Basil, GCB KBE. His Senior Air Staff Officer (SASO) was Air Commodore David Atcherley, the twin brother of Richard (Batchy). David at this time had an arm in a sling because he had injured his shoulder when swinging the propeller of a single-engined aircraft, which had flicked back when the engine back-fired.

Notwithstanding this, he flew as navigator in the two-seater Mosquito bomber when the AOC flew. Everyone was fully aware of this, even the top brass, although they tried officially to ignore it. Basil was almost continually operating, despite his rank and position. Embry would take any opportunity to fly against the enemy, often listing himself as Flying Officer Smith, so as to, (a) keep the records straight, and (b) stop Command HQ from knowing it and therefore prevent them having apoplexy!

The Chief of the Air Staff, Marshal of the RAF, Sir Charles Portal (later Lord Portal, and known to everyone as Peter), heard of David's injury and when he read of a report of an offensive bombing sortie, led by Basil Embry with David as navigator, he sent for Basil and ticked him off. As Portal so rightly pointed out, what would happen if David had needed to bale out.

The upshot of this was that Basil was forbidden to take David on Ops any more; quite apart from the injury, 2 Group were taking the chance of losing their top two commanders in one go, if they were shot down. Of course, there came the usual plea from David to be allowed to take part in one more trip which had already been planned, and which was of the utmost importance. Basil, in turn, of course relented—he was never one for refusing any man who wanted to fly operationally. Most unfortunately, the report of the bombing raid included the fact that David had flown on it. A signal immediately arrived at 2 Group HQ, instructing David to report the next day to the Air Ministry.

Another well known air commander was the Commander-in-Chief of 2nd TAF, Air Marshal Sir Arthur Coningham KCB DSO MC DFC AFC, a successful first war fighter pilot from New Zealand. He was know to everyone as 'Mary', which had started out years earlier as 'Maori'. He visited us fairly often as he and Loel Guiness were old friends. Our own AOC was Air Vice-Marshal E C Hudleston— 'Teddy', later Sir Edmund. He frequently invited us to his Head- quarters for lunch and to meet visiting top brass, such as Marshal of the RAF, Sir John Slessor or our old friend Sholto Douglas.

It seemed to us now, and to our commanders, that the end of the war was in sight although we knew we would have to fight the Germans right to the bitter end. The Allied armies in the West were now on German soil and with the Russians on the Eastern Front knocking on the very door of Berlin, it could only now be a matter of time.

CHAPTER XIII

THE FRENCH FIGHTER WING

Whereas the Poles, Czechs and Norwegians eventually had their own wing leaders, Generals De Gaulle and Valin did not press for this point and I can only surmise that it was because the two Squadrons— 340 and 341—were technically, in the eyes of 345 and 329, military deserters from France. 329 who'd come from Algeria felt superior to the other three while 345, ex-Vichy, felt closer to 340 and 341 because the majority of its pilots had been young civilians when they escaped from the UK. To an outsider it must have seemed very confused, which perhaps it was. It is not surprising, therefore, that only towards the very end of the war did we have a Frenchman as Wing Leader— under training—Commandant Dorrance.

No. 329 Squadron (Les Cigognes—'The Storks') commanded by Jean Ozanne, definitely had a superiority complex, and he was certainly the 'father figure' in the eyes of his pilots. Whilst he didn't in fact argue with me, it was he who very soon informed me what my predecessor, Wing Commander Crawford-Compton, would have done under certain circumstances, as if to say I should do likewise. That gave me the opportunity of stamping on that suggestion very hard and very quickly. Thereafter he was most co-operative. He was in fact, more or less tour-expired and then Marchelidon took over.

Jacques Marchelidon was, as we say in Scotland, very 'dour' indeed and very difficult to get close to. He was, however, a very good and as it turned out, a very brave pilot. When the war finished he returned to Algeria but when De Gaulle was severing France from Algeria, Marchelidon—by now a Colonel in the French Air Force—was foremost amongst the military rebels. I was told that but for his brilliant war record he might have ended up in serious trouble. Instead they gave him early retirement.

I soon discovered that no two French pilots were similar in

character, some being very excitable whilst others were reserved. I put much of this down to the fact that, as already stated, each squadron, in the early stages, was looking somewhat sideways at the other. This changed later when we mixed the men up by promoting people from one squadron to fill command vacancies in the others.

In the air, however, I could not fault them. On the whole they were good press-on types and as a result we had our casualties. But I do not recall a single case of a pilot being accused of LMF—Lack of Morale Fibre—in other words cowardice.

Pilots such as Jacques Andrieux, Oliver Massart, Freddy Hardi, De Reynel de St.Michel DFM (Mike the Killer we called him), Tanguy, Marchelidon, Decroo DFC, de Larminat (who was shot down but evaded and returned), Sergent Kerguelen (a first class dive-bomber pilot), were all very brave. Much to his disappointment, I took Lieutenant P M Decroo, of 345 Squadron, off operations because he was taking unnecessary chances. He had already been shot down three times, each time force landing inside Allied lines, and his CO became anxious that he would inevitably 'buy it'. His third shoot down ended with him walking back on the 8th April, so as his tour was nearing its end, I thought enough was enough. He may have missed a few more shows but at least he survived the war.

Henri de Bordas in 329 Squadron was a first class operational pilot but even he was overtaken by excitement on one occasion. He was flying near Enschede when a Messerschmitt 262 jet, obviously having just taken off from the airfield there in case it was strafed, suddenly popped up right in front of Henri at no more than 150 yards. He was so surprised that he failed to press his gun button and the Me262 pilot, seeing the Spitfire right behind him within killing range, opened up his taps and rapidly disappeared in a cloud of exhaust smoke. (And, undoubedly, more 'exhaust' from the seat of his pants!)

Lieutenant Roger Borne, who flew in 341 Squadron, demonstrated another case of over excitement in an emergency. Near the end of the war I was leading eight Spitfires out on an Armed Recce in the Bremen area. The two sections had split up and I was on the point of leaving what had been a surprisingly hot reception from the Hun flak, when Borne's voice came over the R/T. He had been leading the second four that morning and he was over the Wiesede-Barge area. He said that his Spitfire had been hit and badly damaged, and that he was going to attempt to crash land.

I immediately called him to ask for his height. When he replied he was at 1,000 feet, I told him to, "Bale out, do not risk a crash landing." I then repeated the message which he acknowledged. Soon afterwards and to my surprise, he came on the air again saying he was on the point of making a crash landing. He didn't make it and we lost a really promising leader.

Another pilot in 340 Squadron was Lieutenant 'Blanco' (many French pilots flew under a pseudonym or Nom de Plume in order to protect families if they were captured), son of the Michelin tyre king.

When the Wing or a squadron flew dive-bombing sorties, the 'form' was to release the bombs from 4,000 feet and then climb away as rapidly as possible. Even so, it was not easy to hit the target because strength of wind could take the bombs to one side or the other, and also the bombs were released as the nose of the Spitfire passed though the target, ie: blind.

As I was usually first to bomb I would then climb away in a circle, keeping my eyes on the pilots who followed. I began to notice that Sergent Chef Yves Kerguelen released his bombs somewhat lower than 4,000 feet, was invariably 'spot on' but received a lot of light flak during his attack. I spoke to him about this and whilst not discouraging him, suggested he was unnecessarily courting danger. He listened to me with what I took to be great interest but did nothing to alter his tactics at all.

When I discussed my ideas with the squadron commanders about low level bombing with delay bombs and the fact that it all had to take place at high speed, someone mentioned that there was always a danger of those Spitfires at the back being blasted by the exploding bombs if they happened to lag behind for any reason. This situation could be even worse if more than twelve Spitfires were detailed. We sent for the armament officer and after a discussion there seemed to be no problem in producing a 23-second delay fuse for our bombs and this then became the norm thereafter.

I don't seem to remember many problems in this matter, although I think we had at least one aircraft lost due to a bomb blast. That happened to Warrant Officer F Roberts on 30th March. Four Spitfires on an Armed Recce—Lieutenant P Lanos, Aspirant Y Corveler, Sergent Chef J Davies and Roberts, attacked a train they found in a station just south of Rijssen. Roberts made his attack too soon after Lanos had bombed and the Spitfire was caught in the blast. Roberts pulled up and away, streaming white glycol smoke and then crash landed north of our most forward troops, inside enemy lines, but at least he seemed to be safe if a prisoner. Just over a week later came the welcome news that Roberts was indeed safe, having been liberated by Canadian troops, who had packed him off to hospital as he had suffered some minor injuries in the crash.

The lesson I had learnt from Rolf Berg was that once you identified the target to be attacked, get in there at once and at full speed. If you are the leader, spray the whole area from side to side with all armament as you approached to bomb in order to keep the flak gunner's heads down. The more they had to think about the less chance they had of getting a bead on you.

Sometimes I had to lead a squadron through 10/10ths cloud and then make rendezvous and await bombers, bombing through the cloud. On such occasions I had to rely on Channel 8, which was the 'Fix frequency'. It was really marvellous. "Where am I?", I would ask, and invariably would come the reply, "Over Zwolle," or wherever I happened to be flying.

During March 1945, Loel Guiness told me that we were getting a Commandant Michel Dorrance, who had been in the Italian invasion, and was operationally experienced. Our commanders wanted him to be a Supernumery for a short time to gain some experience in our campaign. He was in fact a first class chap and an excellent pilot. He told me that many eyebrows had been raised when he married an Italian girl, but things were gradually settling down with the situation becoming accepted. He was obviously being groomed for high command and did become a General as did Jacko Andrieux, Henri de Bordas, Tanguy and Billion, although the latter was killed after the war in a flying accident.

For a while after the war, Henri de Bordas flew as a military test pilot which involved him in flying machines before they were fully accepted. In the Toulon area he was scheduled to test a small Air Sea Rescue float-plane; the navigator, he told me, had a pronounced stutter. When they were at 1,000 feet, the single engine failed and Henri instructed the navigator to make a Mayday call whilst he attempted an emergency landing. Henri got it wrong and the aircraft broke up. They were both satisfactorily rescued, but from then on the navigator never stuttered again!

During the 1960s Henri, by then a Colonel, was Air Attache at the French Embassy in London and he once got in touch with me to attend a reunion of 329 Squadron at Dijon. He sent a VIP·jet to pick me up from Glasgow Airport and I stayed the night at his official residence in London. The following day we took off from RAF Northolt for France.

It was good to see General Valin again (as recorded in the next chapter, he presented me with my Croix de Guerre in June 1945). He told me that he had been granted a life-long extension in the French

Air Force, his main job being to attend military re-unions etc—and on full pay.

The French are recognised as being very materialistic and very money conscious. Our Group Captain, Loel Guiness, apart from his obvious ability, was also much admired because he was a multi-millionaire. He owned a large town house adjacent to the British Embassy building in Paris, a villa in Cannes, plus a yacht, as well as a stud farm in Normandy. He also had set-up stores in many towns in France, which he described as similar to Woolworths. He obviously impressed our Frenchmen.

Nevertheless, Loel was not ostentatious. In fact, just the opposite. When I first joined the Wing at Antwerp, Loel informed me that we were to be visited by a contingent of French military and diplomatic personnel from Paris. Among them was to be Philip de Lazlo, the well known portrait painter who was undertaking certain work for him in connection with the property and enterprises owned by Loel in France.

He had a meeting prior to the visit with the Mess Officer and myself and told the officer that he wished to lay on a really good lunch— oysters, Pol Roger 1928 Champagne, Remi Martin, VSOP Brandy, roast beef etc, in fact the full treatment. We were sworn to secrecy that although he was to meet the full cost, it was, as far as the guests were concerned, a Mess party provided by Mess funds. In the event, no one asked any questions.

For his work with the French Wing Loel was later to receive the Legion D'Honneur, presented to him by General Bousquat. At that time, Gaston Guizard, who commanded 345 Squadron, asked me to help him with the official citation.

Those last months of World War II were pretty hectic. The Wing fought on doggedly despite poor weather and none too pleasant living arrangements as we moved forward. Everyone believed that the war would soon be won, but knew equally that it had to be fought to be won. Even so my French pilots, as well as those British boys in 74 Squadron, never let up.

Squadron Leader Reeves led his 74 Squadron on a low level attack on an Army HQ west of Zaltbommel on February 2nd. They met considerable flak fire which hit the Spitfire flown by Flight Lieutenant F Hardman, a New Zealander, and he was reported missing.

We suffered more casualties during that month of February. On the 13th and 14th, 345 Squadron reported two pilots missing, Lieutenant Mareschal de Longville on a morning Armed Recce, probably to flak, then Lieutenant Michel Fleischel who was killed on a similar operation the next morning.

On the 25th, 340 Squadron sent out an Armed Recce led by Henri de Bordas, and Sous Lieutenant F Lagarde was hit by ground fire. His instruments went u/s and he tried to make an emergency landing at B.80 (Volkel) but crashed three miles away. His machine was a write-off but Lagarde was alright.

Then on the 27th, Sous Lieutenant C Chapman was leading a two-man Armed Recce shortly after 9 am, with Sergent Chef J Guichard flying as his No.2. They found and began to shoot up some motor transport but ground fire claimed Chapman who pulled up and baled out. Guichard saw him land alright and later he was known to be a prisoner. On the 28th, Lieutenant R Lambaert of 329 Squadron was hit by flak during another beat-up and had to crash-land at Nijmegen. In a spectacular pile up, both the wings of his Spitfire were ripped off and the machine ended up on its back, but Lambaert scrambled out unhurt.

Sergent Chef Guichard, who had watched Chapman bale out, was himself hit on 9th March and he too had to make a crash landing, but this time at his home base. Like Lambaert, the Spitfire shed both its wings but Guichard was not injured. This was the same day as 329 Squadron left the Wing, flying to Turnhouse. It did not return to France before the war's end.

The ground targets were varied and numerous in those last months. It would be difficult to list everything the Wing pilots had a go at. They ranged from trucks, lorries, tanks, half-tracks, horse-drawn transport of several descriptions, trains, motor trailers, staff cars, gun emplace-ments, buildings in which we would be told troops or HQ staff were housed, as well as troops. Sometimes the pilots, racing along on the deck, would surprise a group of soldiers along a road, a quick burst of gunfire scattering them, possibly leaving some dead or wounded. We must have frightened the hell out of them.

Sometimes we found the odd aircraft on an airstrip—not to mention the famous occasion when one of my Frenchmen went down and successfully strafed six dummy aircraft. Another section one day found and shot up a number of Ju88 fuselages being towed along a road on some trailers. With V1 rockets still being fired into Antwerp, we would often see the odd 'doodlebug'. Flight Lieutenant L S Frost of 74 Squadron shot down one on 28th February and on 25th March, Sergent Chef Girardeau of 340, saw one when flying an Armed Recce and also managed to shoot it down.

I remember the day one French pilot reported seeing seven or eight

V1s flying along in formation and then said that as he turned towards them, they all turned too!

The problem with ground targets, of course, was that one needed to patrol fairly low, say 4,000 feet or so, in order to be able both to spot movement and be low enough to react and make an attack before the target got off the road, or soldiers disappeared behind a wall or in a ditch. Being so low meant that anything and everything able to fire at you generally did so, from the deadly 88 mm guns to rifle and machine-gun fire. The German Army were pretty good at shooting at aircraft—they had certainly had a great deal of practice since 1939.

I had to fly to Lasham on March 20th, and missed a show on the 21st when the Wing sent two waves of Spitfires to dive-bomb some barracks south west of Zwolle. Lieutenant Jacques Carre (340 Squadron) led the second wave off at 2.45 pm, but two of the aircraft immediately developed mechanical problems. Lieutenant Vincent Beraudo, as soon as he realised something was wrong, jettisoned his bombs but they exploded beneath him and he was killed in the resultant crash. The second Spitfire in trouble, flown by Lieutenant Blanc, crashed on the side of the runway but Blanc was not hurt.

On the same day Lieutenant Robert Etlin of 341 Squadron flew an Armed Recce, his wingman being Sergent Chef Davies. Etlin thought he had seen some movement on a road and leaving Davies to cover him, dived down to investigate. He was not seen again and was later reported killed.

The Wing was heavily involved in the Rhine Crossing, but we lost another aircraft, flown by Sergeant Williams, on the 25th when he caught some flak and had to crash land, fortunately on our side of the river. Then we lost two pilots on the last two days of March. On the 30th, Warrant Officer F Roberts was lost in that train attack as mentioned earlier but later returned. The next day Lieutenant J Martin-Prudhomme and Lieutenant Fuchs attacked some MT they found south east of Deventer but Fuchs was hit on breaking away. Prudhomme heard him say that he'd been hit and would have to crash land but saw nothing more of him.

If we had been busy before, we were certainly no less busy as April began. In fact the 1st day of April, the RAF's 27th Birthday, found the Wing heavily involved in attacks which cost us dear. 340 lost two pilots this April Fool's Day. During a late morning sortie, Sergent Chef E Graillot was hit by flak and actually force landed in a minefield near Groesbeek, being seriously injured. Then after lunch, Lieutenant Albert Cavet was involved in an attack on a train but was not seen again after making his third strafing run, later being reported killed.

His No.2 on this mission was Sergent Pierre Lavergne, a future Air Force Lieutenant Colonel. He had joined the French Air Force in October 1939, gaining his wings in March 1940 before he was 18. He recalls:

"I was Cavet's 'weaver' on that fatal day for him. We took off from B.85 (Schijndel) early in the afternoon for an Armed Recce north of the Netherlands and Germany. We discovered a train but I don't remember exactly where, maybe east of Hengelo.

"Cavet attacked the locomotive and I followed him during this attack and the two others, loosing sight of him each time I was myself firing at the train. There was some flak from the train— I remember the tracers—but after the third attack I lost sight of him altogether.

"Meanwhile, I attacked again, alone, and then, when I called Ops, they told me to come back home. The result of our attacks was one goods loco hit and train stopped; one goods truck in flames, one tanker damaged and strikes seen on several MT aboard a flat truck."

Meantime, 341 Squadron lost pilots at almost the exact same times. Sergents G Cristinacce and Gabriel Wolloshing flew an Armed Recce, meeting heavy ground fire. Cristinacce's Spitfire was hit forcing him to make a crash landing at B.78 (Eindhoven) and Wolloshing failed to return. Then on a sortie after lunch Sous Lieutenant Lucien Foissac and Aspirant L Le Flecher were searching for targets near Zutphen when they came under intense flak from a wood ten miles east of the town. Foissac was hit in his long-range tank which burst into flames and his Spitfire dived into the ground and exploded.

No.341's third casualty was Capitaine B de Larminat, leading another two-man Armed Recce. He led an attack on some MT they found in the Coevorden area. As they pulled out, his wingman saw de Larminat's Spitfire climbing up amidst numerous flak bursts, then begin to go down. He made a successful belly landing and a few days later was reported safe in Canadian hands. The weather too had been bad on this day, and following our casualties, Wing operations were cancelled for the rest of the day.

Any loss is a blow to a Wing, but Albert Cavet's loss was particularly sad. He had escaped from France in the summer of 1942 and managed to cross into Spain. After some weeks he was finally picked up by the authorities and imprisoned in Ciudadrodriga prison. He remained in various jails until he finally made a break in March 1943 only to be recaptured and imprisoned in Madrid. In April he was away again, and this time succeeded in reaching Gibraltar. He had, all this time, been pretending to be a Belgian, naming himself Antoine Parse, and he continued using this as his nom-de-guerre after he had joined the RAF and become a fighter pilot. Victor Tanguy recalls:

"I knew Cavet well when I was in the Storks Fighter Group. I knew nothing of his escape from France but I remember his 'thirst' to fight for the liberation of his country.

"When the Storks were detailed to return to Great Britain in March 1945, he took the same attitude as in July 1942—to fight. He did not want himself withdrawn from the theatre of operations and managed to get transferred to the Ile de France Squadron (340). He was shot down just a few days later."

Cavet fell near Bornebrooke in Holland, where he was buried in the local cemetery. It was here his resting place was located after the war. However, the name on the grave was not Cavet, but the name he had on his identity discs—Antoine Parse. He was 26.

We then had nearly a week without any casualties to speak of but the respite didn't last. On the 7th Lieutenant F A d'Aligny of 345 Squadron failed to return while 340 Squadron lost one of the two French Fleet Air Arm pilots they had recently acquired. Le Maitre Francis Delery's name appeared on the list of missing pilots, but there seemed little hope. Hit by flak his Spitfire had dived straight into the ground where it exploded.

The next day we ended up on the credit side, when Lieutenant Decroo reported back from his latest (and last) forced landing, de Larminat too got back and so did Flying Officer Bill Cortis RAAF of 74 Squadron. Cortis had been shot down back in February and wounded. Put into a German hospital which was over-run by American troops in early April, hence his safe return, he was still on the sick list with spinal injuries and a fractured knee.

The following day we were in debit once more. De Reynel and Sergent Lavergne strafed some MT but Lavergne was hit. De Reynel heard him say he was alright but he did not get back, so all we could hope was that he was down safely even if a prisoner. I don't think we heard much of him until the war's end, but Pierre Lavergne remembers:

"The unit diary records that de Reynel and I destroyed a MET at Q7435, which in fact was a very small field, with poplars alongside, near a small village named Holtropp, itself near Aurich, about 20 km ENE from Emden. The time was around 1700 hours.

"I was taken prisoner and during the following days I was transported from jail to jail, by car and foot, often roughly and badly treated, even though I'd been wounded in the heel, and had been knocked about a bit on the face. Obviously the Germans didn't like me being French nor being a French 'Jabo' (Fighter bomber).

"Finally I arrived at Pinneberg, north of Hamburg, and was put into a small POW camp installed in a Luftwaffe station. Probably to justify the large letters 'POW' painted on the roof of the buildings. Only about 30 prisoners were there, all of different Allied nationalities, all air force men, and all but four NCOs, were officers.

"We all finally left this camp on 5th May, most of us by car, although I chose a motorcycle and side car. I was soon back with the Squadron at Drope, B.105. I remember Group Captain Guiness. He congratulated me when I arrived on 6th May, saying, 'Je suis tres content le revoir vous,'—'You are the first back.'"

One of our most experienced pilots was killed on the 10th. Sous Lieutenant Armand 'Fifi' De Saxce of 341 Squadron was out with two other pilots, Sergent J Filliol and Sous Lieutenant J Dabos, flying an armed reconnaissance to north-east Holland. Spotting ground targets 'Fifi' led them in but he was hit by flak. Climbing to around 4,000 feet, he told his companions he'd been hit then his Spitfire began to lose height. At 1,500 feet the canopy was jettisoned and Filliol saw 'Fifi' bale out. However, his parachute snagged on the tail, ripping it badly. At 500 feet, the parachute tore free but it did not deploy and man and machine hit the ground almost together. Filliol circled round but 'Fifi's' body appeared lifeless. As the squadron later wrote, "He had been our best and most experienced pilot, with the heart of a lion. He never failed to answer the call of duty, no matter the odds or how hard the going."

A Section of 74 Squadron lead by Flight Lieutenant Braidwood was bounced by two Me262 jets on the 10th but they were lucky and nobody was hit. One pilot got in a burst at the jets but within seconds they were well out of range as they scooted away over Holland. The next day 74 strafed Ratenburg airfield, claiming five fighters destroyed on the ground with four more damaged. They shot up another airfield at Nordolz on the 18th, scoring more hits on enemy aircraft.

However, it turned out to be third time unlucky for the 'Tigers' on the 19th when they attacked Ardorf aerodrome. Flying Officer Barnes was hit by ground fire and crash landed heavily in enemy territory. His Spitfire was seen to burst into flames as it skidded along the ground before smashing into a wood. His body was later found.

Trains were always a dangerous target, especially if the Germans had stuck a flak waggon or two amongst the trucks. It wasn't always obvious until the attack started, the Germans sometimes hoping to trap the unweary pilot. This is exactly what happened on April 17th. Sous Lieutenant Dabos of 341 led an Armed Recce off at 7.40 am with Yves Corveler, Basin and Pottier. They found a train near Wilhelmshaven but as Dabos approached in a gentle dive, he saw it had a flak waggon on it so wisely broke away. However, Sergent Chef R Pottier, probably due to either inexperience or misunderstanding, went down on the train and was not seen again, although I believe he ended up as a prisoner.

As recorded earlier, Roger Borne was killed on the 20th, and then on the 23rd we lost Jacques Carre of 340 Squadron. It was a dawn show, take-off being at 6.40 am, Lieutenant Andre Tatraux flying on his wing. Before they had flown very far Tatraux (a future French Air Force Lt Colonel) found his radio had failed, so waggled his wings and headed back. Carre must have decided to fly on alone and was not seen again.

That same day, Capitaine A Osmanville of 340 took Lieutenant Rigaud, who had flown as my No.2 on a number of sorties, as his wingman on yet another Armed Recce. Attacking some ground targets, Rigaud's machine was hit by ground fire, but he got it back, only to make a crash landing at base. The Spit caught fire but Rigaud got out, suffering a slight concussion and an injured elbow.

Two days later Aspirant Lois Le Flecher of 341 Squadron was also hit by ground fire while dive bombing near Leer. He baled out over enemy territory and was seen to land safely with men running towards him. He ended the last week of the war as a prisoner. He too has retold his story for us:

"We had taken off at 1500 hours, 12 Spitfires behind our leader, Capitaine Andrieux. Our target was a battery of 88 mm guns and an arms dump, five kilometres south of Emden. There came an announcement over the radio from our leader, 'Target 11 o'clock - it's on fire—form on me, arm bombs—attack!'

"At once we came under heavy flak and shell fire; I followed my leader like a shadow. I saw a gun, took aim but all was not right. My leader went out of sight from my cockpit and my plane was heading for the sky. I pushed the stick but there was no response. I'd been hit. I knew if I stayed with the 'plane I was dead, so decided to jump with my parachute.

"As I descended I could see the North Sea below which caused me some anguish for two reasons; one I couldn't swim, and for once I didn't have on my Mae West. With bullets still whistling past my ears, and in fear of my parachute being cut in two, I was relieved a little to find the breeze was pushing me inland and not out to sea. The ground approached fast, and thanking God I was still alive, I landed safely.

"The Germans were 100 metres away and they shot at me as if I was a rabbit. The shots missed, hitting the mud some 20 metres away, then the soldiers caught me. Here I was, in an RAF pullover but without any boots! I could not understand anything they said but a shaken Wehrmacht officer—our 36 bombs had caused much damage—drew his pistol and took me prisoner.

"I demanded a drink, and water to clean the mud off my face and head, but they kept kicking me with their boots, at first thinking I was an English pilot. I kept going, thinking that in a short time the Canadians would arrive. At last the officer of my captors, said, 'For you it's your second chance today.' We followed the river south of Emden, then crossed the river by boat and for the first time saw other prisoners.

"Suddenly came the sound of Spitfires, which were bombing the same targets as we had attacked earlier. I recognised them as from my 145 Wing. It was a great sight and again success. After ten minutes the turmoil created was terrific.

"Arriving at an army prison cell I was again interrogated. They did not believe me when I said I was a Canadian and I finally had to admit I was French. The interrogator was extremely correct and proper and had no doubts that the war would soon be over.

"I was not so lucky with other bullies who used me like a punch-bag, but I was not badly marked. I was taken to a cell, being both thirsty and hungry, but went without food or drink for three days, during which time I mostly slept. Then one morning the door opened and I was told to get up. Two armed guards put me in the back of a lorry, from where I could see nothing, but I was then surprised to find I was now with the Luftwaffe.

"Another interrogation followed, by an officer wearing the Iron Cross, who asked me a lot of silly questions. We also discussed our respective aeroplanes. He apologised as I was placed once more in a cell, guarded by two old Germans. I could have been their son. I was later moved on, using a bicycle, guarded by an army corporal. Eventually we arrived at a prisoner of war camp, met by a very correct commandant. The guards were all very old.

"On the 7th of May 1945, we were liberated by Canadian troops. We requisitioned German lorries and celebrated with whisky. I arrived back at 341 Squadron, 145 Wing, at Lingen a few days later."

I seem to remember out last wartime casualty occurred just a few days before the war ended. Sergeant Francis Donovan took off to make an air test or some such thing, on 3rd May 1945. Soon afterwards came word that he had crashed into a mill. It was believed he was doing some low aerobatics. Such a waste so near to the end of hostilities.

Sadly this chapter does not really convey the full story of No.145 Wing, but just gives a brief summary of some of its activities. I was proud to have led them and flown with them. They will always be in my memory and I will never forget their bravery and achievements.

CHAPTER XIV

VICTORY IN EUROPE

We were now pushing further into Hitler's Germany, each day dominating the once hostile skies. Escorts and Armed Recce sorties came thick and fast but despite our dominance, the main danger was the ever-present enemy ground fire.

My first sortie in April was on the evening of the 4th, when I led 340 Squadron as Target Cover to 24 Mitchells bombing gun concentrations east of Deventer. A couple of days later I flew as leader of the second section led by Lieutenant Freddy Hardi of 340. We flew over the areas of Zwolle, Leeuwarden and Groningen, shooting up trucks and lorries.

Then it was back to Close Escort on the 8th, leading 341 in a raid upon the German town of Sogel. The next day it was a two-hour Recce of Oldeburgh-Emden, flying with Lieutenant Rigaud of 340 Squadron. We found some German road transport, our strafing attack destroying a motor trailer, an attached trailer and damaging another. Then we strafed an ammo dump causing some explosions. Flak fire was pretty accurate north of Papenburgh and my 'SS' took three hits in the cowling, but I was flying her again the next day.

The Germans were now using more and more mobile Ack-Ack, so that their military vehicles were usually accompanied by these flak waggons, so hot or very hot receptions were the norm. I was hit again on the 10th, flying another Armed Recce with Sergeant Nixon of 341 as my wingman. Again we found fleeing German transport and we left one destroyed and two severely damaged and smoking. I caught a bullet in the spinner, despite attacking at very high speed with a bit of weaving to make it more difficult for the flak gunners.

My wingman on the 11th was again Freddy Hardi. He came from the island of Madagascar, was very well educated and but for his uniform, might easily have been taken as British, for his English was spoken without any sign of a French accent. On this day, Army Intelligence had reported that military vehicles were on the move in the north of occupied Holland. At a moment's notice I decided to investigate and so took Freddy as my No.2.

We came across a column of mixed Hun vehicles and a number of them quickly slipped into roadside pens which the Germans had erected on most main roads so as to avoid, if possible, being strafed in the middle of the road, thereby blocking it. However, some were not quick enough and we both made several attacks without opposition, which after the previous two days was a pleasant change. We both expended all our ammunition and returned well satisfied. As Freddie climbed down from his Spitfire, he grinned at me and said in his best English/RAF accent, "That was wizard fun."

On the whole my French boys were pretty much on the mark and very press-on types. I flew out on the 12th just to watch them, as 340 and 341 dive-bombed targets around Arnhem. They achieved good results and as I noted in my log book at the time, "These French boys have plenty of clues."

Although busy with any number of things as Wing Leader, including paper work which seemed never ending, I was managing almost one sortie per day at this stage. I took Freddie again as my No.2 on the 13th when we again shot up some road transport north of Zwolle. Then on the 16th the Wing moved again, but this time to Germany.

Our new airfield was at a place called Drope, a former German base some 10 miles east of the Dutch border. As I touched down on German soil for the first time, I had a feeling that now the end of the war was only a matter of time. Every German house without exception had a white flag hanging out of a window and such Germans as we saw in the vicinity of the airfield were very docile.

After settling in, it was back to the job in hand on the 18th, escorting 60 Mitchells early that afternoon. The target was some barracks at Oldenbergh which being heavily defended, seemed to be holding up the Army considerably. I led 341 and 345 Squadrons as Close Escort, making rendezvous with the bombers over Sogel but we only met some slight heavy flak on this raid.

By this time 74 Squadron had joined the Wing, plus the Dutch Squadron—322—commanded by Squadron Leader Bram 'Bob' Van der Stok. Bob was one of the three men who were successful in reaching home following the mass escape from Stalag Luft III in March 1944. This was the occasion when Hitler ordered fifty of the recaptured British officers to be shot. He made it back after four months of hiding and travelling, finally reaching Portugal. The other two were both Norwegian pilots, Jens Muller and Per Bergsland, so all three obviously had the added advantage of language, and in Bob's case, of being able to hide for a while in his native Holland.

Obviously Bob was forbidden to fly on operations again, an instruction emphasised by Sholto Douglas himself. However, Bob pleaded with Prince Bernhardt of the Netherlands, who in turn was strong enough to over-rule Sholto. He ended up flying with 74 Squadron before taking command of 322 in early March. The danger of course, was for Bob to be again shot down and recaptured, although I imagine by this late stage in the war German records would have taken too long to establish who he was, before hostilities ceased. Nevertheless, he was a pretty unique guy to have in the Wing. After the war he went to America where he became a doctor. He lived in Honolulu from 1970 where he also joined the US Coastguard service, assisting in 162 rescues. He died in 1993.

No. 485 Squadron was to join the Wing at the beginning of May, commanded by Squadron Leader K J Macdonald. They had been scheduled to re-equip with Tempests, but this idea was then abandoned, so they returned to the Continent, arriving at Drope.

I led seven Spitfires of 74 Squadron, still commanded by Squadron Leader A J Reeves DFC, who had been with the Squadron as pilot and flight commander, on a dive-bombing sortie south of Oldenbergh on 20th April. We found a train pulling more than 40 petrol waggons near Varel, just south of Wilhelmshaven. Flight Lieutenant W W Peet, a New Zealander soon to receive the DFC, was actually leading 74. We achieved some good bombing on this vital target—vital for the German tanks and so on—scoring seven direct hits. We left the train burning well, our direct hits causing part of the train to blow up. No.198 Typhoon Squadron later confirmed it as totally destroyed. Flak fire was again pretty intense, so much so that we did not return for a follow-up strafing run, which was perhaps just as well, for I had already heard the by now familiar sound of metal hitting my Spitfire.

It had been suggested that I pay a courtesy visit to the French Air Ministry to make my number with some of the Staff, many of whom had been with me either in 340 or 341 Squadrons. I asked Freddy Hardi to fly me in a captured Messerschmitt 108 two-seat communications aircraft. We flew off on 21st April, heading for Le Bourget. However, we ran into some bad weather near Amiens and I suggested to Freddy that we land at Glisy until the weather cleared, which it did a couple of hours later. We returned on the 24th—in better weather.

During the visit we were entertained by various French senior officers. At one party which was mixed with some very good looking and attractive girls, I noticed Freddy in the middle of four young ladies. As I approached he saw me and said, "I will introduce you." When he came to the last, and the most attractive, he mentioned her name and added, "I think you will agree that she is a nice bit of frippet." She then asked me, "Frippet, what is that?" Quick as a flash I responded, "Very good looking and charming." Then turning to Freddy, I said in English, "You really are a fucking idiot!" To which she said, "Oh Colonel, your language!" That was the first time I discovered that the word 'fuck' is understood in every language.

I should perhaps mention that I now had a new 'SS' marked Spitfire. Although the Wing was mainly equipped with Spitfire XVIs, I liked to fly a Spitfire IXB. Unfortunately the airfield commander had over-heard one of my French pilots saying that they found it difficult to keep up with me sometimes in their Mark XVIs, so I was quietly asked to change my IXB for a XVI.

During my operational career I flew first the Spifire Mark Vb, which while a beautiful aeroplane, did not quite match up to the Me109F or FW190. Next the Mark VI with pointed wing tips and pressurised cockpit, which we used in the Orkneys to try and catch the photo-graphic recce aircraft. We could fly this to 41,000 feet.

When I was at Skeabrae in 1942, Wing Commander A H 'Tony' Rook DFC (who had won the Order of Lenin when serving in Russia with 151 Wing) on the Staff at 14 Group, Inverness, contacted the Squadron. He said that the AOC, Air Vice-Marshal Ray Collishaw DSO DSC DFC, the famous Canadian WW1 Naval 'ace', wished to see a demonstration of how quickly a pilot could get into the Spitfire VI, get airborne and how long it took to get to maximum height of anything over 40,000 feet. I was detailed to fly a Spit VI to Longmans aerodrome, Inverness, to give the said demonstration.

With everyone watching, I got airborne very rapidly and climbed at maximum speed to 41,000 where the Spitfire just kept on sinking; I could not get it higher. It was a marvellous day and I remember being able to see the Shetlands to the north and Newcastle to the south. The demonstration proved that the Spit VI could never reach the Hun photo recce Heinkels or Ju88s which were stripped of all unnecessary clobber such as guns, etc.

With the Mark IXA and IXB, we had an aircraft designed to operate in excess of 30,000 feet where it had the edge on both the Messerschmitts and Focke Wulfs. Unfortunately when it came into full use in 1943, operational heights seldom reached beyond 25,000 feet. The IXB was in full use by 1944, had all the answers and was superior in all conditions to the German day fighters.

During 1944 the Exeter Wing was equipped with Spitfire VIIs, to all intents and purposes very similar to the IXA. The five-bladed Spitfire XIV with the Griffin engine as opposed to the Merlin 66 in the Mark IXs, was used operationally by the photo-recce wing for low-level photography and had all the characteristics of the IXs, although bigger forward of the cockpit to house the larger engine. I only flew this machine when at the GSU.

The Mark XVI, which equipped the Wing in February 1945, was said to be the same as the IXB with the exception that the Merlin 66 engine was produced in the USA by Packard. The AFDU, now under Air Commodore Dick Atcherley, with Wing Commander Francis Blackadder DSO, as I/C Flying, received a report from me disagreeing with their findings that there was no difference between the Merlin 66 produced in the UK and that produced by Packard. As I was so adamant, Loel Guiness arranged for one of the engineers from Rolls-Royce, Derby, to visit us and I expressed my opinion forcibly. The engineer told us that over the period there had been very many minor alterations to the original Blue Print, which all the Production Team understood. The fact that the Blue Print had been sent to the US, showing none of these minor adjustments, might possibly make a slight difference. He also, rather with his tongue in cheek, suggested that as Wing Leader, my IXB probably received much more polish which would make a difference. I made a somewhat rude response.

The day after my return from Paris, we were ordered to fly another dive-bombing show (25th April). Group Ops were aware that we had two squadrons bombed-up and gave us an oil storage tank farm south of Bremen. I decided that 74 Squadron, led by Reeves, would dive-bomb first followed by myself, leading 341 Squadron. Group Captain Loel Guiness wanted to accompany us so I suggested that he, plus a No.2, Capitaine Victor Tanguy of 341 should fly above our formation at say, 15,000 feet, to observe whilst we approached at 10,000 before bombing.

I was about 1,000 yards behind 74 and I must say I could not believe that they had all come out unscathed by the amount of flak that came up to meet them. But then, we were also fortunate. When I commenced my dive from 10,000 feet, to the release point at 4,000, I seemed to be surrounded by bursting AA shells. I could also hear Capitaine Tanguy, at 15,000 feet, warning Loel to turn to starboard to avoid the gunfire which they too were receiving.

It was a pretty frightening experience, but we again achieved good results, were completely successful and everyone got back. After landing, Loel admitted to having been very shaken. Loel was never one to stay on the ground, but it was always useful for a commander to see and experience what his men were going through.

The following day, Group Captain Johnnie Baldwin DSO DFC— one of the famous exponents of Typhoon operations now at Group Ops, telephoned to say that Army Intelligence had located a German Army HQ in what appeared to be a farming complex, to the south east of Oldenbergh and wanted it obliterated. He went on to say that it would have been an ideal Typhoon rocket attack but all were otherwise engaged. Johnnie continued, "I see from the Readiness state that you've got a squadron bombed-up and ready, but is the CO a good, press-on type, because it's extremely important that this Headquarters is taken out completely." To this I replied, "All my COs are good, press-on types, but I personally will lead the raid." I then went on to say that I should like to take a No.2 with me first to have a look over the target from a suitable distance, in order to decide the best direction from which to approach and attack. To this Baldwin said, "No—there is no time and in any case they must not be alerted. How soon can you go, so that I can advise Army Intelligence?" I told him half an hour.

My Wing Intelligence Officer and the Army Liaison Major examined the map very thoroughly and I decided on 23-second delay bombs for a low level attack from a north to south direction. This would be followed by one, possibly two, low level strafes.

I led with 340 Squadron, flying a Spitfire XVI of 74 Squadron, coded 4D-A, taking off just before 3 pm. It was very hazy with 8/10ths cloud at 5,500 feet. Approaching the target from the south as planned, passing by at 8,000 feet, some 600 yards to the starboard of it, I called the pilots on the R/T, pointing out the target with just a brief, "Nine o'clock below!" Having passed by to some 1,000 yards or so, I then ordered all aircraft to close up as we turned to port and started our dive to zero feet.

At about 500 yards I began firing all armament, spraying the area from left to right, kicking my rudders as I headed in and down, in the hope of keeping any alert gunners' heads down. We did in fact get some light flak fire on the final 100 yards and when I said, "Bombs gone!", I hauled back on the stick and started to climb to port to about 5,000 feet.

As we climbed, Capitaine Aubertin led in his section of four at low level, his wingman being Lieutenant Tatraux. With all the Spitfires screaming up after me, I reformed the Squadron then ordered them to spread out and strafe the buildings which we could see were already burning.

As soon as I passed over, I released the gun button, climbed once again, while calling, "Same again!" Climbing to our attack height, it was then another wing-over and down towards the smoke and flames. Pulling out from this second strafing run, we left the whole area a burning inferno. There must have been mobile Ack-Ack guns in some woods quite some distance from the buildings because these began to fire at us as we formed up to head back, but nobody was seriously hit.

Soon after landing I telephoned Johnnie Baldwin who said the Army were full of praise for the attack. As soon as we had departed they had made a ground attack and had captured the remnants of the Staff who were still alive. I was well pleased with the performance of the Squadron and the accuracy of both bombing and strafing. At our de-briefing we claimed 27 direct bomb hits, having seen my own three bombs score bullseyes. I think in many ways that this was my most successful Wing show.

I flew 4D-A again on 28th April, which proved to be my last operational sortie during the war. This time I led 345 Squadron, bombing a target at Oldersom, south of Emden, with excellent results. We met some heavy flak but caused many fires to start burning, the smoke still rising from them as we reformed and headed back to base.

We felt that the end of the war was near, but I had no idea that as I curved in towards the grass runway at Drope, lowering flaps and undercarriage, that for me personally it was all over. I suppose I would have liked to have flown these last Ops in my personal Spit 'SS', but it was being serviced, so it was not to be. I also see from my log book that by the end of April 1945, I had topped one thousand flying hours, since my first tentative dual control flights back at Cambridge in August 1941.

On the 5th of May, at 0800 hours, on the instructions of Field Marshal Montgomery, the Armies ceased fighting and as far as we were concerned the war with Germany was over. Within two days or so I decided to go into Berlin to see for myself the results of Bomber Command's concentrated and continuous bombing raids. Having seen the results of the German 'Blitz' on London three years earlier, I felt complete satisfaction with Air Marshal Sir Arthur Harris' reply; after all the Germans started the bombing raids on non-military targets in our towns and cities, such as Coventry, Exeter and Bath.

Three of us drove to the British Sector and spent one night in the Ritz Hotel (no comparison to our own Ritz in London) and two days sight seeing. In the Russian Sector we entertained some Russian soldiers in our large staff car which was loaded with alcohol, and one of the Russians stole my Leica camera which failed to impress me!! We also visited the Reich Chancellery and were taken into Hitler's famous Bunker which was adjacent. We were shown a pile of ashes outside the Bunker which were said to be the remains of Hitler, Eva Braun and the Goebbels' family.

When we went into the American Sector we saw a number of large signs erected at the side of the roads. In typical fashion we read of such information as—"G.I's beware—they all now say that they never were Nazis!" Another read, "G.I's beware—flies spread disease. Keep yours buttoned!" The final one noted—"G.I's—we won the war, we must now win the peace. Do not fraternise with the creepy crawlies!"

Just as the war ended I received notification that I had been awarded a bar to my DFC, while the French had awarded me their Croix de Guerre and Palm. I was very surprised when the AOC, Teddy Hudleston, came out to inspect the Station and said to me, "I am sorry about the bar to your DFC. I had you up for a DSO and Wing Commander Harries for a bar to his DSO. Unfortunately I was told that we were rationed to one and it so happened that Harries's name was above yours so he got it." That little piece of information somehow didn't improve my feelings for Ray Harries.

I received my French medal when General Valin, the senior Free French Air Force officer visited the Wing at Drope, on 5th June. There were a number of French officers being awarded their country's Legion of Honour while others, including myself received the Croix de Guerre. I had noticed that the men who received the Legion of Honour were kissed on both cheeks by the General, in typical French fashion. However, as he pinned my medal on my left breast he must have seen the expression on my face for he said, "Don't worry, you don't get kissed for this one."

In June I managed to have a couple of flights in a Tempest V, finding it an aeroplane that 'moves slightly!', and then had a flight in an American L5, the Vultee-Stinson 'Sentinal' high-wing monoplane, similar to our Austers.

On the 10th I led 145 Wing in a fly-past for the Russian, General Zhukov, over Berlin. One could be forgiven for thinking that this was not so much as an honour for him, but a show of strength by the Allies, for 3,000 aircraft were in the show, practically every Allied aeroplane stationed on the Continent, which we hoped shook him and made him think. A few days later we were in another fly-past over Paris for the benefit of General De Gaulle. This must have impressed him too, but the difference was that the French people were led to believe that the majority of the aircraft taking part were French and mainly responsible for winning the war.

To undertake the Paris fly-past we had to move for a week to Dreux airfield which was occupied by the Americans. The US Colonel in command told us that there was no decent restaurant in the town so that we would have to put up with American food. However, our Intelligence Officer visited the Gendarmarie (Police Station) and was told by the Chief that the best eating house around was the Brothel on the edge of the town, although it was out of bounds (off limits) for the Yanks.

We were advised that the women of the establishment were not up to much but the food was very good. So that first evening off we went to this house of ill-repute where we found the cooking superb as promised. Just for fun, we asked the Madame if she would parade the girls for us, and I can confirm that there were no takers.

Once victory was ours it was decided to send one of my French squadrons on a month's training visit to RAF Exeter, each squadron taking a turn. On one of my visits to them I landed in dubious weather at RAF Tangmere and was delighted to find my friend Pete Brothers at tea in the Mess. Also with our party, I met for the first time the recently released POWs whose names were to become so well known, although they had both been famous in the early war years. They were Douglas Bader and Bob Stanford Tuck.

During June, Wing Commander Douglas Watkins, by now on the Staff at No. 84 Group HQ, rang me to say that the AOC of 83 Group, AVM Harry Broadhurst, had the use of a villa at Cannes and that six wing commanders were invited to have it for 14 days—and would I like to accompany him with four others? Would I? It was simply out of this world, all found and plenty of it, plus the use of two cars as well as two motor boats in the harbour. It proved to be a continuous round of parties in the various British and American villas.

As soon as Loel knew I was off to Cannes, he asked me if I would drop in a note at his villa for his Chief Executive, looking after his interests in the south of France and to wait while it was read. This I did and after the man had read the letter, he said to me, "The Group Captain says you are bound to need some money and that I am to give you whatever you require." This was typical of Loel Guiness, but I told the chap it was not necessary.

When Loel finally retired from the RAF the French wanted to give him a farewell present. I asked him what he would like and he said a silver cigarette box with the four Squadron crests and the signatures of every person who contributed. Having acquired all the signatures etc, I asked the Adjutant, Flight Lieutenant Arthur Dunsford, an experienced businessman to arrange everything and eventually he and I met Loel in the Ritz Hotel in London, his favourite watering place, where we presented the box to him.

In 1989, after his death, there was a memorial service for Loel, held in the Guards Chapel, Wellington Barracks. During a gathering afterwards at the Ritz, I was told by his grandson, also named Loel, (his father was Loel's eldest son Patrick) that he now had the cigarette box and it was his proudest possession. Patrick was unfortunately killed in a motor accident in France not long afterwards.

It was in July that Zulu Morris called me up from Group and told me that he wished me to Chair an investigation into an accident to the Group Comm. Flight Anson which had landed on a disused airstrip in Kent in foggy conditions, finishing up in a ditch with a written off under-carriage. The pilot had said that the CO had forced him to fly against his will in poorish conditions. I was assisted by a Squadron Leader Engineering Officer.

The CO of the Comm Flight was a Canadian Flight Lieutenant, DFC. Having heard his evidence I then asked him what he was flying when he won his DFC. He told me he had been part of a Mosquito squadron in 2 Group stationed at RAF Benson. The Squadron had been briefed to carry out a low level bombing raid on a marshalling yard south of Paris. In his briefing the Squadron CO had told them that as there was cloud cover at 4,000 feet all the way to the target, take-off would be at two-minute intervals and each aircraft should fly on dead reckoning, descending to ground level some two miles from the target. Because of the cloud there would be no fighter escort. However, there was a possibility of the weather clearing so if the crews found themselves in the open before descending to bomb, they should abort immediately and return home.

It appeared that the Flight Lieutenant was in the last Mosquito to take off and when some three miles from the target they ran into clear weather. His navigator said he could see the target ahead but there was no evidence of bombing. The pilot decided to carry on, dropped his bombs, and returned to the cloud. When he landed his CO had asked him where he'd been and when the pilot told him, asked him why on earth he hadn't turned back when the weather cleared like everyone else? As it was he had been reported as missing, and even Basil Embry had been told.

The next thing was that he was told to report to Embry himself who, by the next day, had before him the photographic evidence from PRU of a succesful bombing attack. Embry dished out a lengthy rocket for placing his aircraft, not to mention his navigator, in serious danger, but the Flight Lieutenant was then surprised a few weeks later by the award of his DFC. With it came a flowery citation mentioning things like, above and beyond the call of duty.

In the event we found that the CO did not force pilots to fly if weather conditions were poor—it was always up to the pilot to make the final decision.

In early July we moved to Fassberg, a large airfield to the north east of Hannover, about midway between this city and Hamburg. During the war the Luftwaffe had used it as an experimental airfield similar to our own Farnborough. It was full of every type of aircraft, including a number of Messerschmitt 262 jets. The whole set-up was very well appointed. The Officer's Mess possessed a swimming pool and a large vegetable garden, and also a Brothel which was soon closed at the request of the Padre. Most of the girls became employed in the kitchens and as waitresses.

The nearest town was Celle, adjacent to the notorious Belsen Concentration Camp. We were regularly visited by senior officers wishing to see the camp. It was incumbent upon me to take an Australian Air Vice-Marshal to it on one occasion and I was so ill for days that I detailed the Admin Squadron Leader to take future visits.

The airfield was an airman's dream come true with all the various aircraft types, most of which had been but names and photographs to us. As I recall there were at least six Me262s, and a couple of Heinkel four-engined bombers which never flew operationally. There was great excitement one day when a Squadron Leader arrived to fly off one of the Me262s. He spent a long time sitting in the cockpit with a crib manual on his knees. Group Captain Guiness finally told him that everything was all clear for take-off and did he need anything. The Squadron Leader replied, "Yes please, the Fire and Blood wagon at the end of the take-off area." In the event there was no problem.

Lieutenant General Sir Brian Horrocks, commander of 30 Corps, flew in and out of the airfield and after his first appearance, when I laid on a Guard of Honour, said, "Please don't. I shall be a frequent visitor 'en passant' and I know you've got enough to do without doing this sort of thing." A very charming man. Also that summer we were warned that Lieutenant Mary Churchill would be arriving on the airfield by car from where she was stationed further north, as she was to be picked up by a Mosquito and flown to the UK to accompany the Prime Minister on a visit to meet up with Stalin and Roosevelt. A delightful young lady whom my wife and I subsequently met on a cross channel steamer a couple of years after the war.

There were other distractions too. We received an order which emanated from Montgomery to the effect that there was to be, "No fraternisation with the Germans, especially the women." I soon received a deputation from the four French commanding officers. Their spokesman, Gaston Guizard, said that they didn't like that order because the French philosophy was that when they were victors, the spoils included the women! I promised to have a word with the Group Captain and when I saw Loel he quite sympathised. He agreed with their feelings on the matter and told me to tell them that provided it was done discreetly and with no fuss, they could continue. He added to me, "There is an old Yorkshire expression; what the eye doesn't see the heart doesn't grieve, or as Mrs Patrick Campbell said to George Bernard Shaw, 'It doesn't matter what they do so long as they don't frighten the horses!'"

The French are very keen on shooting and of course, as there had been little or none by Germans for a year or more we were in an area where wild boar, red and roe deer, black game (grouse) and wild duck were more than plentiful. Two occasions are worth mentioning.

Both wild boar and deer feed in the safety of night so we evolved a system where we rigged up a strong searchlight on the back of a jeep and got a young German farmer to operate same after he had guided us to the area where boar or deer were feeding. I would drive and there would be three other guns, one next to me and two in the back. I would approach the potential area using only side lights and at the given moment the farmer would switch on and rotate the light until it focused on the prey. I would then drive like mad, only halting literally short of contact. We would all then jump out and in line abreast pick off the boars, the searchlight following them as they tried to scatter.

On one occasion our young farmer told us that there was a female boar with some dozen or so offspring, which although well past the suckling stage were still with the mother rooting in a potato field. When the light was triggered I instructed the boys to take the female first and then the young. Once we had accounted for the young, one of the French boys said the female was snorting so the searchlight was turned on to the sow which was starting to rise onto its front legs. I said I would go forward to finish her off; she was some 20 yards from the jeep. I approached and when literally two feet away I carefully aimed the .303 rifle at the brain-box and fired one shot. To my surprise the sow immediately rose up, shook herself and proceeded to move towards me! I quickly turned and started to race back towards the jeep and my companions.

Meantime, the three Frenchmen were blazing away at the sow and I could literally feel the wind as the bullets zipped past me just inches away. I was deafened for many days. Even so the sow managed to make it to a wood some 50 yards away before finally passing out.

On a second occasion we were passing along a track adjacent to a wood and the side lights of the jeep picked up at 100 yards, what appeared to be the eye of a large deer. As we approached slowly the light kept disappearing and then reappearing. At, I suppose, 70 yards, Felix Jacquemet, a very good and experienced shot, told me that he reckoned he could hit the target. I said no, let's get closer and told him he could have a shot as soon as the searchlight was switched on.

So I instructed Felix to get ready and then said, switch on. To our surprise the light showed an old man wheeling his bicycle with an old fashioned oil lamp flickering! I shudder to think what would have happened if I had given Felix the go-ahead in the first instance.

Loel Guiness was demobbed in July and I was told by Teddy Hudleston that he wished me to take command of the Station. He added that as I would be demobbed myself in November, I could not be promoted to Group Captain. During September, Sholto Douglas, by now Marshal of the RAF, came to inspect the Station and asked me if I was going to apply for a permanent commission. I replied in the negative for the simple reason that I was now in my 30th year and most of my wing commander contemporaries who were applying were about 25. After reflecting he agreed with me.

There is an amusing story following an invitation I received from Air Marshal Sir Charles Steele, the AOC of 82 Group, to visit him at his HQ in the Hertz Mountains. As the RAF now had a leave centre at Bad Hartsburgh in the same mountain range, I decided to, 'kill two birds with one stone'. I organised a weekend leave at the centre and Sir Charles' ADC confirmed a dinner date during my visit. Squadron Leader Taylor and I arranged to go by car with a driver.

The day before leaving I received a call from 84 Group HQ asking if I would be kind enough to take two SRN nursing sisters, members of the RAF Nursing Service, who had also been booked in for the same weekend. This I agreed to and when we finally arrived at the centre I told our driver to find out where his accommodation was and then to bring up our luggage. Our room numbers would be on the information board in the main hallway.

A flight lieutenant met us and took us upstairs to our rooms. The room Taylor and I were to share was large, well furnished, had twin beds and a private bathroom. We then went off to see if the two nurses were settling in. However, one of the Sisters expressed some disappointment as there was no private bath. Being a couple of gallant officer gentlemen we offered to swop our rooms with them. We did this and then suggested we meet downstairs in the bar for a drink in about half an hour.

When the girls eventually joined us one of them remarked that we really had a marvellous batman, and we asked why. She told us that he was obviously not aware of the room swop when he suddenly came into the room with our luggage. One of the girls was, due to the sound of running water, audiby in the bathroom, while the other was standing in the middle of the bedroom, quite naked, drying herself from her bath. The man obviously thought he could hear me in the bath, and without turning a hair said, 'Excuse me Miss, which is the Wing Commander's bed?'

CHAPTER XV

APRES LA GUERRE

My last day of service was to be 31st December, 1945. I was invited by Air Vice-Marshal Hudleston, towards the end of September, to lunch, where I asked for and was granted permission to leave early in October in my own Spitfire as I wished to pay a number of flying visits to UK airfields and various officer friends.

Thus I said farewell to the Wing on October 8th, and flew 'SS' off to Lasham the next day. From there I went to Exeter, at least that was the flight plan, but it took me till the 13th to arrive, as I flew via Brussels, Ghent, Liege, Paris, Amiens, Glisy and Dreux. I had then to fly to RAF Hendon as very close to the airfield was the warehouse from which we drew a civilian suit and other items. I remember the RAF Warrant Officer saying, as I tried on the suit, "Don't get caught in the rain Sir, or it will roll right up your back like a Swiss roll.'

My main concern at Hendon, however, was how to get back into the airfield without my Military I/D card , for I was going to fly back to Lasham, having been, to all intents and purposes, demobbed. It worried me slightly but as I went through the Main Gate at Hendon to go to the demob centre I made a point of saying to the sergeant on duty, "I shall only be out for a while, will you still be here when I return?" When he confirmed he would, I walked off, my problem having been solved, for I knew I would not have to produce my, by then, non-existent card when I returned.

I had flown to Hendon in bad weather and my last flight in 'SS' was also terrible due to fog. It would have been nice to have had a pleasant empty blue sky to, perhaps, have a last fling, but this was denied me. As it was I had to be homed into Lasham, but I made it.

I handed over my Spitfire to Capitaine Felix Jacquemet on the 15th. He was going to fly it back to Fassberg. Unfortunately he ran into bad weather, crashed and was killed. A sad end to a very fine chap and an ignominious end to my Spitfire which had been in so many and varied offensive actions over the last weeks of World War II.

Both the Sampson boys had been lucky in the war, for brother Victor too had survived. He had a full operational war, first in Abyssinia, then the Desert, Italy, and finally Germany, which included the Elbe River crossing with the Seaforth Highlanders, to which he had been posted as a Major. He returned to England towards the end of 1945 almost six years after leaving his wife of just two weeks. Unfortunately the marriage broke up but he remarried a Peruvian lady he met whilst working in South America after the war. They have a daughter and now live in Lincolnshire.

But, at the end of 1945 the months and years of peacetime loomed before me. After six years of war, what would lay ahead. The extraordinary thing was, at first, the problem of sleeping. While I had managed to sleep soundly at night on the various airfields and billets, especially Antwerp where nightly we received V1 Buzz bombs and V2 rockets, I simply could not sleep in a comfortable peacetime bed for about a month. Almost each night I awoke amidst some terrifying dreams. However, my future father-in-law, being a doctor, soon put that right with various experimental medicines, whilst saying, "You are my most interesting patient."

In 1952 I was living and working for a Printing Ink manufacturing company near Paisley, west of Glasgow. I was on a business trip to London, staying as usual in the Royal Air Force Club, Piccadilly. Also staying there was Group Captain R J Clare-Hunt, who had been Senior Admin Officer at 10 Group when I was on the Staff. When he heard that I lived and worked near Glasgow he told me that there was a vacancy for a Wing Commander I/C the Glasgow and West of Scotland Air Training Corps (ATC) Wing, which had 23 squadrons and some 750 young air cadets.

Apparently the CO, a retired RAF acting Group Captain, had become ill and was also struggling to maintain a small holding. I agreed to visit him at Turnhouse, the Scotland Home Command set-up, under Air Vice-Marshal Peter Craycroft. I was told I would just be a father figure visiting each squadron, say, once a year, so I agreed to become the new ATC Wing Commander for that part of Scotland.

I soon discovered that as the Wing was bottom of the 52 UK Wings in Efficency Examinations, a hell of a lot needed doing. I got rid of the existing Wing Admin Officer, a retired flight lieutenant, and Wing Commander W R Dunlop MBE arrived. He had been an Engineer Officer and was very efficient and hard working. We gradually got rid of some elderly and not very effective squadron COs, and picked Flight Lieutenant Joe Robertson, a secondary school headmaster, as Wing Staff Squadron Leader I/C the Exams Syllabus, etc. It was a hard grind and we had to do a tremendous amount of evening and weekend visits. It took us about six or seven years for the Wing to win the Foster Trophy—an annual award for being Top in Efficiency and the Wing won this annually for the next eleven or so years.

The Commander-in-Chief, Home Command was now Air Marshal Sir Douglas MacFadyan and about 1955-56 Home Command was disbanded and a new Air Cadet Corps set-up was formed, based at RAF White Waltham, in Berkshire. The Command was over-seen by Flying Training Command and the first ATC Commandant promoted to Air Commodore was Nigel (Flossie) Farmer DFC.

During my eighteen years service with the Corps (I received the OBE [military division] after 11 years), we had as Commandants, James Coward AFC, a former Battle of Britain Spitfire pilot who had had a leg blown off during the battle, then E J 'Teddy' Morris DSO DFC (and American DFC), the brother of my old commander, Zulu Morris. Teddy Morris had also been a pilot in 1940, ramming a German bomber with his Hurricane on one occasion. Others were A G Dudgeon DFC, who had flown light bombers in the war, and John Stacey DSO DFC, later an Air Vice-Marshal, who retired in 1974.

During 1962 the C-in-C of Training Command was Air Marshal Sir Augustus Walker (GCB CBE DSO DFC AFC MA) known to everyone as 'Gus'. I knew Gus very well because in 1938-39 he played rugby as a fly half for Blackheath and I was in the London Scottish XV. We were both on the annual Easter Tour to Wales, having been selected by the Barbarians RUFC. Gus also played for England that year as I played for Scotland.

In 1948 I was again selected to play for Scotland. Gus, as is well known, after completing a tour on Hampden bombers, commanded a RAF bomber Station and whilst trying to rescue the crew of a bombed-up Lancaster that crashed on take-off, lost an arm above the elbow when the machine blew up. When he recovered he was determined to continue flying and had a metal arm specially made which allowed him to fly any normal aeroplane. When he was C-in-C Flying Training Command he had No.38 Group under his command which flew heli-copters. He had to have a new special arm made so as to fly them, but he did it.

In due course he arranged with the CO of RAF Odiham to receive instruction and was allocated a squadron leader who took off and flew a circuit, explaining the routine and then landed. Gus then took off and as he was coming in to land the Squadron Leader quickly took over and landed the 'chopper'. There is a special form which has to be filled in by the Instructor when such an emergency takes place. The question which asked: "Why did you take over?", was answered with—"The pilot's arm fell off!"

Gus still kept up an interest in rugby after the war and in fact became a first class referee as well as a member of the Rugby Union. Personally, before returning to Scotland in late 1948 I captained the Middlesex County Rugby Union, and the London Counties (Middlesex, Surrey, Kent and Eastern Counties). One annual game was against a Paris XV and I played games versus such touring sides as the All Blacks, Wallabies, etc. I also captained the Barbarians in 1948.

During the late 1950s the Air Ministry put on a small exhibition in Londonderry House, in Park Lane, to publicise the flying branches and aimed especially at young men and potential flyers. On one occasion I believe, at an opening ceremony they had on parade, so to speak, the following. Air Chief Marshal Sir Theodore McEvoy, who has a very pronounced stoop (curvature of the spine), Sir Gus Walker, with one arm, Air Vice-Marshal George Lott DSO DFC, who'd lost an eye commanding 43 Squadron in 1940, and Group Captain Douglas Bader, who had no legs. One young chap was asked what he thought of the show and said he thought it was marvellous. "But I'm not so sure," he continued, looking at the line of distinguished aviators, "now that I've seen all those battered warriors."

Battered warriors they might have been, but it had been my privilege to know them and to fly with many others during World War Two, whether battered or otherwise. I would not have missed it for the world.

POSTSCRIPT

In Chapter 11 we read of how some of the French pilots came to England to continue the fight against the occupation of their country. Many had stories of great interest which would make a book in themselves but in 1990, 45 years after the war had ended, one of my French pilots received a much belated French Medaille Militaire.

It says much for the French Air Force and their old comrades, that even after such a long period of time, it was not too late to present this medal to one who had spent most of the war actually getting to the war. His name is Roger Bethon, who was a young Sergent Pilot with 341 Squadron in 1945. The medal was presented to him following a short ceremony at Chinon, on 16th February 1990, pinned to his chest by non other than General Victor Tanguy, himself holder of the Legion d'Honneur, and former pilot with 341 Alsace Squadron.

I cannot recall if I ever heard the full story of Roger Bethon's fight to get to the war, but Victor Tanguy has now told it to me and I offer it here, in shortened form, as an example not only of gutsy courage, but as a final tribute to the determination of all those Free Frenchmen who made it to England to fight.

When the war began, Bethon was just 19 years old, too young for call-up, but on 9th December he enrolled himself as a student pilot. He went to Cholet No.I pilot school at Angers, and from there to Marrakesh where he began his training in January 1940. He got his wings in June just as France was about to fall.

At this stage, France had lost the war with Germany and Bethon was a pilot without an Air Force. He was demobilised in Montpellier and sent home to Paris. However, with his country occupied, his eager ears heard the call of General de Gaulle in London, and became enthused to join the fighting Free French in England.

There were various possible ways of reaching Britain, and he chose an elegant but hazardous one—by aeroplane. With his flying club friend Denis Lavogade, he decided to steal a Goeland light twin-engined aeroplane from the airfield as Issy-les-Moulineaux, to the west of Paris. After some weeks of careful planning, they decided to get into the base at night, hide in the back of one of the aircraft, then await the arrival of the crew. The plan then would be to chloroform them, dump them on the airfield and take off.

Another friend thought the scheme too risky and finally persuaded Roger to try instead to get over the Pyrenees into Spain, and then make for Gibraltar. It was now late 1942, but by early February 1943 he had crossed into Spain, only to be arrested in the town of Isaba and put into the local prison. He was then transferred to the civil jail at Pamplona for two months, then interned at Santander. It was now he learned the fate of Denis Lavogade.

His friend had recruited another friend to join in the aeroplane hi-jack, and in due course got onto the airfield and into an aeroplane. However, before they could overcome the crew the next morning, they were discovered and taken by German guards. On being searched, the chloroform was found as well as a revolver. They also found the names of Bethon and another man, who was the pharmacist who had supplied the chloroform. Bethon of course was well out of it in a Spanish prison, but the other named person was arrested and spent two years in Dachau. Lavogade and his companion were both tried, condemned to death and shot in July 1943.

Bethon remained in Pamplona prison until May 1943, from where he made his way to Casablanca, and went to Meknes where the Stork Fighter Group was based. Commander Fleurquin, who was in charge, secretly allowed him to take up his aerial training and he was then officially enrolled at the pilot school at Kasba-Tadla, also in Morocco. He completed his training at the Fighter Training Centre at Meknes.

Now a fully fledged fighter pilot he was posted to one of the French Fighter Groups attached to the RAF. From May 1944 to February 1945 he trained as a British fighter pilot at Kirton-in-Lindsay, from where he was posted to 341 Squadron. Roger Bethon had finally got to the fighting war. In those last weeks of the war he flew a number of fighter and fighter-bomber missions, attacking numerous ground targets with both bombs and cannon fire. He took part in the fighting which accompanied the Rhine crossings and the battle to take Bremen. It was also at a time when the French Wing took some of its heaviest casualties of the whole war.

On 8th May 1945, he was with those of us who had been fortunate enough to see and be a part of the defeat of Nazi Germany, but as a Frenchman, he took pride in the liberation of his country and the freeing of his people from occupied domination.

On 18th June 1945, Roger was with his Squadron at the head of about 300 aircraft, having the honour of taking part in the grand flypast above the Champs Elysees, Paris, flying in a huge Cross of Lorraine formation. For him, the struggle had been well worth it. We all knew how he must have felt, for we had thought along similar lines in those days immediately after the war ended. We had fought and won. Thought of defeat had never entered our heads.

APPENDIX A

RAF Record of Service

No.2 ITW	Cambridge	12 Jun 1941	–	1 Aug 1941
No.22 EFTS	Cambridge	11 Aug	–	24 Sep
No.17 EFTS	Peterborough	11 Oct	–	18 Oct
No.15 SFTS	Kidlington	18 Oct	–	19 Feb 1942
No.53 OTU	Llandow	17 Mar 1942	–	8 Jun
No.602 Sqdn	Redhill	9 Jun	–	16 Jul
" " "	Peterhead	16 Jul	–	16 Aug
" " "	Biggin Hill	16 Aug	–	20 Aug
" " "	Peterhead	20 Aug	–	10 Sep
" " "	Skaebrae	10 Sep	–	14 Dec
No.131 Sqdn	Westhampnett	14 Dec	–	29 Dec
" " "	Martlesham Heath	29 Dec	–	11 Jan 1943
" " "	Westhampnett	11 Jan 1943	–	20 Jan
" " "	Castletown	20 Jan	–	26 Jun
" " "	Exeter	26 Jun	–	16 Aug
" " "	Redhill	16 Aug	–	17 Sep
" " "	Culmhead	17 Sep	–	10 Feb 1944
SGO	Exeter	10 Feb 1944	–	14 Mar
CGS Course	Catfoss	15 Mar	–	18 Apr
SGO	Exeter	18 Apr	–	2 Jun
GGS Course	Southend	2 Jun	–	10 Jun
10 Group HQ	Exeter	24 Jul	–	22 Oct
No.84 GSU	Thruxton	22 Oct	–	24 Nov
No.84 GSU	Lasham	24 Nov	–	8 Dec
No.127 Sqdn	B.60 Grimbergen	9 Dec	–	21 Dec
" " "	B.79 Woensdrecht	21 Dec	–	17 Jan 1945
No.145 Wing	B.70 Derne	17 Jan 1945	–	6 Feb
" " "	B.85 Schijndel	6 Feb	–	16 Apr
" " "	B.105 Drope	16 Apr	–	5 Jul
" " "	B.152 Fassberg	5 Jul	–	1 Sep
" " "	B.152 as OC	2 Sep	–	13 Oct

Distinguished Flying Cross	London Gazette, 19 May 1944
Bar to DFC	London Gazette, 30 May 1945
French Croix de Guerre & palm	London Gazette, 10 May 1945

APPENDIX B

Combats and Sorties

1942

Date	Unit	Aircraft	Result	Location	Aircraft	Code
19 Aug	602 Sqdn	FW190	Probable	N Dieppe	Spitfire Vb	EP249 'K'
" "	" "	Do217	Damaged	" "	Spitfire Vb	EP249 'K'
" "	" "	Do217	Damaged	" "	Spitfire Vb	EP249 'K'
" "	" "	FW190	Destroyed	Dieppe	Spitfire Vb	EP244 'B'
1943						
31 Jul	131 Sqdn	FW190	Destroyed	N St Omer	Spitfire Vb	BM121 'X'
19 Aug	" "	FW190	Damaged	N Poix	Spitfire Vb	BM121 'X'
" "	" "	FW190	Damaged	N Poix	Spitfire Vb	BM121 'X'
26 Nov	" "	FW190	Damaged	Martinvast	Spitfire IXA	MA807 'M'
1944						
7 Aug	" "	FW190	Destroyed	NE La Fleche	Spitfire VII	MD165 'M'
1945						
13 Mar	145 Wing	Me109G	Destroyed	N Bocholt	Spitfire IXB	'SS'

− plus one Me109 destroyed on the ground on Laval airfield.

Operational sorties flown:

Defensive patrols over UK	−	41
Offensive sorties over France	−	83
Offensive sorties over Germany	−	31
Offensive sorties over Holland	−	29
Offensive sorties over Belgium	−	3
Offensive sorties over Luxembourg	−	2
Total:	−	189

Adams, SL D: 18-19
Andrieux, Gen J: 4, 138, 144, 146, 153
Andrews, FS: 76
Atcherley, AVM D F W: 30, 141-2
Atcherley, AVM R L R: 29-30, 31, 32, 37, 41, 64, 141, 160
Aubertin, Capt: 161
Austen, Dr: 20
Austen, Miss M: 20, 65
Aves, FO B: 19-20
Avon, Gen M: 117

Bader, GC D R S: 4, 24, 60, 164, 173
Baldwin, GC J R: 102, 104, 161
Barnes, FO: 153
Barthrop WC P P C: 5
Barton, Miss P: 79
Barwell GC P R: 37
Basin: 153
Bateman, PO: 76
Baynham, FL G T: 23, 25-7, 28-9
Beard, SL J: 85
Bearman, FL P: 93-5
Beamish, GC F V: 24, 30
Bell, PO N: 14, 15, 18
Benson, Mr: 29
Beraudo, Lt V: 149
Berg, WC R A: 105, 107, 110, 132-3, 145
Bergsland Sgt P: 158
Bernhardt, Prince: 158
Bethon, Sgt R G: 174-6
Beytagh, SL M L ff: 54, 56
Billon, Gen: 146
Bird-Wilson AVM H A C: 89
Blackadder, WC F: 160
Blanc, Lt: 149
Brignell, GC J A: 18
Bocock, SL E P W: 29, 30, 31, 37-41, 48-51
Boisot, M: 115
Borne, Capt R: 113-4, 134, 140, 144-5, 153
Boudard, S-Chef: 138
Boudier, Col M: 113
Bousquet, Gen R: 147
Bower, FO A W: 57, 103
Boyer de Bouillane, Col F: 123-8
Boyd, WC R F: 31
Bradley, Gen O: 107
Braidwood, FL: 152
Brandt, J: 12-13
Brereton, Gen L H: 97
Broadhurst, ACM Sir H: 24, 31, 52, 64, 164
Broadhurst, FO: 31
Brothers, AC P M: 4, 6, 34-5, 39, 41, 44, 46, 47, 50-1, 53-4, 56, 89, 92-8, 164

Brown, FL D: 41-3, 63, 64, 72, 99
Brunschwig, Lt M F: 113

Caldecott, Sgt W E: 49
Campbell, J: 10
Campbell-Orde, WC I R: 94
Carlson, FL: 54
Carre, Lt J J M: 138, 149, 153
Cavet, Lt A P E: 149-151
Chamberlain, Neville: 10
Chapman, S/Lt C: 148
Chapman, SL R H: 89
Checketts, WC J M: 52, 85
Churchill, Mary: 166-7
Churchill, Winston: 13, 19-20, 32, 35, 77, 167
Clare-Hunt, GC R J: 171
Cobham, Sir A: 14
Colbeck-Welch, AVM E L: 139
Cole-Hamilton, AVM J B: 91, 97
Collishaw, AVM R: 159
Coningham, AM Sir A: 142
Corkett, SL A H: 21-3
Corner, GC H W: 40
Cornwallis, Lord: 58, 69, 79
Cortis, FO W: 151
Corveler, Asp Y: 145, 153
Covington, FL: 109
Coward, AC J B: 172
Craig, FL: 136-7
Crane, FL: 7
Crawford-Compton, WC W V: 109, 116, 121, 129, 143
Craycroft, AVM P: 171
Crayford, WO: 95
Croke, AC L: 19

Dabos, S/Lt J: 152, 153
d'Aligny, Lt F A: 151
Dalton-Morgan, GC T: 84, 89, 90, 139
Daoules, H: 115
Davey, PO P: 44
Davies, S/Chef J: 145, 149
Deacon-Elliot GC R: 102
de Bordas, Lt H: 57, 144, 146, 148
Decmar: 29
de Colasse, C-B: 23
Decroo, Lt P M: 144, 151
De Gaulle, Gen C: 113, 115, 130, 143, 164, 174
Deere, AC A C: 85, 102
De Labouchere, Capt F: 115
de la Torre, SL B E: 45, 52
de Larminat, Capt B: 144, 150, 151
de Longville, Lt M: 147
Delery, Le M F: 151
Dennehey, FO J: 29, 33

Denville, FO: 26
De Saxce, Lt A: 152
Doll, FL C: 57, 59-60
Donovan, WC C: 23
Donovan, Sgt F P A: 155
Dorrance, Gen M: 145
Dowding, ACM Sir H: 32
Dubourgel, V: 115
Dudgeon, A G: 172
Dudgeon, Lt E: 132
Dunlop, WC W R: 171
Dunsford, FL A: 165

Edge, SL A: 23, 25, 28
Eisenhower, Gen D D: 107, 132
Embry, ACM Sir B: 25, 68, 141-2, 165-6
Etlin, Lt R R E: 149
Evatt, Dr H V: 35

Farmer, AC N: 172
Fifield, SL J S: 39, 56, 57, 59, 60, 62
Filliol, Sgt J: 152
Finley, GC D O: 99, 100
Finucane, WB B: 6, 28-9, 30, 34, 35, 39-41
Fitzalan-Howard, Lt M: 11
Fleishel, Lt M: 148
Fleurquin, Cdt: 175
Flick, FO C S: 72
Foissac, Lt L: 150
Fraser, Adm Sir B: 66
Frost, FL L S: 148
Fuchs, Lt: 149

Gilbert, M: 32
Gillam, GC D E: 104
Girard, S/Chef G: 113, 114
Girardeau, S/Chef: 148
Giraud, Gen: 130
Gledhill, Sgt: 44
Godsell, Sister A: 24-5
Gonay, SL H: 89
Goodchap, PO M: 49
Gort, Lord: 11, 25
Gouby, Lt R: 115
Graillott, S/Chef E: 149
Gran: Maj M Y: 4, 85
Grant, SL R J C: 30
Grant-Peterkin, Maj: 11
Guichard, S/Chef J: 148
Guiness, GC T L E B: 7, 68, 109, 110, 116, 130, 132,
    134, 136, 140, 146-7, 152, 160, 164-5, 166, 167,
    168
Guiness, P: 165
Guizard, Cdt G: 128, 130, 147, 167

Hallings-Pott, GC J R: 45
Hallowes, SL H J L: 57
Hardi, Lt F: 144, 156-7, 158-9
Hardman, FL F: 147
Harries, WC R H: 57, 102, 103, 163
Harris, MRAF Sir A: 162
Harrison, PO: 15
Harvey, Lord: 91, 97, 98
Hauser, Sgt P L: 49
Helies, Lt C: 115
Hill, AM Sir R M: 96
Hillwood, FL P: 105, 108
Hitler, A: 13, 163
Hlado, FO: 62
Hodgkinson, FO C: 4, 60-1
Holman, R: 10
Holme, Mrs J: 112
Holmes, GC J W E: 84
Honington, R de: 115
Hope, GC Sir A: 86
Hope, Bob: 87
Horrocks, Gen Sir B: 166
Horseburgh, G: 10
Hubidos, S/Chef P: 115
Hudleston, AVM Sir E: 102, 142, 163, 168, 170
Huin, Adj R: 115
Hylton, Jack: 87

Igoe, SL W A K: 51
Inglis, A: 10
Innes-Jones, FO: 39

Jacquemet, Capt F: 168, 170
Johnson, AVM J E: 24, 61
Johnson, S: 58
Johnston, B: 5
Johnston, SL H A S: 69
Johnstone, N: 13
Jones, GC J I T: 20-1
Jongblood, FO G: 66

Kellett, WC R G: 24, 31
Kelly, FL L: 103
Kemp, Maj Gen: 54
Kerguelen, S/Chef Y: 144, 145
Kimlichka, FO: 61
Kingcome, GC E B C: 41
Krebbs, Col: 87
Kruml, FL T: 59, 62

Lagarde, S/Lt F: 148
Laurent, Gen P: 113-4
Lambaert, Lt R: 148
Lanos, Lt P: 145

Lavergne, Col P: 150, 151-2
Lavogade, D: 175
Lazlo, P de: 147
Lea, FL H: 108
Le Flecher, Col L: 114, 150, 153-5
Leigh-Mallory, AVM T: 32, 104
Lentz, Lt G: 113, 114
Le Page, Lt H: 141
Leslie, Sgt D: 77
Leslie, Mrs: 77
Lewis, R: 12-13
Lott, GC G C: 173
Loud, WC W W J: 9, 30, 33, 36, 49, 53
Lovat, Lord: 45
Luckhoff, PO L: 72

Mackie, SL J: 19
Magrot, S/Chef P: 115
Mailfert, M: 113
Malan, GC A G: 24, 31, 32, 37-8, 104, 116, 121
Malcolm, WC H G: 132
Malcolm, Toppy: 132
Malfroy, WC C E: 65, 68-72, 74-5, 79-80, 130
Mallet, Sgt J: 115
Manners, Lady I: 68
Marchel, S/Lt: 129
Marchelidon, Col J: 117, 120, 136-7, 143, 144
Maridor, Capt J-M: 111-2, 113, 118
Marples, WC R: 110, 120, 121
Martel (see Montet)
Martin-Prudhomme, Lt J: 149
Massert, Gen O: 115, 116, 131, 137-8, 139, 144
Mathillon-Croizet, Adj P: 115
May, WC P: 14-16
Michelin, Lt H: 115, 145
Mitchell, R J: 8
Mitchell, Maj: 137
Mollison, Jim: 100
Monnier: 115
Montbron, X de: 115
Montet, Cdt C: 119, 131
Montgomery, Viscount: 9, 107, 132, 140, 162
Morris, AM Sir D: 103-4, 107, 109, 133, 165, 172
Morris, AC E J: 172
Morris, SL R E: 30
Muir, H: 10
Muller, Lt J: 158

MacDonald, SL K J: 158
MacDougall, SL I N: 92, 94
MacFadyan, AM Sir D: 172
MacGuire, FO P: 89
MacIntyre, SL A S: 73
Mackenzie, W: 63

McEvoy, ACM Sir T: 98, 102, 173
Nettleton, WC J D: 70
Newbury, SL R A: 89
Newlands, J: 10
Niven, SL J B: 29, 30, 34, 39, 40, 44, 46-8,
    50-1, 53, 56
Nixon, Sgt: 156

O'Meara, WC J J: 6, 62, 63, 67, 71, 75, 81, 86, 89
Osmanville, Capt A: 153
Ouches, Lt J de: 124-5
Oxspring, GC R W: 37
Ozanne, Cdt J: 130, 136, 143

Park, ACM Sir K: 32
Parry, FS K: 76
Parse (see Cavet)
Payne, FS: 26, 27
Peacock, FL M: 65
Pearson-Rogers, GC H W: 99
Peet, FL W W: 158
Perdrizet, Gen M: 128-9
Pickering, FL T G : 62, 69, 71, 79, 87
Pledger, PO: 15
Porchon, S/Lt: 129
Portal, Lord: 77, 141
Pottier, S/Chef R: 153
Powell, WC R P R: 64, 65
Poype, Lt R de la: 29
Pringle-Paterson, Col 11, 12

Quill, J K: 58

Rankin, GC J: 31, 38
Reeves, SL A J: 130, 147, 158, 160
Reynel, S/Chef M de: 138, 144, 151, 153
Rigaud, Lt: 141, 153, 156
Rippon, FO: 41
Roberts, WO F: 145, 149
Robertson, FL J: 172
Rogers, Sgt: 18
Rook, WC A H: 159
Rosa, S/Lt: 138
Rosier, ACM Sir F: 102

Sampson, C: 20
Sampson, J: 20
Sampson, S: 20
Sampson, Maj V F: 10-12, 97, 171
Sanders, WC J G: 65
Saunders, AM Sir H: 35
Saunders, WC: 55, 62-3
Scott, FL: 85
Scott, FL: 134

Selway, AM Sir A: 100
Sheen, WC D F B: 64
Sholto-Douglas, Lord: 24, 32, 142, 158, 168
Sinclair, Sir A: 32, 63
Sinclair, Miss K: 63
Slesser, MRAF Sir J: 139, 142
Smallwood, ACM Sir D: 80-2, 89
Smik, SL O: 57, 103-4
Smith, FO C: 61, 71-2, 73
Smith, FO E: 61, 73
Souviat, Gen J: 117-123
Sparrow, Sgt: 15
Stacey, AVM J N: 172
Stalin, J: 13
Steele, AM Sir C: 79, 84, 87, 168
Strudwick, FS A: 30, 33
Strugnell, GC W V: 19-20
Swindon, SL W W: 89

Tait, FO C K: 29
Tanguy, Gen V: 116, 144, 146, 151, 160, 174
Tatraux, Col A: 153, 161
Taylor, SL: 168
Tedder, Lord: 132
Thomas G: 54
Thorne, Gen Sir A: 11, 25
Trenchard, MRAF Lord: 25
Trinder, Tommy; 87
Trueman, Sgt: 17

Truscott, SL K W: 28, 40
Tuck, WC R R S: 58, 164
Turnbull, Sgt N A A: 70, 72

Valin, Gen M: 143, 146, 163
Van der Stock, SL R: 157-8
Vaux, Col: 12-13

Walker, AM Sir A: 172-3
Walker, GC P R: 102, 104
Wallaker, FO: 22
Waterhouse, FL J C R: 93, 96
Watkins, SL D H: 30, 32, 47, 99, 100, 101-2, 164
Watts, SL L W: 89
Wellesley, Lady C: 13
Wells, WC E P: 30, 34
West, FL R: 82, 87-8
Winskill, AC Sir A: 85
Williams, Sgt: 149
Wolloshing, Sgt G: 150
Wood, FS: 82
Woodall, GC A B: 68
Woolger, FO H: 89
Worsthorne, P: 23
Wykeham, AM Sir P: 73
Wymeersch, PO R van: 115

Yorke, Miss A M: 132

Zhukov, Gen G: 163